# Dialogues with Ethnography

**MIX**
Paper from
responsible sources
**FSC® C014540**
www.fsc.org

# ENCOUNTERS

*Series Editors:* Jan Blommaert, *Tilburg University, The Netherlands*, Ben Rampton, *Kings College London, UK*, Anna De Fina, *Georgetown University, USA*, Sirpa Leppänen, *University of Jyväskylä, Finland* and James Collins, *University at Albany/SUNY, USA*

The Encounters series sets out to explore diversity in language from a theoretical and an applied perspective. So the focus is both on the linguistic encounters, inequalities and struggles that characterise post-modern societies and on the development, within sociocultural linguistics, of theoretical instruments to explain them. The series welcomes work dealing with such topics as heterogeneity, mixing, creolization, bricolage, crossover phenomena, polylingual and polycultural practices. Another high-priority area of study is the investigation of processes through which linguistic resources are negotiated, appropriated and controlled, and the mechanisms leading to the creation and maintenance of sociocultural differences. The series welcomes ethnographically oriented work in which contexts of communication are investigated rather than assumed, as well as research that shows a clear commitment to close analysis of local meaning making processes and the semiotic organisation of texts.

All books in this series are externally peer-reviewed.

Full details of all the books in this series and of all our other publications can be found on http://www.multilingual-matters.com, or by writing to Multilingual Matters, St Nicholas House, 31–34 High Street, Bristol BS1 2AW, UK.

ENCOUNTERS: 10

# Dialogues with Ethnography

## Notes on Classics, and How I Read Them

**Jan Blommaert**

MULTILINGUAL MATTERS

Bristol • Blue Ridge Summit

## For Aaron Cicourel and Johannes Fabian

DOI https://doi.org/10.21832/BLOMMA9504
Library of Congress Cataloging in Publication Data
A catalog record for this book is available from the Library of Congress.
Names: Blommaert, Jan, author. | Hymes, Dell H., honouree.
Title: Dialogues with Ethnography: Notes on Classics, and How I Read Them /
Jan Blommaert.
Description: Blue Ridge Summit, PA: Multilingual Matters, [2018] |
Series: Encounters: 10 | Includes bibliographical references and index.
Identifiers: LCCN 2017038807| ISBN 9781783099498 (softcover : alk. paper) |
ISBN 9781783099504 (hardcover : alk. paper) | ISBN 9781783099511 (pdf) |
ISBN 9781783099528 (epub) | ISBN 9781783099535 (kindle)
Subjects: LCSH: Ethnography—Social aspects. | Language and culture. |
Sociolinguistics.
Classification: LCC P40 .B46 2018 | DDC 306.44—dc23 LC record available at
https://lccn.loc.gov/2017038807

British Library Cataloguing in Publication Data
A catalogue entry for this book is available from the British Library.

ISBN-13: 978-1-78309-950-4 (hbk)
ISBN-13: 978-1-78309-949-8 (pbk)

**Multilingual Matters**
UK: St Nicholas House, 31–34 High Street, Bristol, BS1 2AW, UK.
USA: NBN, Blue Ridge Summit, PA, USA.

Website: www.multilingual-matters.com
Twitter: Multi_Ling_Mat
Facebook: https://www.facebook.com/multilingualmatters
Blog: www.channelviewpublications.wordpress.com

WOODBROOKE
LIBRARY

306· 44

The policy of Multilingual Matters/Channel View Publications is to use papers that are natural, renewable and recyclable products, made from wood grown in sustainable forests. In the manufacturing process of our books, and to further support our policy, preference is given to printers that have FSC and PEFC Chain of Custody certification. The FSC and/or PEFC logos will appear on those books where full certification has been granted to the printer concerned.

Typeset by Nova Techset Private Limited, Bengaluru and Chennai, India.
Printed and bound in the UK by Short Run Press Ltd.
Printed and bound in the US by Edwards Brothers Malloy, Inc.

# Contents

# Acknowledgments

With one or two exceptions, the material collected in this volume has been published in the period between 1997 and the present. Most versions presented here, however, are earlier drafts or abridged and revised versions of the final published texts:

- Chapter 2 was published as 'Obituary: Dell Hymes (1927–2009)'. *Journal of Sociolinguistics* 14 (5): 682–686, 2010. I am grateful to Wiley for permission to use this publication.
- Chapter 3 was published as 'Ethnography and democracy: Hymes' political theory of language'. *Text and Talk* 29 (3): 257–276, 2009. I am grateful to de Gruyter for permission to use this publication.
- Chapter 4 was published as 'Ethnopoetics as functional reconstruction: Dell Hymes' narrative view of the world. Review article'. *Functions of Language* 13 (2): 229–249, 2006. I am grateful to John Benjamins for permission to use this publication.
- Chapter 5 was published as 'Grassroots historiography and the problem of voice: Tshibumba's "Histoire du Zaire"'. *Journal of Linguistic Anthropology* 14 (1): 6–23, 2004. I am grateful to Wiley for permission to use this publication.
- Chapters 6 and 7 were published as Chapters 2 and 3 of my *Ethnography, Superdiversity and Linguistic Landscapes: Chronicles of Complexity*. Bristol: Multilingual Matters, 2013.
- Chapter 8 was published as 'Pierre Bourdieu: Perspectives on language in society'. In Jan-Ola Östman & Jef Verschueren (eds) *Handbook of Pragmatics*, 2015 (pp. 1–16). I am grateful to John Benjamins for permission to use this publication.
- Chapter 9 appeared as paper 65 in the Tilburg Papers in Culture Studies (2013), https://www.tilburguniversity.edu/research/institutes-and-research-groups/babylon/tpcs/
- Chapter 10 appeared as Chapter 4 in my *Workshopping: Professional Vision, Practices and Critique in Discourse Analysis*. Ghent: Academia

Press, 2004. I am grateful to Academia Press for permission to use this publication.

- Chapter 11 was published as 'Chronotopes, scales and complexity in the study of language in society'. *Annual Review of Anthropology* 44: 105–116, 2015. I am grateful to Annual Reviews Inc. for permission to use this publication.
- Chapter 13 was published as 'Commentary: On scope and depth in linguistic ethnography'. *Journal of Sociolinguistics* 11 (5): 682–688, 2007. I am grateful to Wiley for permission to use this publication.

Chapters 7 and 9 were originally co-authored by colleagues April Huang and Fons van de Vijver, respectively; I gratefully acknowledge their input and contribution here. The individual texts will offer further acknowledgments of the support and contributions of the numerous colleagues and friends with whom I have shared and debated many of these thoughts over the years.

However, I must emphatically thank a number of people for pushing me toward completion of this particular book, and for taking me seriously whenever I discussed ethnographic theory with them: Rob Moore, Michael Silverstein, Asif Agha, Gunther Kress, Karel Arnaut, David Parkin, Jim Collins, Jeff Bezemer, Charles Briggs and Aaron Cicourel. Ben Rampton deserves my deep gratitude in a great variety of roles: as my preferred sparring partner for debates on ethnography, as a member of the superb InCoLaS team where so many fundamental discussions were held over the past number of years, as a good and caring friend, and as the one who got the idea for this book. Karin Berkhout, finally, made this bunch of papers and scribbles into a manuscript, and I have come to increasingly appreciate such assistance over the years. Karin: bedankt!

*Tilburg and Antwerp*
March 2017

# Preface

Academics read, and reading defines a very large part of their professional habitus and ethos – it is through reading that we establish intertextual intellectual lineages connecting our own empirical work with that of previous generations of scholars or contemporary peers, all of this in search of a potential for adequate generalization or, as some prefer, theoretical validity for our own findings. We read, thus, instrumentally, but to actually put our finger on this 'instrumental' value is far from easy – we read in search of a broad and not too precise thing called 'inspiration', often also in search of a less focused form of intellectual fellowship, and quite often also just for pleasure, because reading is fun. Subjective filters occur at every moment of reading: every reading of someone else's text reflects our own concerns, priorities, curiosities or frustrations. This is a truism, but it is this truism that encourages me to publish my own readings of texts and oeuvres written by others.

My own reading has rather consistently been filtered and biased by a search for *ethnographic relevance*. My work is and has been ethnographic throughout, but ethnographic in a particular sense: not that 'ethnography' found in most textbook descriptions of it (a 'method', in other words), but a general programmatic *perspective* on social reality and how real subjects, in real conditions of everyday life, possessed by real interests, make sense of it. This broader understanding of ethnography pushed and pushes me to seek, translate and apply elements in the work of others that could strengthen and validate the theoretical and epistemological foundations of this ethnography-as-perspective. This quest drove me, at times, deeply into the work of people not often considered as canonical sources in ethnography, where ideas, metaphors and empirical insights could be found that were useful for my own theoretical 'bricolage'. The present collection reflects this quest.

Several authors have profoundly influenced the quest, and this book will discuss just a handful of them. I must, first, recognize two major *maîtres à penser* in my search for a more broadly grounded ethnographic theoretical perspective: Dell Hymes and Johannes Fabian. In their work,

I found the major directions for my own thinking and research; my inter-pretation of their work – their influence on me – permeates everything I have to say on the subject, and Chapter 1 – an early coherent formulation of my views – codifies their pervasive influence. Dell Hymes is discussed in the next three chapters. Chapter 2 is an obituary that I wrote after his passing away, in which I attempt to concisely reformulate the key insights that I gained from his work and consider to be of lasting programmatic value for any ethnographic and sociolinguistic project. Of major impor-tance, in my reading, is Hymes' humanist politics of science: he saw eth-nography not just as a scientific occupation but as a political-democratic project in the Enlightenment and Marxist tradition – an ethics of science that I am happy to endorse (Chapter 3). Hymes' most developed, but also least understood, ethnographic endeavor was ethnopoetics, and it was in his ethnopoetics work that his humanist ethos was most clearly imple-mented. Ethnopoetics was a project of restituting voice to people who, for a variety of reasons, remain voiceless – a point that proved very productive in my own work, notably in what was to become *Discourse: A Critical Introduction* (Cambridge University Press, 2005) (Chapter 4).

A similar direction is present in Johannes Fabian's oeuvre. Fabian doubtlessly counts among the most influential critical theorists of ethnog-raphy-as-epistemology, and this epistemology pushed him toward unique analyses of the historical situatedness of voice and the impact of such historical conditions on contemporary articulations of it. Fabian applied this tactics throughout his career to documents from Central Africa, designing in the process a highly sensitive ethnographic semiotics which I discuss and apply to similar materials in Chapter 5. My decades-long dialogue with Fabian was the direct prompt for what became *Grassroots Literacy* (Routledge, 2008).

Sociolinguistics, as I saw and see it, is a tradition offering great analyti-cal purchase but often rather poor theory, notably on issues such as space and time. The next two chapters discuss the work of, respectively, Ron and Suzie Scollon (Chapter 6) and Gunther Kress (Chapter 7) as productive sources for a more sophisticated sociolinguistic semiotics of spacetime. I developed the interpretations of their work reported in these chapters during a sustained struggle to shed the synchronic, localist and static ana-lytical frameworks derived from structuralism and offered in mainstream scholarship, and to replace them by a dynamic view of sociolinguistic mobility (leading to *The Sociolinguistics of Globalization*, Cambridge University Press, 2010, and later work on the complexity of contemporary linguistic landscapes in contexts of superdiversity: *Ethnography, Superdiversity and Linguistic Landscapes*, Multilingual Matters, 2013).

Further chapters will re-engage with issues of spacetime, but before we can return to these issues, a third major influence on my own thinking needs to be identified: Pierre Bourdieu. I became very interested in the often overlooked, but in my view determining, ethnographic dimensions of Bourdieu's epistemology and methodology, an effect of his deep engagement with the work of US symbolic interactionists such as Goffman, Cicourel, Garfinkel and Blumer. It is, in my opinion, impossible to grasp the full depth of Bourdieu's views of language in society unless this influence is acknowledged (Chapter 8). And it is again this influence, notably that of Aaron Cicourel and his fundamental critique of naïve statistics, that enables us to detect the creative methodological loop from ethnography to statistics and back that defines so much of Bourdieu's work (Chapter 9). This methodological loop is, I think, an extraordinarily valuable resource for studies of the complexity of social change.

Aaron Cicourel already figured in the previous chapters; I consider him one of the most powerful social-theoretical methodologists of the post-Second World War era, and it is regrettable that so much of his work remains confined to the margins of the humanities and social science at present. It was my encounter with Cicourel's principled methodological austerity that withdrew some of my earlier illusions about research and committed me to ethnography in the 1990s, and his influence on scholars such as Charles Goodwin spawned the critique on mainstream Conversation Analysis as a methodological inadequacy written up in Chapter 10. Cicourel's own rejection of Conversation Analysis on theoretical and methodological grounds is well known; I add my own critique of some of the infra-methodologies of Conversation Analysis, infused with insights from the work of Michael Silverstein, Gregg Urban, Charles Briggs and others in Chapter 10 (part of what later became *Workshopping*, Academia Press, 2004).

The challenges of an adequately theorized and methodologically sound approach to spacetime in sociolinguistics and adjacent sciences were described earlier; in the next two chapters I return to these issues, drawing on the work of authors not generally considered as sources of ethnographic theory: Mikhail Bakhtin (Chapter 11) and Henri Lefebvre (Chapter 12). Both discussions, we can see, are deeply influenced by my own adoption of some central insights from symbolic interactionism – recall Cicourel's influence – and both can be read as appeals to draw the metaphorical qualities of concepts such as 'chronotope' (Bakhtin) and 'the urban' (Lefebvre) into the orbit of ethnographic feet-on-the-ground research and exploit them profitably there. My discussion of Lefebvre's theoretical interventions in Chapter 12 also offers a small glimpse of what is undoubtedly the largest, most pervasive and most enduring general intellectual influence on me: Marx. Perceptive readers will have already understood that most of the influences I gratefully acknowledge derive from scholars whose work was at least sensitive and responsive to the Marxian scholarship that pervaded and saturated the intellectual history of the 20th century.

I conclude this collection with Chapter 13, a short commentary piece on a newly emerging and very creative branch of 'linguistic ethnography' that grew out of UK-based applied and sociolinguistics under the guidance of Ben Rampton, a scholar of formidable erudition and creativity. Rampton's work draws heavily on the Gumperz–Hymes tradition of ethnography of communication, and it enriches it with contemporary insights in superdiversity and practice-based communicative complexity. The argument I build in Chapter 13 is merely an invitation for people involved in the development of linguistic ethnography to use the full richness of the intellectual and analytical pedigree offered by ethnography, to which this collection hopes to bear testimony.

I apologize to readers for the at times repetitive character of the text. It documents a dynamic but consistent trajectory of intellectual exploration sustained over a couple of decades, and thus inevitably returns to the same large issues, dominant influences and arguments.

# 1 Ethnography as Counter-hegemony: Remarks on Epistemology and Method

## Introduction

Ethnography is a strange scientific phenomenon. On the one hand, it can be seen as probably the only truly influential 'invention' of anthropological linguistics, having triggered important developments in social-scientific fields as diverse as pragmatics and discourse analysis, sociology and historiography, and having caused a degree of attention to small detail in human interaction previously unaddressed in many fields of the social sciences.[1] At the same time, ethnography has for decades been under fire from within. Critical anthropology emerged from within ethnography, and strident critiques by e.g. Johannes Fabian (1983) and James Clifford (1988) exposed immense epistemological and ethical problems in ethnography. Their call for a historization of *ethnographies* (rather than a singular *ethnography*) was answered by a flood of studies contextualizing the work of prominent ethnographers, often in ways that critically called into question the epistemological, positive-scientific appeal so prominently voiced in the works of e.g. Griaule, Boas or Malinowski (see e.g. Darnell, 1998; Stocking, 1992). So, whereas ethnography is by all standards a hugely successful enterprise, its respectability has never matched its influence in the social sciences.

'True' ethnography is rare – a fact perhaps deriving from its controversial status and the falsification of claims to positive scientificity by its founding fathers. More often than not, ethnography is perceived as a *method* for collecting particular types of data and thus as something that can be added, like the use of a computer, to different scientific procedures and programs. Even in anthropology, ethnography is often seen as a synonym for description. In the field of language, ethnography is popularly perceived as a technique and a series of propositions by means of which something can be said about 'context'. Talk can thus be separated from its context, and whereas the study of talk is a matter for linguistics, conversation analysis or discourse analysis, the study of context is a matter for ethnography (see Blommaert, 2001a, for a fuller discussion and references). What we notice in such discussions and treatments of ethnography is a reduction of ethnography to *fieldwork*, but naïvely, in the sense that the critical epistemological issues buried in seemingly simple fieldwork practices are not taken into account. Fieldwork/ethnography is perceived as *description*: an account of facts and experiences captured under the label of 'context', but in itself often un- or undercontextualized.

It is against this narrow view that I want to pit my argument, which will revolve around the fact that ethnography *can as well* be seen as a 'full' intellectual program far richer than just a matter of description. Ethnography, I will argue, involves a *perspective* on language and communication, including an ontology and an epistemology, both of which are of significance for the study of language in society, or better, of language *as well as* society. Interestingly, this programmatic view of ethnography emerges from critical voices from within ethnography. Rather than destroying the ethnographic project, critiques such as the ones developed by Fabian (1983, 1991a, 1995) and Hymes (1986 [1972], 1996) have added substance and punch to the program.

## Ethnography as a Perspective

A first correction that needs to be made to the widespread image of ethnography is that, right from the start, it was far more than a complex of fieldwork techniques. Ever since its beginnings in the works of Malinowski and Boas, it was part of a total program of scientific description and interpretation, comprising not only technical, methodical aspects (Malinowskian fieldwork) but also, e.g. cultural relativism and behaviorist-functionalist theoretical underpinnings. Ethnography was the scientific apparatus that put communities, rather than human-kind, on the map, focusing attention on the complexity of separate social units, the intricate relations between small features of a single system usually seen as in balance.[2] In Sapirian linguistics, folklore and descriptive linguistics went hand in hand with linguistic classification and historical-genetic treatments of cultures and societies. Ethnography was an approach in which systems were conceived as non-homogeneous, composed of a variety of features, and in which part–whole relationships were central to the work of interpretation and analysis. Regna Darnell's book on Boas (Darnell, 1998) contains a revealing discussion of the differences between Boas and

Sapir regarding the classification of North-American languages, and one of the striking things is to see how linguistic classification becomes a domain for the articulation of theories of culture and cultural dynamics, certainly in Boas' case (Darnell, 1998: 211ff). It is significant also that as ethnography became more sophisticated and linguistic phenomena were studied in greater detail and nuance, better and more mature theories of social units such as the speech community emerged (Gumperz, 1968).

So there always was more than just description in ethnography – problems of interpretation and indeed of ontology and epistemology have always figured in debates on and in ethnography, as did matters of method versus interpretation and issues of aligning ethnography with one discipline or another (linguistics versus anthropology being, e.g. the issue in the Boas-Sapir debate on classification). In fact, it is my conviction that ethnography, certainly in the works of its most prominent practitioners, has always had aspirations to *theory* status. No doubt, Dell Hymes' oeuvre stands out in its attempt at retrieving the historical roots of this larger ethnographic program (Hymes, 1964, 1983) as well as at providing a firm theoretical grounding for ethnography itself (Hymes, 1986 [1972], 1996). Hymes took stock of new reflections on 'theory' produced in Chomskyan linguistics, and foregrounded the issue in ethnography as well, and in clearer and more outspoken terms than before. To Hymes, ethnography was a 'descriptive theory': an approach that was theoretical because it provided description in specific, methodologically and epistemologically grounded ways.

I will discuss some of the main lines of argument in Hymes' work at some length here, adding, at points, important elements for our understanding of ethnography as taken from Johannes Fabian's work. Fabian, like Hymes, is probably best known for his documentary work (e.g. Fabian, 1986, 1996), while his theoretical reflections have not received the attention they deserve.

To start with, a crucial element in any discussion of ethnography should be its history, for inscribed in its techniques and patterns of operation are numerous traces of its intellectual origins and background. Ethnography has its origin in *anthropology*, not in linguistics nor in sociology or psychology. That means that the basic architecture of ethnography is one that already contains ontologies, methodologies and epistemologies that need to be situated within the larger tradition of anthropology and that do not necessarily fit the frameworks of other traditions. Central to this is *humanism*: 'It is anthropology's task to coordinate knowledge about language from the viewpoint of *man*' (Hymes, 1964: xiii). This means that language is approached as something that has a certain relevance to man, and man in anthropology is seen as a creature whose existence is narrowly linked, conditioned or determined by society, community, the group, culture. Language from an anthropological perspective is almost necessarily captured in a functionalist epistemology, and questions about language take the shape of questions of how language works and operates for, with and by humans-as-social-beings.[3]

Let us immediately sketch some of the implications of this humanist and functionalist anthropological background to ethnography. One important consequence has to do with the ontology, the definition of language itself. Language is typically seen as a socially loaded and assessed tool for humans, the finality of which is to enable humans to perform as social beings. Language, in this tradition, is defined as a *resource* to be used, deployed and exploited by human beings in social life and hence socially consequential for humans. Further implications of this will be addressed below. A second important implication is about context. There is no way in which language can be 'context-less' in this anthropological tradition in ethnography. To language, there is always a particular function, a concrete shape, a specific mode of operation and an identifiable set of relations between singular acts of language and wider patterns of resources and their functions. Language is context, it is the architecture of social behavior itself, and thus part of social structure and social relations. To this as well I will return below.

Let me summarize what has been said so far. Central to any understanding of ethnography are its roots in anthropology. These anthropological roots provide a specific direction to ethnography, one that situates language deeply and inextricably in social life and offers a particular and distinct ontology and epistemology to ethnography. Ethnography contains a *perspective* on language which differs from that of many other branches of the study of language. It is important to remember this, and despite possible relocations and redeployments of ethnography in different theoretical frameworks, the fact that it is designed to fit an anthropological set of questions is important for our understanding of what ethnography can and cannot perform. As Hymes says, 'failure to remember can confuse or impair anthropological thinking and research, setting up false antitheses and leaving significant phenomena unstudied' (Hymes, 1964: xxvii).

## Resources and Dialectics

Let us now get a little deeper into the features identified above: the particular ontology and epistemology characterizing ethnography.

Language is seen as a set of resources or means available to human beings in societies. These resources can be deployed in a variety of circumstances, but when this happens it never happens in a neutral way. Every act of language use is an act that is assessed, weighed, measured socially, in terms of contrasts between this act and others. In fact, language becomes the social and culturally embedded thing it is because of the fact that it is socially and culturally consequential in use. The clearest formulation of this resources view on language can be found in Hymes' essay 'Speech and language: On the origins and foundations of inequality among speakers' (Hymes, 1996: Chapter 3). In this strident essay, Hymes differentiates between a linguistic notion of language and an ethnographic notion of speech. Language, Hymes argues, is what linguists have made of it, a concept with little significance for the people who actually use language. Speech is language-in-society, i.e. an *active* notion and one that deeply situates language in a web of relations of power, a dynamics of availability and accessibility, a situatedness of single acts vis-à-vis larger social and historical patterns such as genres and traditions. Speech is language in which people have made investments – social, cultural, political, individual-emotional ones. It is also language brought under social control – consequently language marked by sometimes extreme cleavages and inequalities in repertoires and opportunities.

This has no small consequences to the study of language. For one thing, studying language means studying society; more precisely, it means that all kinds of different meanings, meaning effects, performativities and language functions can and need to be addressed than those current (and accepted) in mainstream linguistics.[4] Second, there is nothing static about this ethnographic view of language. Language appears in reality as performance, as actions performed by people in a social environment. Hence, strict synchrony is impossible as the deployment of linguistic resources is in itself, and step by step as sentences and utterances are interactionally constructed, a process. It is this process, and not its linguistic product (statified and reified sentences or utterances), that needs to be understood in ethnography. In order to acquire this understanding, as much attention needs to be given to what is seen from the statified and reified perspective mentioned as 'non-linguistic' matters as needs to be given to strictly 'linguistic' matters. It is at this point that one can understand how ethnography triggered important developments both in general sociology – Bourdieu's work is exemplary in this respect – as well as in kinesics, non-verbal communicative behavior and indeed social semiosis in general – Goffman, Garfinkel and Goodwin can be mentioned here. From an ethnographic perspective, the distinction between linguistic and non-linguistic is an artificial one since every act of language needs to be situated in wider patterns of human social behavior, and intricate connections between various aspects of this complex need to be specified: the ethnographic principle of *situatedness*.

It is also relevant to underscore the *critical* potential which ethnography derives from these principles. The constant feedback between communicative actions and social relations involves, as said, reflections on *value* of communicative practices, starting from the observation that not every form of communication is performed or performable in any situation. Society imposes hierarchies and value-scales on language, and the looking-glass of linguistic practice often provides a magnified image of the workings of powers and the deep structures of inequality in society. It is telling that some of the most critical studies on education have been produced by scholars using an ethnographic perspective (Cook-Gumperz, 1988; Gee, 1996; Heller, 2000; Rampton, 1995). Similarly, it is an interesting exercise to examine the critique formulated from within ethnography against other language scholars involved in the study of language and power. These critiques are not merely critiques of method; they are about the nature of language–power relationships (see Blommaert & Bulcaen, 2000; Blommaert *et al.*, 2001). And central to this critique is often the notion of language ideologies (Kroskrity, 2000; Woolard *et al.*, 1998): metalinguistic and hence deeply sociocultural ideas of language users about language and communication that not only appear to direct language behavior and the interpretation of language acts, but also account for folk and official 'rankings' and hierarchies of linguistic varieties.

Object-level (the 'acts' themselves) and metalevel (ideas and interpretations of these acts) cannot be separated in ethnography, for the social value of language is an intrinsic and constituent part of language usage itself; that is, in every act of language people inscribe and mark the social situatedness of these acts and so offer patterns of interpretation to the others. These patterns of interpretation are never fixed, of course, but require acknowledgment and interactional co-construction. So here also, strict synchronicity is impossible, for there is both a processual and a historical dimension to every act of language-in-society (Silverstein & Urban, 1996a), and the rankings and hierarchies of language are themselves an area of perpetual debate and conflict (Blommaert, 1999a). The social dimension of language is precisely the blending of linguistic and metalinguistic levels in communication: actions proceed with an awareness of how these actions should proceed and can proceed in specific social environments. And to be clear about this point, this means that every language act is intrinsically historical.

This brings me to the epistemological level of ethnography. Knowledge of language facts is processual and historical knowledge, lifting single instances of talk to a level of relevance far higher than just the event. They become indexical of patterns and developments of wider scope and significance, and these wider dimensions are part of ethnographic interpretation. Static interpretations of context – 'setting', 'speech community' and so forth – are anathema and to the extent that they occur in ethnographic writing they should be seen as either a rhetorical reduction strategy or, worse, as a falsification of the ethnographic endeavor (Fabian, 1983, 1995). Fabian stresses the dynamic process of knowledge gathering in ethnography, emphasizing the fact that ethnographic work also involves active – very active – involvement from the ethnographer himself (a fact known from the days of Malinowski and emphasized, e.g. by Edmund Leach, but often overlooked). This provides ethnography with a peculiar, dynamic and dialectical epistemology in which the *ignorance* of the knower – the ethnographer – is a crucial point of departure (Fabian, 1995). Consequently, ethnography attributes (and has to attribute) great importance to the history of what is commonly seen as 'data': the whole process of gathering and molding knowledge is part of that knowledge; knowledge construction *is* knowledge, the process is the product (see Blommaert, 2001a; Ochs, 1979).

Summarizing, language in ethnography is something very different from what it is in many other branches of language sciences, and so is the status of gathering knowledge. There is no way in which knowledge of language can be separated from the situatedness of the object at a variety of levels, ranging from microscopic to macroscopic levels of 'context' and involving, reflexively, the acts of knowledge production by ethnographers themselves.

## Ethnography as Counter-hegemony

Walter Benjamin once wrote that the task of historians was to challenge established and commonly accepted representations of history. History, in his view, was necessarily critical and counter-hegemonic, and a science such as history only had a *raison d'être* to the extent that it performed this role of challenging hegemonies. Exactly the same suggestion can be made with respect to ethnography: it has the potential and the capacity to challenge established views, not only of language but also of symbolic capital in societies in general. It is capable of constructing a discourse on social uses of language and social dimensions of meaningful behavior which differs strongly from established norms and expectations, and indeed takes the concrete functionings of these norms and expectations as starting points for questioning them; in other words, it takes them as problems rather than as facts.

Central to all of this is the mapping of resources onto functions: the way, for instance, in which a standard variety of a language acquires the function of 'medium of education' while a non-standard variety does not. This mapping is socially controlled; it is not a feature of language but one of society. Ethnography becomes critique here: the attributed function of particular resources is often a kind of social imagination, a percolation of social structure into language structure. Ethnography deconstructs this imagination and compares it with observable real forms and functions.

What does this mean for the study of literacy? The lack of an ethnography of writing has been lamented in the past, but in the meantime, thanks to scholars such as Brian Street, David Barton and others, a considerable body of scholarship has been composed and has become influential. It seems to me that the peculiarities of ethnography could induce a *materialist* approach to writing, in which the social-resources and social-evaluative aspects of literacy in relation to empowerment or disempowerment can be favorably studied. To the extent that such an approach to literacy draws attention away from statified and reified concepts such as 'literacy = written text', and delves into the conditions of production and the process of production so to speak, rather than to the product, I believe that this approach has an enormous critical potential.

## Acknowledgments

This paper benefited from illuminating comments by Dell Hymes. The gist of it was presented in the form of discussant's comments during a workshop on ethnography organized by BAAL and Cambridge University Press in Leicester, March 2001. Further down the road, many of the points offered here have been (and still are) the topic of conversations and debates with my associates in the FWO research group on 'Language, Power and Identity': Jim Collins, Monica Heller, Ben Rampton, Stef Slembrouck and Jef Verschueren. I gratefully acknowledge their input and influence.

## Notes

(1)  The journal *Ethnography,* launched in 2000, testifies to the impact of ethnography in a wide range of social sciences. An important, and frequent, contributor to the journal was Pierre Bourdieu, operating alongside sociocultural and linguistic anthropologists and micro-sociologists.

(2) Cf. Hymes (1980: 89): 'The earliest work that we recognize as important ethnography has generally the quality of being systematic in the sense of being *comprehensive*.'

(3) It may be interesting to point out that this view has percolated contemporary pragmatics. In the introduction to the *Handbook of Pragmatics* (Verschueren, 1995), pragmatics is defined as a functional perspective on language and communication. Verschueren refers, significantly, to Sapir (1929) as a source of inspiration for this view.

(4) At a very basic level, this pertains to the assumption that language *has* a function, and that its main purpose is *communication*. Truistic as it now may seem, at various points in the history of the language sciences these points required elaborate arguing.

# 2  Obituary: Dell H. Hymes (1927–2009)

Upon the passing away of Dell Hymes in November 2009, several obituaries appeared in major journals documenting his life and career in great chronological detail. Several special issues were recently published paying tribute to Hymes, and more are in the making. It seems that Dell Hymes' death triggered a wave of sympathy and recognition that he did not receive in the last stage of his life – an effect of the controversies and sensitivities surrounding this figure of power and influence during large parts of his career. It is good that the *Journal of Sociolinguistics* devotes space to him too. After all, Hymes was one of the genuine founding fathers of sociolinguistics, and his work remains an influence on what most of us practice today.

I only got to know Hymes personally during the very final days of his career as an almost retired professor at the University of Virginia. I was never part of the generation of scholars that had intense contact with Hymes during his heyday, when he gathered an extraordinary group of students and scholars around him at the University of Pennsylvania as Dean of Education in the 1970s, founded *Language in Society* and was President of the American Anthropological Association, the Linguistic Society of America, the American Folklore Association and the American Association for Applied Linguistics. In those days, I was merely a student who avidly read his works, struggled with the theoretical and methodological complexity in them, and became devoted to an ethnographic and critical paradigm because of them. Hymes to me was an early discovery; I read him as an early undergraduate and in retrospect always considered that an advantage. I could not claim to understand much of his work at that point, but later when I developed myself in linguistics and anthropology, these early readings of Hymes' work provided me with a model of synthesis, a frame in which so many things could fit and begin to make sense not as isolated themes and approaches but as elements of a broad programmatic vision, sketched by Hymes, of the study of language in society.

This is how I prefer to remember him and to use his legacy: as a framework that enables the incorporation of a vast field of social-scientific angles, tools and instruments. Hymesian sociolinguistics – which he himself used to prefer to call ethnography – is a full-blown theoretical program, designed and constructed as an alternative for the Chomskyan hegemony in the 1970s, grounded in the traditions of anthropology, folklore and linguistics, and thus concerned not with language in and for itself, but with language because it offers us a privileged understanding of society. Hymes' anthropological roots are crucial for an understanding of the scope of his program and ambition. Hymes took anthropology literally as the 'study of man', and language studies had to tell us something about man, about human nature and human society, and in particular about that link between human nature and human society which we call culture. Hymesian ethnography is therefore profoundly humanistic, in the sense that it takes human life as its object and target, and it allows us to address the producers of language not just as 'speaker/hearers', but as *subjects* in the anthropological and broader social-scientific sense of the term. How people understand one another, why they want such a thing and why they spend such monumental efforts doing so, those were the questions Hymes took as his central heuristics. Voice – the capacity to make oneself understood – was always a central concern in this: understanding is never just a practical and instrumental phenomenon, it is a social, cultural and political praxis that creates, sustains or changes subjects, and places them in relations to one another. As a Marxist, Hymes would qualify these relations invariably as unequal, and both his ethnopoetic reconstructions of defunct native oral poetry from the Pacific Coast and his work in education were inspired and driven by a recognition that language is not just an opportunity but a problem for many people. His sociolinguistics was targeted at real and critical problems of language in society; it was, in other words, a fundamentally political approach to language. The humanism that was central to his work was a Marxist humanism that had an emancipatory and liberating political struggle as its finality. And just like Marx' humanism, Hymes' fundamental commitment to human development, nor his implicit view of what people are and how they relate to one another, have received the attention they deserved.

This, alas, counts for so much of his work. Hymes was not always an engaging author, and as a public speaker, I have rarely come across anyone worse. I chaired the plenary lecture he gave at the 1998 International Pragmatics Conference in Reims, and I found myself sitting next to an utterly nervous, almost incapacitated speaker who delivered superb, fantastic contents in the most inadequate style of public oratory – a problem of voice he himself had so often documented in his own work, and of which, apparently, he had his own rich experiences. In a recent issue of *Language in Society*, several of Hymes' former students testified about his challenging lecturing style, saying that unless one took a front-row seat and concentrated hard, much of what Hymes delivered during his lectures would be lost.

His written work, too, is often dense and complex. Hymes, of course, has written highly readable, sometimes almost pamphlet-like texts. The editorial notes (or rather, essays) he added, for instance, to the readings in his 1964 collection *Language in Culture and Society* are a marvel in didactic terms, and students interested in linguistic anthropology will find there a clear definition and delineation of the scope of this discipline. The same goes for the introduction to *Reinventing Anthropology*: the text is combative, almost militant, and brings fundamental insights to readers in an accessible, user-friendly way. A little-known brochure from 1963, in fact a published version of a lecture for the Voice of America called 'A perspective for linguistic anthropology', is a text that should be on the compulsory reading list of every Sociolinguistics 101 course. In just a dozen pages, Hymes summarizes the history of language as an anthropological object and of linguistics as a 20th-century science. Having stated the gap between this object and the science that should address it, he then sketches a programmatic view for the approach he was then designing, linguistic anthropology. It is a jewel of solidly intellectual didactic writing, and it is my secret hope that some journal will reprint it in the near future.

But even in such accessible work, there is a layer of tremendous complexity, because Hymes draws on a massive amount of knowledge of the Boasian anthropological tradition, of philology and of linguistic structuralism, a phenomenal control of linguistic and narrative analytic detail, and a broad range of large theoretical and political issues palatable only for the very erudite. My second year undergraduates of some years ago will forever remember (and curse) me for having assigned Hymes' essay 'Two types of linguistic relativity' to them – a paper of immense value for understanding that foundational point Hymes made, that languages are not just linguistic systems but also, and foremost, sociolinguistic systems. The paper was, to put it bluntly, unreadable. And consequently, it was not read. The same goes for other landmark papers of his. 'Models of the interaction of language and social life', in the epochal *Directions in Sociolinguistics* that Hymes edited with John Gumperz, is another case in point, as is the invaluable 'Breakthrough into performance', a paper that revolutionized the field of narrative analysis and, *en passant*, also makes some superb points about ethnographic technique and modes of research.

I will not mention *In Vain I Tried to Tell You*, a book everyone should read regardless of race, class, age or gender, but which demands quite an effort to digest. The point is that those who really wish to enter into the theoretically more developed parts of Hymes' oeuvre must come equipped and prepared, because it is tough reading.

Such work has laid the foundations for what we now know as linguistic anthropology, and in fact for what we now understand as the ethnographic branch of sociolinguistics. Those who thoroughly read and studied it were invariably profoundly influenced by it, and it is impossible to read contemporary work without hearing the resonances of Hymes' fundamental insights, even if such resonances are muffled or kept implicit. We see an increasing interest in ethnographic approaches in our fields of study, and one hopes that this increasing interest will be articulated in a renewed and serious attention to Hymes' oeuvre. That means that people will have to talk about more than that S.P.E.A.K.I.N.G. mnemotechnic when they talk about Hymes, and do justice to the fullness of his work. That includes, in my view, at least the following points.

*One*, language needs to be seen as a sociolinguistic system, i.e. a system that only exists and operates in conjunction with social rules and relations.

*Two*, this sociolinguistic system needs to be understood not by reference to 'Language' with a capital L (the things that have a name, such as Latin, French, Russian), but by reference to repertoires. Such repertoires are an organized complex of specific resources such as varieties, modes, genres, registers and styles.

*Three*, in every social unit, such resources are unevenly distributed; there are no identical repertoires among speakers, and inequality is the key to understanding language in society. Nobody is the perfect native speaker, because nobody possesses all the resources any language makes available. No one speaks *all* of the language. And, no, not all languages are equal. They should be, but they are not in actual fact.

*Four*, repertoires can only be understood by attending to their functions, i.e. to their actual and contextual deployment, not to any abstract or *a priori* assessment of what they mean or of what they are worth. A standard variety of language is not always 'the best' variety, and a 'substandard' variety is not always a 'bad' variety (as Hip-hop makes so clear). The function of particular forms of speech is a contextual, empirical given, not an *a priori*.

*Five*, this is why a sociolinguistic system requires ethnographic inspection, in which particular and unique instances can be related to larger patterns and to social structure – the key to finding out what there is to find is not to ask, but to observe and describe in relation to a general theory of social behavior. Ethnography is a 'descriptive theory' in Hymes' words.

*Six*, such an ethnography requires a historical awareness, and this clashes with the synchronic view of contemporary linguistics since Saussure. If we want to understand the actual functions of forms of language, we have to know where they come from, how they entered people's repertoires, and how they relate to larger patterns of social and cultural behavior.

*Seven*, all of this is situated in a real world of real problems and issues, not in an abstract or ideal universe. Ethnography has mud on its boots.

And *eight*, no social cause is served by poor work. Critical commitment demands never-ending attention to theoretical and methodological improvement. If we believe that languages and their speakers should be equal, we have to understand their actual inequalities precisely and in detail, and not be satisfied by reiterating the slogans of equality. We have to do the hard work of describing, understanding and explaining, and we have to do that over and over again.

I could add several other points, but the eight I have listed may do as an alternative for the eight points listed under S.P.E.A.K.I.N.G. If people (re)turn to Hymes' work with these points in mind, which I firmly hope, I am convinced that they will find a treasure there – a theoretical and methodological treasure, surely, but also a selection and motivation of topics and fields of activity worth considering, and an ethos of being a student of language in society. No one who has ever ventured into his work left without nuggets in his/her pocket. May that tradition survive the man.

# 3 Ethnography and Democracy: Hymes' Political Theory of Language

## Introduction

Dell Hymes' work is, like that of Bourdieu and Bernstein, but also that of Gumperz and Goffman, highly political. Texts such as the essay 'Speech and language' (Hymes, 1996: Chapter 3), or the introductory essay to his *Reinventing Anthropology* (2002 [1969]) explicitly testify to that. Most of his oeuvre, however, can be read as a political statement, an attempt toward a critical science of language in social life, toward 'a union of knowledge and social values' (Hymes, 2002 [1969]: 51). Hymes would often mention his own background as an explanation for this, especially his experiences as a GI enlisted so as to gain access to college education under the GI Bill, and stationed in the Far East. Hymes saw Hiroshima shortly after the bomb; the madness and scale of human rage witnessed there turned him into someone whose main concerns were peace, equality and solidarity, a man of the left. And his program was an oppositional response to the direction taken by linguistics after the Second World War: an opposition that he would compare with that of Marx to Feuerbach (Hymes, 1996: 99, 189; Marx appears with amazing frequency in the introductory essay of *Reinventing Anthropology* as well). It was an approach in which the proclaimed ('idealist') equality of the Chomskyan universal language faculty was countered by an empirical and contextually grounded ('materialist') focus on real existing conditions of use, marked by inequalities. Political affinities between Hymes and Chomsky did not interfere with robust disagreements over the intellectual programs that both advocated. Hymes defined the goal of the ethnography of speaking as 'to explain the meaning of language in human life, and not in the abstract, not in the superficial phrases one may encounter in essays and textbooks, but in the concrete, in actual human lives' (Hymes,

1986 [1972]: 41). That was an academic and intellectual program, but also a political one. He also consistently underscored the importance of broader ethical and political values in anthropological work. Anthropology, to him, needed to make general statements on human societies, and such statements would need to have a critical and radical edge:

> I would hope to see the consensual ethos of anthropology move from a liberal humanism, defending the powerless, to a socialist humanism, confronting the powerful and seeking to transform the structures of power. (Hymes, 2002 [1969]: 52)

In what follows, I want to discuss one of the implicit political dimensions of Hymesian ethnography: the way in which, to Hymes, it could be a *democratic* and *anti-hegemonic* science. Ethnography would be a science 'of the people' in the sense that it would keep its two feet in the lived experience of those whom it studied, and that it therefore would abstain from pontificating and *a priori* theorizing but instead offer voice to those it studied. In that sense, it would also be an anti-hegemonic science, one that destabilized accepted views by allowing different voices to speak: a science that constantly called into question the status of 'truth', and constantly negated what is known by going out to find more (see the discussion in Fabian, 2001). Ethnography, to Hymes, was the study of 'the interaction of language and social life' (Hymes, 1986 [1972]): an approach in which language and society blended, and which consequently could yield more precise understandings of language *and* of society. It was the critical science *par excellence*.

I will develop these points first by looking at the larger theoretical edifice of Hymesian ethnography. Often, ethnography is presented in an absurdly reductionist way, as a complex of methods for data collection and description (many, for instance, would speak of 'ethnography' as soon as a piece of research is based on *interviews*, as if interviews would be *per se* ethnographic). Yet Hymes' oeuvre and that of other leaders of the tradition in which he included himself are littered with theoretical statements that show that ethnography is a theory complex, a paradigm, and not just a method. It is this *theory* (not the method) that makes ethnography critical and democratic in Hymes view.

After that, I will turn to Hymes' ethnopoetic work as an example of the critical and political aspects of Hymesian ethnographic theory. Even if ethnopoetics can be seen as a form of philology, it is aimed at a reconstruction of voice – of silenced voices to be precise, in an act that 'liberate[s]' them (Hymes, 2003: 11).[1] The reconstruction is again more than a refined philological method: it is an *ethnography of text*, a theoretically dense and complex approach that re-creates the text not for the analyst, but for its original community of users.

## Ethnography as a Democratic Science

Hymes held a firm belief in the critical potential and the emancipatory value of ethnography. According to him, 'good ethnography ... will be of perennial importance' for at least two reasons:

> On the one hand, there is much that ethnographers do that is wanted done by local communities, from preservation of languages and traditions ... to help with problems of schools. On the other hand, where social transformation is in question, Anna Louise Strong once said that if Lenin himself came to your town, he would have to know what you know about it before he could plan a revolution there. (Hymes, 2002 [1969]: 56)

So ethnography was the key to his political vision, and he saw an immense political benefit to spreading ethnography beyond the small community of anthropologists who practiced it. This has not been materialized. Ethnography is more often than not misunderstood, and I need to return to the points I developed in Chapter 1.

'True' ethnography is rare, I argued there, and much too often it is perceived as a *method* for collecting particular types of data and thus as something to be added to different scientific procedures and programs – 'ethnographic interviews' thus presented are therefore very often entirely un-ethnographic interviews. Furthermore, ethnography is often seen as a synonym for description, for *fieldwork*, and in the field of language, ethnography is often presented as a technique and a series of propositions by means of which something can be said about 'context'. All of these views are tremendously reductionist and bypass the critical epistemological issues buried in seemingly simple fieldwork (see Blommaert & Dong, 2010, for an extensive discussion).

Hymes has been a victim of such reductions. His theoretical program is hardly ever fully addressed and the coherence between various key parts of his oeuvre – between, e.g. his views of communicative competence and those on function and form – is hardly ever highlighted. The effects of such reductions are that many students in linguistics and adjacent disciplines only get to know Hymes through that silly mnemotechnic acronym 'S.P.E.A.K.I.N.G.', often presented as a definition of ethnography. Or they are given the version of communicative competence that became widely used among psycholinguists and applied linguists as a shorthand for that bit of pragmatic skill that people fortunately have in addition to their Language Acquisition Device – a version of communicative competence that bears only the vaguest and most distant traces of its Hymesian origins (see Hymes, 1992, for comments on this topic). The previous chapter should, I hope, have addressed some of these caricatures and replaced them with an invitation to explore and address the full scope and complexity of Hymes' theoretical efforts.

Hymes was deeply convinced that ethnography has the potential and the capacity to challenge established views, not only of language but also of symbolic capital in societies in general. It is capable of constructing a discourse on social uses of language and social dimensions of meaningful behavior, which differs strongly from established norms and expectations. As we saw earlier, it takes the concrete functioning of these norms and expectations as starting points for questioning them in relation to the really available linguistic means that people actually have. In other words, it takes them as problems rather than as facts; 'The fundamental vantage point must be what means of speech are available to a group and what meanings they find in them and give them' (Hymes, 1996: 83). The social and political dimensions of the distribution and stratification of linguistic and communicative resources (discussed more fully in Chapter 1) are central to this.

Hymes' ethnography is also critical in another sense. Whereas in most other approaches, the target of scientific method is *simplification and reduction of complexity*, the target in ethnography is precisely the opposite. Reality is kaleidoscopic, complex and complicated, often a patchwork of overlapping activities. Compare it with a soccer game. Usually, when we watch a soccer game on TV, we are focused on the movement of the ball and on a limited number of players in the area where the ball is. We rarely see all 22 players in the same shot on TV: the lens directs our attention to a subset of the space, the actors and activities. What we miss is the movement of the other players, the way they position themselves in anticipation of what comes next; we also miss the directions they give to one another, by shouting, pointing, pulling faces or making specific gestures. The 22 players perform all sorts of activities simultaneously. All of the players are constantly monitoring each other, and the coach does the same, shouting instructions to players from the sideline whenever he spots a potential problem. All of this happens at the same time, it is a series of seemingly unrelated – but obviously related – activities, very hard to describe in a linear and coherent narrative, *because as an activity it is not linear and coherent* but multiple, layered, chequered, unstable.

A full account of a soccer game – and think of Goffman here – should include all of that, for all of it is essential in understanding what happens during the game. Players usually do not arrive at particular positions by accident or luck; they are there because of the complex interlocking activities that produce the game. Ethnography tries to do just that: describe the apparently messy and complex activities that make up social action, not to reduce their complexity but to describe and explain it. This is what makes ethnography a demanding approach: it is not enough (not by a very long shot) to follow a clear, pre-set line of inquiry and the researcher cannot come thundering in with pre-established truths. The procedure is what Hymes (1980: 89) calls 'democratic': 'a mutual relation of interaction and adaptation' between ethnographers and the people they work with, 'a relation that will change both'. Or to be more precise:

> The fact that good ethnography entails trust and confidence, that it requires some narrative accounting, and that it is an extension of a universal form of personal knowledge, make me think that ethnography is peculiarly appropriate to a democratic society. It could of course be reduced to a technique for the manipulation of the masses by the elite. As envisioned here, ethnography had the potentiality for helping to overcome divisions of society into those who know and those who are known. (Hymes, 1996: 14)

Ethnography relies on 'a mutuality not only of trust, but also of knowledge' (Hymes, 1969 [2002]: 53) and is in that sense a science that can emancipate by sharing knowledge with those who usually are left out of the circulation of knowledge. That too is counter-hegemonic.

## Democracy and Voice: The Politics of Ethnopoetics

Throughout his career, one of Hymes' foremost empirical concerns was the analysis of Native American narrative. Many of his theoretical reflections on communicative competence, function and functional relativity, language–culture relationships, repertoires and linguistic inequality emerged out of questions encountered in the kind of analysis that is now known as ethnopoetics. Some of his most theoretically innovative essays present elaborate ethnopoetic analyses: 'Two types of linguistic relativity' (Hymes, 1966) and 'Breakthrough into performance' (Hymes, 1975) are cases in point. And his *Ethnography, Linguistics, Narrative Inequality* book (Hymes, 1996) – his theoretically most powerful statement – has ethnopoetic analysis as its engine. Ethnopoetics was the topic of *In Vain I*

*Tried to Tell You* (Hymes, 1981) and of his latest *Now I Know Only so Far* (Hymes, 2003) – more on this in Chapter 4.

Hymes's efforts in ethnopoetics can be seen from one angle as deviating from his other work, which focused on the ethnography of situated, contextualized speech events (Hymes himself flags this 'deviation' and amply motivates it (2003: 11); compare also Hymes (1981: Chapter 1)). Yet there is more that ties ethnopoetics into his other work than separates it. Hymes' ethnopoetic work is one way of addressing the main issue in ethnography: to describe (and reconstruct) languages not in the sense of stable, closed and internally homogeneous units characterizing parts of mankind, but as ordered complexes of genres, styles, registers and forms of use: *languages as repertoires or sociolinguistic systems* (not only linguistic systems), in short. And ethnopoetics is urgently needed, because many languages are not only endangered as linguistic systems, but also, and perhaps even more critically, *as sociolinguistic systems* – genres, styles, ways of speaking becoming obsolete or unpracticed.[2] In Hymes' own words: 'sociolinguistic systems disappear before their languages, perhaps several generations before. If salvage linguistics is urgent, salvage sociolinguistics is doubly urgent' (Hymes, 1966: 158).

Ethnopoetic analyses attempt to unearth culturally embedded ways of speaking – materials and forms of using them, that belong to the sociolinguistic system of a group (or groups), and that have a particular place in a repertoire owing to their specific, characteristic form–function relationships. Such form–function relationships, Hymes argues, are complex and display 'second linguistic relativity' – a relativity of *functions* rather than form (as in Whorf's 'first' relativity; Hymes, 1966), causing a need to investigate functions empirically, that is ethnographically.[3] In that sense, ethnopoetics fits into the general theoretical ambitions of the ethnography of speaking.

It also fits into Hymes' more general concerns with language functions, notably with narrative and performance. Hymes starts from what he calls 'a narrative view of the world' (Hymes, 1996: 112), in which narrative is 'a universal function' of language, subject, however, to all kinds of constraints and socioculturally framed restrictions on use: narrative is a way of using language which possesses limited legitimacy and acceptability (Hymes, 1996: 115). Furthermore, it is rarely seen as a vehicle for rational, 'cognitive' communication, and often stereotyped as affective, emotional and interpersonal (remember Bernstein's restricted codes). In contrast to this widespread view (both lay and specialized), Hymes sees narrative as a central mode of language use, in which cognitive, emotional, affective, cultural, social and aesthetic aspects combine (see especially Hymes, 1975).

They combine in *implicit form* – and here Hymes' approach to narrative starts to differ from that of many others (e.g. Labov), who focused on *explicit* form and *explicit contents*, and who saw narrative largely as a repository of explicitly voiced facts, images and concerns. Consequently (and this defines much of the tradition of folklore studies) stories could be asked for and elicited, and performance could be invited, while the results were seen as *the* tradition, folklore, even 'culture' of the performers. Hymes' approach differs fundamentally. To Hymes, the essence of narrative – what makes it poetic – is an implicit level of structure: the fact that stories are organized in lines, verses and stanzas, connected by a 'grammar' of narration (a set of formal features identifying and connecting parts of the story) and by implicit organizational patterns, pairs, triplets, quartets etc. This structure is only partly a matter of awareness: it is the 'cultural' dimension of narration. Most speakers produce it without being aware of its functions and effects, and good narrators are those who can stage a performance organized through 'the synchronization of incident and measure' (Hymes, 1996: 166).

Consequently, narration involves the blending of at least two kinds of 'competence': the competence to organize experience, events, images in a 'telling' way, and the competence to do so in a sequentially organized complex of measured form (Hymes, 1996: 198). This is not a random thing: narratives are 'organized in ways that make them formally poetry, and also a rhetoric of action; they embody an implicit schema for the organization of experience' (Hymes, 1996: 121). More precisely, 'the relationships between verses ... are grouped in an implicit cultural patterning of the form of action, a logic or rhetoric of experience, if you will, such that the form of language and the form of culture are one and the same at this point' (Hymes, 1996: 139).

So implicitness – its recognition and interpretation – is central to Hymes' concerns. It is by recognizing that a lot of what people produce in the way of meaning is implicit that we can reflect more sensibly

on the general problem of assessing behavioural repertoire, and [alert] students to the small portion of cultural behavior that people can be expected to report or describe, when asked, and the much smaller portion that an average person can be expected to manifest by doing on demand. (Some social research seems incredibly to assume that what there is to find out can be found out by asking.) (Hymes, 1981: 84)

In other words, it is through investigating implicit form that we get to a vastly wider, richer and complex domain of cultural-linguistic organization, one that has been overlooked by much of 20th-century linguistics. This more complex domain is also a domain of more complex functions, the aesthetic (or 'presentational', in Hymes' terms) functions being central to it. And for Hymes, narrative is the mode of language use in which such presentational functions coincide with denotational, cognitive, affective and interpersonal ones.

Hymes' ethnopoetics addressed oral traditions that were, or were about to become, defunct. Many of his analyses address stories originally recorded, edited and published by Sapir and other anthropologists of that generation. According to Hymes, the way in which such stories were recorded and later presented – as *prose not poetry* – had made them 'function-less': they no longer had the capacity to fulfil the cultural and social roles they had in the societies that produced them. Ethnopoetics, then, was a technique used to restore such defunct traditions, a form of *functional reconstruction* (Blommaert, 2006a; cf Chapter 4 below).

This could easily be read as a classic instance of salvage linguistics or salvage sociolinguistics, and nothing would be wrong with that. But once again, now that we know a thing or two about Hymes' overtly political approach to ethnography, there is more. The effort of reconstruction is inspired by an acute awareness of inequality and a desire for equity. Reconstructing the functions of narratives is not just a matter of reconstructing latent cultural heritage, it is a politics of recognition that starts from a restoration of disempowered people as bearers and producers of valuable culture, over which they themselves have control: recognizing one's language, to Hymes, means recognizing one's specific ways of speaking, one's voice. It is, thus, an attempt to avoid an anthropology that only provides 'a defensive source of knowledge about the exploited of the world for those who exploit it' (Hymes, 2002 [1969]: 51). This is how Hymes concludes *In Vain I Tried to Tell You*:

> We must work to make visible and audible again that something more – the literary form in which the native words had their being – so that they can move again at a pace that is surer, more open to the voice, more nearly their own. (Hymes, 1981: 384)

*Voice* – this is what functional reconstruction is about. Ultimately, what ethnopoetics does is to show voice, to visualize the particular ways – often deviant from hegemonic norms – in which subjects produce meanings. As mentioned earlier, in Hymes' view (most eloquently articulated in Hymes, 1996), voice is the capacity to make oneself understood in one's own terms, to produce meanings under conditions of empowerment. (Note that Hymes' notion of voice differs from, and in many ways functions as a more flexible alternative to Bakhtinian notions of voice.) In the present world, such conditions are wanting for more and more people. The Native American storytellers are obvious victims of minoritization, but Hymes (1996) extends the scope of ethnopoetic reconstructions to include other marginal groups in society – African Americans, working-class college students, other minorities. Interestingly, such groups frequently appear to be the victim of a very Bernsteinian phenomenon: the negative stereotyping of part of their repertoire, the dismissal of their ways of speaking as illegitimate, irrational, not-to-the-point, *narrative* rather than factual (Bernstein would say: restricted rather than elaborate), and 'one form of inequality of opportunity in our society has to do with rights to use narrative, with whose narratives are admitted to have a cognitive function' (Hymes, 1996: 109).

More in general, Hymes observes (alongside many others, e.g. Gumperz, Labov, Bourdieu) that 'making sense' often, concretely, is narrowed to 'making sense *in particular ways*', using very specific linguistic, stylistic and generic resources, thus disqualifying different resources even when they are perfectly valid in view of the particular functions to be realized. It is in this world in which difference is quickly converted into inequality that attention to 'emic' forms of discursive organization takes on more than just an academic import and becomes a political move, aimed at the recognition of variation and variability as 'natural' features of societies, and at recognizing that variation in cultural behavior can result in many potentially equivalent solutions to similar problems.

This, consequently, radicalizes the issue of diversity, because it shifts the question from one of latent potential equivalence to one of effective disqualification and inequality. If all languages are equal, how come some (many!) are not recognized even as languages? How come that the latent and potential equivalence of languages, in actual practice, converts into rigid language hierarchies? That potential equality is matched by actual inequality? That 'unfamiliar pattern may be taken to be absence of pattern' (Hymes, 1996: 174)? Part of Hymes' answers is that diversity still requires deeper understanding as to its actual forms, structures and functions. Misunderstanding of such aspects of diversity, often resulting from errors in past work or sloppiness in current work, precludes appreciation of diversity *as a solution*. It also precludes a critical understanding of diversity in society and of the power relations in which it is couched. It fails to live up to the emancipatory potential of ethnographic work and allows work to 'drift backwards into the service of domination' (Hymes, 2002 [1969]: 54).

In this respect, he is particularly hopeful that a different universal dimension of human sense-making may be found in the numbered patterns he discovers in Native American texts. Such patterns, he submits, could recast visions of diversity:

> In sum, there lies ahead a vast work, work in which members of narrative communities can share, the work of discovering forms of implicit patterning in oral narratives, patterning largely out of awareness, *relations* grounded in a universal *potential*, whose *actual* realization varies. To demonstrate its presence can enhance respect for an appreciation of the voices of others. (Hymes, 1996: 219)

This is no longer just about developing a better, more accurate philology of native texts; ethnopoetics here becomes a program for understanding voice *and the reasons why voice is an object and instrument of power* with potential to include as well as to exclude. It becomes a critical *sociolinguistic* method that offers us a way into the concrete linguistic shape of sociocultural inequality in societies. Here is democracy again in Hymes' program, and ethnography is again the instrument for that.

## Conclusions

Hymes' oeuvre is heartening to its readers, and those who get drawn to it are often attracted by the intensity of the argument he presents and by the clear opportunities he offers to build bridges between academic practice, social values and political principle. It was a critical discourse analysis long before anyone laid claim to that term. It is a pity that its readership is so small. As mentioned before, students often only come across it in a massacred form devoid of the depth and scope it offers. And even among more sophisticated academics, his theoretical oeuvre is rarely explored – a fate he shares with one of his sources of inspiration, Benjamin Lee Whorf.

The effect is that his oeuvre, much like that of Whorf, remains an untapped source of theory of significance of current studies of language in society. Susan Ervin-Tripp's repeated claim that 'we have no fully developed contextual theory of language' is correct, but the different pieces we find in Hymes' oeuvre and in that of scholars inspired by his work offer already quite a lot in that direction. The theory he offers is contextual and is therefore critical. The link between both may be surprising to those who see context as a neutral canvass, as 'background' to linguistic phenomena. It is not surprising to those who accept Hymes' view that context is a lived environment full of inequalities and constraints. Consequently, his ethnography does not just address text, it addresses and questions context. It does so from within an elaborate epistemology and methodology in which the political is a fundamental feature, not an *a priori* or *a posteriori* claim to relevance by the analyst. This mature view of text and context, language and culture, speech, voice and social life makes Hymes a theoretical source of fundamental importance to what we do.

## Notes

(1)   Hymes has no problems whatsoever with the qualification of 'philology'. Defining ethnopoetic analysis, Hymes (1966: 141) writes: 'In aim, the method is structural, but in execution it must also be philological'. Note the 'structural' here: Hymes (2003: 123) talks of ethnopoetics as a form of 'practical structuralism'.

(2)   Moore (2000: 67) has more recently noted the emphasis 'in the "endangered languages" discussion ... on languages qua grammatical systems (and/or systems of nomenclature), as artefacts ... of cognition: something akin to the Elgin Marbles, perhaps, in the realm of conceptualization'. See also Blommaert (2005c) for an ethnographic critique of such views of language endangerment. Hymes (1996) provides rich discussions of this point.

(3)   According to Hymes, modern linguistics has consistently overlooked the problem of functional relativity, often wrongly taking functional stability and formal variability as the central assumption of analysis. This point is forcefully developed in Hymes (1996); see also Hymes (1980: Chapter 1). The need to empirically establish relations between forms and functions is what led Hymes to speak of ethnography as a 'descriptive theory' (1986 [1972]).

# 4 Ethnopoetics as Functional Reconstruction: Dell Hymes' Narrative View of the World[1]

*In Vain I Tried to Tell You* was published by the University of Pennsylvania Press in 1981; it quickly gained recognition as an important book. It also quickly gained recognition as one of the most difficult books to read, complex in structure and argument and replete with long and extremely detailed analyses and re-analyses.[2] Consequently, it is doubtful whether it was widely read, and it went out of print some years ago. I considered this a tragic defeat for scholarship, for there are books that deserve to remain in print simply because they are good and important, not because they sell well. In light of this, the new edition of *In Vain I Tried to Tell You* by the University of Nebraska Press (Hymes, 2004) should be warmly welcomed, and one hopes that this new edition will be treated with more courtesy by the readership than its predecessor.

There are very good reasons to be hopeful, for whereas the first edition (Hymes, 1981) of *In Vain I Tried to Tell You* (henceforth IV) was a rather lonely book on any shelf, the second edition can be read alongside two other major publications by Hymes on ethnopoetics: the small study *Reading Takelma Texts* (Hymes, 1998, henceforth RT) and the rather more monumental *Now I Know Only So Far* (Hymes, 2003, henceforth NK). Taken together, they now constitute a voluminous, complex and rich oeuvre demonstrating the tremendous linguistic and anthropological skill, the capacity for meticulous, scrupulous analysis of detail, and the unstinting, challenging theoretical and historical insight of Hymes. One could add Hymes' *Ethnography, Linguistics, Narrative Inequality* (Hymes, 1996; henceforth EL) to the pile of must-reads, for there as well the theoretical argument is underpinned by copious, detailed and rich ethnopoetic analyses, and ethnopoetic analysis is predicated explicitly on concerns for justice and equality. I will refer to EL in what follows, because it can now be read as an introductory volume to the more 'technical' ethnopoetic publications IV, RT and NK.

In addition to the expansion of Hymes' own work, there is now a much more widespread appreciation of implicit form in language, of poetic patterning in narrative and of the indexical (i.e. implicit, often iconic) organization of speech, and prominent scholars have published magnificent surveys and analyses (see, e.g. Bauman & Briggs, 1990; Moore, 1993; Ochs & Capps, 2001; Haviland, 1996a, 1997; Silverstein, 1985b, 1997, 2005b). There is thus now an infinitely richer environment for reading Hymes' ethnopoetic studies than there was at the time of the publication of IV. This does not mean, to be sure, that the reading is any easier than it was 20 years ago. Having ventured into ethnopoetic analysis on some occasions, I can testify to the fact that it is a demanding, tough kind of analysis requiring skill, patience and analytic insight in a variety of technical domains, from phonetics over grammar to discourse and narrative analysis, sociolinguistics and cultural anthropology. This complexity in analytical process converts into complexity in presentation, and this in turn demands concentrated and careful reading. Ethnopoetic studies are not exactly novels. In addition, ethnopoetics itself is often misunderstood and misrepresented, and unless the fundamental assumptions are well understood, works such as these may be perceived as overly detailed, technical and dull. Ethnopoetics suffers from the same curse as phonetics: unless one understands its function, value and potential applicability, it is a very unattractive thing.

In what follows, I will introduce ethnopoetics in general terms, avoiding a technical exposé (for which, anyway, there is no substitute to reading Hymes' work) but focusing on the main theoretical assumptions underlying it. Next, I will engage in a discussion of the way in which Hymes sees ethnopoetic analysis as a tactic for restoring, reconstructing and repatriating the functions of narratives. Finally, I will turn to the critical and humanist dimensions of Hymes' ethnopoetics, arguing for a political reading of his ethnopoetic work. But before that, let us have a quick look at the books.

## Books and Oeuvres

Throughout this essay, the books will be treated as an oeuvre: not a complete one and even less a closed one, but a consistent scholarly effort resulting in different books. It is recommendable – because immensely rewarding – to read the three volumes in one effort, as an oeuvre and a serious introduction-and-immersion into ethnopoetic theory and analysis. When such is impossible, it is still worth keeping in mind that the books are connected by common lines of argument, visions of what narrative is, and ideologies of research – elements that I will try to spell out in the sections below.

Chronologically, IV is the precursor of the two other ones, and Hymes sets out, step by step, to define the challenges, purposes and possibilities of ethnopoetics. The pivot of the book is the essay 'Breakthrough into performance' (Chapter 3) – a text of fundamental importance even decades after its first circulation. In 'Breakthrough', Hymes defines the central theoretical preoccupations of ethnopoetics; he sketches the field in which ethnopoetics plays. It involves issues of competence, real versus potential ability, the development and 'bringing about' of genres, different kinds of performance, and the way in which linguistic form (e.g. code- and style-shifting) is mobilized in performance. Around that central essay, Hymes collects studies that describe the state of affairs in scholarship of Native American folklore and studies that re-analyze and retranslate pre-viously published texts from the North Pacific coast of North America, in Clackamas Chinook, Wasco Chinook, Takelma, Kwakiutl and Haida.

In IV, Hymes repeatedly emphasizes that there is very little work on Native American oral tradition going on, and that what there is often suf-fers from serious methodological defects; Hymes repeatedly insists that there is some urgency here, as the materials, speakers and occasions for performance are disappearing fast. RT and NK both express this sense of urgency: in contrast to the more theoretical ambitions of IV, they both seem to have mainly documentary goals, to present a maximum of eth-nopoetically analyzed texts. RT is a careful edition and analysis of a Takelma myth, 'Coyote and frog', narrated by Frances Johnson in 1906 and recorded, later published by Edward Sapir. As a stand-alone study of a single text, it is exemplary, and it can serve as a pocket-format summary of ethnopoetics. Hymes takes us all the way up from 'discovery' of the text, the identification of the problematic nature of its first edition, and the careful reconstruction of the story as a poetically organized narrative, oriented toward local and universal motifs and organizing principles. NK is far wider in scope, and it represents Hymes' second attempt at summa-rizing his views on ethnopoetics and accomplishments in analysis. Like IV, it is again organized around central essays, two in this case: 'Use all there is to use' (Chapter 3) and 'When is oral narrative poetry?' (Chapter 5). Whereas in IV, Hymes focused strongly on issues of competence and per-formance, the focus in NK has shifted toward the potentially universal patterns that Hymes starts identifying in several of the stories he analyzes. The 'poetic' – identified as a central function of language use in IV – now becomes a potential universal of human conduct. The range of languages he addresses in NK is, consequently, also wider; Hymes still works from within the Pacific Northwest, but he now also discusses at length the stud-ies done by others on Native American languages and, elsewhere, on

European languages. He even concludes the book with a chapter on the work of the American poet Robinson Jeffers – a chapter that includes important reflections on what one understands by a poetic 'line'.

As I said before, one should not expect easy reading when picking up these books from the library. Even for someone relatively at ease with Hymes' style, lexicon and arguments, NK is a book that takes time to read. It is packed with data and transcripts, and story profiles fill many, many pages; Hymes also attempts to incorporate and address almost all issues that have arisen in the study of oral narrative – methodological and historical issues, issues of method emerging from discussions with other scholars, the emergent work done on other communities and traditions, etc. Thus, it needs to be read in conjunction with IV, for the fundamental issues discussed in IV are presupposed in NK.

## Ethnopoetics

Ethnopoetics, to Hymes, is part of a larger theoretical vision revolving around narrative and performance and ultimately embedded in a view of language in society. Ethnopoetic analyses, as we shall see, attempt to unearth culturally embedded ways of speaking – materials and forms of using them, that belong to the sociolinguistic system of a group (or groups), and that have a particular place in a repertoire owing to their specific, characteristic form–function relationships. Such form–function relationships, we have seen, display 'second linguistic relativity' (a relativity of *functions*) and are therefore complex and relatively unpredictable: we need to investigate functions ethnographically and realize that they strongly depend on larger issues of repertoire structure and the distribution of linguistic and communicative resources.[3] In that sense, ethnopoetics fits into the general theoretical ambitions of the ethnography of speaking.

Hymes sees ethnopoetics as a form of structural linguistics, more precisely of 'practical structuralism' – 'the elementary task of discovering the relevant features and relationships of a language and its texts' (NK: 123).[4] It is about describing *what exists* in language and texts, and when applied to texts, it is a form of *philology*. But even if '[t]his kind of linguistics is old, known as philology ..., [t]he kind of discoveries it makes are new' (RT: ix), because

> To the recording of texts as massive documentation, with linguistics as a means to the ends of ethnography and aesthetic appreciation, we can now add ... the influence of structural linguistics on our ability to perceive poetic structure. (IV: 59)

It is an eclectic and composite philology, though, one that has been composed out of classical philological principles (the collection and meticulous analysis of texts), anthropological heuristics (the Boasian and Whorfian emphasis on cultural categories, on culture as an organizing principle for linguistic form), ethnographic epistemology (the principle that things can only be found out by structured attention to situated contextualized behavior) and the influence of two important predecessors to whom we shall turn in a moment. This philology is oriented toward discovering verbal *art*, organized in a (structurally described) 'grammar' of discourse which yields implicit patterns and principles of organization, allowing us to see 'artistry and subtlety of meaning otherwise invisible' (NK: 96).[5] It comes down to

> considering spoken narrative as a level of linguistic structure, as having consistent patterns – patterns far less complex than those of syntax, but patterns nonetheless. (NK: 97)

This level of linguistic structure revolves around three 'universal principles' (NK: 340, also 95). The first principle is that narratives do not consist of sentences, but of *lines and relations between lines* (verses, stanzas ...). Identifying such lines and relations is the bread and butter of ethnopoetics, and considerable skill and technique are required to do so.[6]

Lines and verses are often marked by particular formal linguistic features, from discourse markers and particles to syntactic parallelisms and intonation contours, where all of this is subject to what Roman Jakobson (Hymes' first important predecessor) called 'equivalence' (Jakobson, 1960). Equivalence is the second 'universal principle' that governs this form of art: 'a variety of means is employed to establish formal equivalence between particular lines and groups of lines' (NK: 340). Thus, repetitions of (parts of) lines, similarities in length, number of syllables, intonation contours, grammatical concord and so on can all mark lines and groups of lines, and sudden changes in pattern indicate new episodes in the story – new verses, stanzas, refrains, etc. Finally – the third universal principle – there is always a general aesthetic organization to the story, a more global form of organization that connects the story to culturally embedded understandings of the logic of activities and experiences. This is the level where a story can become a captivating one, a joke a good one, a poem a beautiful one, and here, Hymes draws on insights from his second important predecessor, Kenneth Burke (e.g. 1969 [1950]). Attention to this level of structure leads to a higher level of abstraction in ethnopoetic analysis. After the identification of lines and groups of lines, a 'profile' of the story needs to be drawn which brings out the intricate and delicate correlations between linguistic form, thematic development (scenes, episodes) and the general ('cultural') formal architecture of the story. In the appendix to this paper, I will provide an illustration of such an architecture.

Comparatively investigating such architectures, Hymes argues, could yield universal insights. Especially in NK, Hymes insists that stories are usually organized around numbers of lines – he talks of *measured* instead of *metrical* to denote forms of non-metrical formal internal organization of stories: 'There are regularities in the relations among measured lines, just as there are regularities in metrical lines' (NK: 96). And these regularities, Hymes suggests, are a limited set:

> These regularities have to do with cultural patterns, but also with the explorations and skill of narrators. In terms of cultural patterns, communities appear to build upon one of two alternatives: relations in terms of two and four or relations in terms of three and five. (NK: 96)

Thus, stories can be organized along series of two and four lines, verses or stanzas, or alternatively along series of three and five – with all sorts of permutations occurring within both alternatives. Hymes here argues for a different kind of universal: an aesthetic-formal universal that simultaneously may be a universal of the discursive sedimentation of human experience.

Summarizing, Hymes sees ethnopoetics as a descriptive (structural-philological) tactic capable of addressing (and analytically foregrounding) implicit formal patterns in narratives that can help identify them as ways of speaking within a culturally embedded speech repertoire. Such patterns are responsible for the poetic, artistic, aesthetic qualities of such narratives, and these qualities are a central part of their meaning and function. At the same time, these aesthetic qualities are deeply cultural, and they may reveal the cultural 'grammar' of human experience, both at the level of specific communities (repertoires) and at the level of universals of language and culture. In that sense, ethnopoetics fulfils (or attempts to fulfil) the promises of linguistic anthropology in the Boas–Sapir–Whorf tradition: to detect and make understood the cultural in language, the relation between culture and linguistic form, and the way in which language use feeds into culture. *En passant*, we take on board conceptions of language form, function and usage that are fundamentally different from those of mainstream linguistics, and we venture into an exciting new world of theory and analysis.

## Ethnopoetics as Functional Reconstruction

But there is more: ethnopoetic analysis, to Hymes, is a form of restoration:

> The work that discloses such form can be a kind of repatriation. It can restore to native communities and descendants a literary art that was implicit, like so much of language, but that now, when continuity of verbal tradition has been broken, requires analysis to be recognized. (RT: vii)

In order to understand this argument, the *décor* of our discussion needs to be slightly changed, from the texts themselves to the tradition of recording and analyzing them. Hymes is critical of the linguistic and folkloristic traditions of scholarship on 'oral tradition', claiming that they produced a record that has dismembered the very traditions *as traditions*, i.e. as something deeply connected to culture and cultural activity – as performable, poetically organized narrative, operating as a cognitive, cultural, affective way of handling experience. Losing that dimension of language means losing the capacity to produce voice – to express things on one's own terms, to communicate in ways that satisfy personal, social and cultural needs – to be communicatively competent, so to speak. Consequently:

> The fact is that one cannot depend upon most published versions of Native American myth. Even if the native language is preserved, its printed form is two steps away from what was said. The first step, from what was said to what was written down, cannot be transcended. We are dependent on what did get written down. But we can transcend the step between what was written down and what was published. Choices were made, mistakes sometimes made, in the course of that step. And words may be given a form they did not have. For generations they have been assumed to be prose and put in paragraphs ad hoc. Experience in recent years has shown that such narratives had an organization of their own, an organization not of paragraphs, but of lines and groups of lines. (RT: vii)

The stories, in other words, were not represented as *poetry* – a form which bespeaks artistry and aesthetic intentions (Burke's 'arousal and satisfaction of expectation' – NK: 340) – but as denotational, linearly organized, 'sense-making' text. Features of narration such as repetition (one of the most common forms of Jakobson's equivalence, hence usually revealing emphasis or insistence) were often dropped from printed editions; codeswitching or borrowing were similarly often edited out; likewise with 'nonsensical' sounds or utterances, audience responses and so forth – the model for native text was that of literature in European languages. And as a consequence, little was learned about how such stories fitted into local speech repertoires, how they functioned *in contrast to* other forms of language use, how they operated in a group as a culturally legitimate, relevant, useful way of speaking.[7]

A lot of what Hymes does in IV, RT and NK, consequently, is retranscribing and critically retranslating texts previously published by the likes of Edward Sapir and Melville Jacobs, organizing them in a different presentational format. This is methodologically essential:

> questions of mode of presentation arise because ethnopoetics involves not only translation but also transformation, transformation of modality, the presentation of something heard as something seen. The eye is an instrument of understanding. (NK: 40)

In other words, the stories need to be presented not as denotational text but as aesthetically organized *poetic* text, text containing the implicit forms of organization that make it meaningful culturally as myth, popular story, anecdote or experiential narrative – where such genre differences are a matter of implicit poetic organization triggering generic recognizability. Using old-fashioned anthropological terminology, the ethnopoetic transformation of texts is aimed at visualizing the *emic* organization of the text, the text as organized in terms of culturally embedded genre features. And such features, it should be underscored, are primarily *aesthetic* features, features of narrative-poetic *shape*, not only linguistic form.

We could reformulate Hymes' point of view as the primacy of the aesthetic functions of narrative, and the primacy of narrative as a cultural genre (or genre complex). Analytic interventions of the past, Hymes insists, have erased these aesthetic features, focusing on form instead of on shape, and reducing narrative to surface-segmentable (explicit) denotational expression organized in graphic units belonging to the language-ideological repertoires of the describers, not of the narrators. The essence of the object of inquiry – its implicit, cultural organization – was thus erased from the record, effectively precluding an accurate understanding of such texts as cultural artifacts, as forms of language use having complex, multiple functions, rather baffling degrees of (non-random) variability, and a unique situatedness in the act of telling.[8] Since '[n]arratives answer to two elementary functions of language, presentational as well as propositional' (EL: 205), deleting presentational aspects from the record means the loss of the narrative (behavioral, cultural) aspects of the texts.

This is not only a problem for analysts; it is an even greater problem for members of the communities from whom these narratives were taken. For them, the written, published versions of stories are often the only remains of an endogenous oral tradition, and given the functional dismembering of such stories in scholarship, stories are no longer oral and can no longer be performed *as poetry*, i.e. as texts organized according to community-specific poetic conventions. Thus:

> One merit of verse analysis (as this work can be called) is that it helps recognize the worth of oral traditions for which we have only written evidence. ... When lines, verses, and relations are recognized, one can venture to perform the narratives again, given appropriate circumstances. (NK: 98)

And in that way, by showing the implicit structure of such narratives, the rules of such implicit art forms could be learned anew, so that narrators can acquire again the tacit, implicit knowledge of form and the conventions of telling culturally appropriate, useful, functional stories.

I already pointed to the political dimensions of these restorative aims of ethnopoetics in the previous chapter. At this point, however, a theoretical argument deserves to be underscored, one that leads us back to Hymes' 'narrative view of the world'. Ethnopoetics, to Hymes, is about reconstructing the aesthetic functions of narratives, thus reconstituting them as a culturally recognized and valid complex of genres combining cognitive, affective, emotive, aesthetic and other aspects of language. This, then, goes back to his view of functional relativity – the fact that the function of language forms is a matter of their place within culturally configured repertoires, which cannot be posited *a priori* but need to be determined ethnographically (EL: 44ff). The scholarly tradition of investigating narrative has assigned particular functions to such narratives: those commonly ascribed to denotational, linearly organized, written/printed explicit prose text. And by doing that, such narratives have lost their 'meaning' – their usefulness, their functionality *as narrative* in particular communities. Ethnopoetics is the technique by means of which some of these functions could be restored. Rather than just as repositories of 'wisdom' or 'customs', such texts could now again become objects of aesthetic pleasure, of entertainment, opportunities for the display of narrative skill and virtuosity, for endless variation and renewal, for negotiating and enacting norms, conventions, standards – for culture in the sense of dynamic social-semiotic transmission.

## Conclusions

There are many instances in this world where people lose everything, and where the only thing they have left is culture. This is, Hymes consistently underscored, at once an incredibly valuable and a vulnerable possession – valuable because it provides them with the capacity to uniquely and authentically express their predicaments, their stories of who they are and what their life is like. It gives them voice. Vulnerable because of these very qualities, which might render their stories hard to understand and, thus, easy to dismiss, disqualify or reject. This was one of the main reasons why Hymes saw language as a human *problem*: it takes someone else to understand, and such understanding rarely develops in a field of equals. Especially in domains where other factors contribute to extreme inequality, voice is an extraordinarily fragile thing. I myself took this core insight from his work and developed it in a great deal of my work, because, to me, it provided the key to understanding sociolinguistic globalization as a field of real and potential inequalities emerging from mobile processes of voice (e.g. Blommaert, 2005b, 2008, 2010), and Chapter 5 will provide an illustration.

In this chapter, I focused on the theoretical and methodological, programmatic character of Hymes' ethnopoetic work. This part of his oeuvre, ironically, suffers from a problem of voice: it is too often dismissed (and too easy to dismiss) as an aridly technical toolkit of bewildering complexity, aimed at developing more 'authentic' or 'accurate' (philological) readings of badly edited Native American texts. In the final years of his life, Hymes was consumed by a desire to publish as much ethnopoetic work as possible, and frustrated because of the manifest lack of enthusiasm for it in his peer community. He enjoyed talking about the intricate verse structures he had found in a variety of stories, and was eager to underscore the significance of such findings, but not too many people enjoyed listening to that. It was tedious, arcane and cryptic stuff for most of his interlocutors.

It is, to be sure, far more than that, and it has been my attempt to bring out and foreground some of the fundamental assumptions underlying ethnopoetics. These fundamental assumptions are in line with other lines of work in Hymes' large and complex oeuvre. Even if ethnopoetics *looks* like a very different type of language study than, say, Hymes' papers on communicative competence or the ethnography of speaking, it is inspired by precisely the same fundamental preoccupations. These include an ethnographic epistemology and a concern with language-as-praxis, as a socially and culturally conditioned form of human behavior subject to constraints and developments that cannot be predicted *a priori* but need to be established empirically. The aim of ethnopoetics, furthermore, is to arrive at a reconstruction of languages-as-sociolinguistic-systems: of language as composed of culturally embedded ways of speaking. The fact that language is often misunderstood because its role in societies is often only superficially addressed is another thread that shoots through his ethnopoetic work as well as his other work. And here perhaps more than elsewhere, he illustrates the unpredictability of form–function relationships in the structure of language-in-society, as well as the – real, effective – dangers of taking form–function relationships for granted. It not only leads to misunderstanding, but it also leads to disqualification, dismissal and erasure for those who produce 'strange' patterns. A book such as EL clearly, and convincingly, demonstrates the ways in which ethnopoetics fits into a larger sociolinguistic-programmatic edifice, both of theory and of commitment.

There is thus room for exploring 'applied' topics for ethnopoetic analysis – for taking it beyond the study of folkloric oral tradition and into other spaces where narrative matters: service encounters, police interviews, asylum applications, trauma narratives, social welfare interviews, political speech, advertisements and promotional discourses, and so forth.[9] It would be a great pity if a powerful analytic tool such as ethnopoetics remained under-used because of it stereotypically being pinned on a small set of particular analytic objects.

## Appendix: 'I Walked for Seven Hours'

By way of illustrating ethnopoetic analytic technique, I will try to show how implicit structure can be made visible in a small story, an anecdote. The anecdote is part of a long interview recorded in late 1997 with a 75-year-old man, a former District Commissioner in the Belgian Congo. The man spoke Flemish Dutch with clear regional (dialect) accent. The topic of the interview was life in the colony and the practice of professional conduct in colonial service – the theme of a fieldwork project for students of African Studies, Ghent University in 1997–1998.[10] The interview was transcribed by the students in 'field transcript style', i.e. using minimal codes and focusing on general patterning of talk. Present during the interview were the interviewee, his wife and three female students who performed the interview. During the interview, many anecdotes were told. These are generically marked and usually start with an explicit generic framing device ('once ...', 'there ...').

Let us start from the field transcripts. The Dutch field transcript is the original transcript provided by students; I have provided an approximate English equivalent.

*Dutch*

ik heb daar eens zeven uur gemarcheerd om in een dorp te komen/... en euh/... als ik dan hoorde ik ze lachen/... en ik verstond nie wa da ze zeiden maar ik had altijd ne jachtwachter Kalupeshi heette die die had ik bij en die was van de streek en ik zei wat wat is 't groot plezier hij zei dat dat oud vrouwke wat daar zit hij zei die zei/... ik moest al ik had al jaren gene blanke meer gezien en ik wou absuluut nog eens ne blanke zien ik moest dus naar de weg waar dat ik van kwam daar è/. en nu heb ik hem gezien/. nu hoef ik nie te gaan zei ze.

*English*

I once walked for seven hours there to get to a village/and ehr/when I then I heard them laugh/and I didn't understand what they were saying but I always had a gamekeeper with me Kalupeshi was his name that that one I had with me and he was from that region and I said what what is the big fun he said that that old lady who sits over there he said she said/... I had to I hadn't seen a white man for years and I desperately wanted to see another white man so I had to go to the road where I came from right/and now I've seen him? now I don't need to go she said.

This is a short, at first sight unremarkable micro-narrative, certainly when represented as prose organized in sentences. However, when we deploy an ethnopoetic apparatus focusing on line, verse and stanza organization, relations of equivalence and general aesthetic/poetic patterning in the story, we get an amazingly complex and delicate narrative, which shows how the narrator deploys content and form in synergetic, aesthetic moves.

In the ethnopoetic transcript of this anecdote (which is the *outcome* of analysis – see Blommaert & Slembrouck, 2000), I am using several procedures and codes.

(1) *Indentation and clustering* of lines indicating the relations between lines. Some lines are subordinate to others; groups of lines can be identified.

(2) *Boldface* elements in the transcript indicate particularly salient markers, often identifying lines and signaling relations among lines. Thus, the difference between '*en*' and '*maar*' signals a change from one group of lines to another.

(3) *Underlined* fragments mark parallelisms: repetitive constructions that suggest themes and emphases on parts of the story, and contribute to the overall aesthetic organization of the narrative. *Arrows* further mark such repetitive poetic constructions.

(4) Single or grouped lines can be *verses*, marked by a, b, c in the transcript. A verse is typically a line identified as a main proposition (and marked by a line-initial narrative marker such as 'and'), potentially complemented by dependent, subordinate lines.

(5) Several verses can form a narrative unit – a *scene* – in which part of the narrated event is developed. In the transcript, scenes are marked by (I)–(IV)

Taken together, we get the 'architecture' of this story, and it looks like this:

| | | | |
|---|---|---|---|
| *ik heb daar eens* zeven uur gemarcheerd om in een dorp te komen /. | | a | (I) |
| ...**en** euh /... als ik dan hoorde ik ze lachen /.. | | b | |
| **en** ik verstond nie wa da ze zeiden | | c | |
| | | | |
| **maar** <u>ik had</u> altijd ne jachtwachter   ⇐ | | a | (II) |
| Kalupeshi heette die | | | |
| die <u>had ik</u> bij   ⇐ | | b | |
| en die was van de streek | | | |
| | | | |
| **en** *<u>ik zei</u>* wat wat is 't groot plezier | (T1) | | (III) |
| *<u>hij zei</u>* dat=dat oud vrouwke wat daar zit *<u>hij zei die zei</u>* /... | (T2) | | (IV) |
| **ik** moest al <u>ik had al jaren gene blanke meer gezien</u>   ⇐ | | a | |
| en <u>ik wou absoluut nog eens ne blanke zien</u>   ⇐ | | | |
| **ik** moest dus naar de weg waar dat ik van kwam daar è/. | | b | |
| en <u>nu heb ik hem gezien</u> /.   ⇐ | | | |
| **nu** hoef ik nie te gaan *zei ze* | | c | |

In this brief anecdote, three actions are put in a sequence. Together, they form the 'stuff' of the story:

(1) I arrive in a village, hear them laugh and don't know what it means.
(2) I ask the gamekeeper what it is about.
(3) He translates the words of an old lady.

Actions 2 and 3 are both narrated communicative events: dialogues with two turns each. Between actions 1 and 2, the narrator inserts an out-of-sequence scene: 'I had a local gamekeeper'. This part provides contextual information, it complements the sketch of the situation and introduces a character for actions 2 and 3. These actions are narratively organized in four *scenes*, marked by numbers (I)–(IV):

(I) Generic framing: deictic anchoring and sketch of the situation. First action: I heard them laughing and did not understand them.
(II) Out-of-sequence contextual element: I had a local gamekeeper.
(III) Second action and first part of dialogue turn: I asked him what it was about.
(IV) Third action and second part of dialogue turn: gamekeeper translates the words of the old lady (reported speech framed by 'she said', 'he said').

Whereas the actions are, so to speak, 'content' elements of the story, the scenes are *narrative* elements in which form and content are blended into a poetic organization of lines and relations between lines. Let us have a closer look at the different scenes.

## Scene I

This scene comprises three verses (a, b, c) marked by (a) a generic framing device for the very first verse of the narrative – explicit deictic anchoring of the story and sketch of the setting ('I once walked there for seven hours' – in italics in the transcript); and (b) the use of the connective *'en'* ('and') for verses b and c, which both contain the first action of the story.

## Scene II

This scene is an out of sequence scene with two verses (a, b) in which contextual information is given: 'I had a gamekeeper there – his name was Kalupeshi – I had him there – he was from that region'. Note the parallelism: proposition–elaboration//proposition–elaboration. This scene is introduced by *'maar'* ('but'), an adversative discourse marker that marks a break with scene I as well as with scene III – both are identified by the use of *'en'*.

## Scene III

The action sequence of the story is resumed by means of the connective *'en'*, which establishes cohesive links with Scene I. In this one-line scene, we get the first turn of the dialogue (T1): the narrator asks Kalupeshi what the big fun was all about. The dialogue action is framed by an explicit metapragmatic signal: the phrase *'ik zei'* ('I said').

## Scene IV

This complex three-verse scene is the second turn of the dialogue (T2). Like the first turn, it is introduced by a metapragmatic phrase *'hij zei'* ('he said'). The reported speech of the old lady is framed initially as well as finally ('sandwiched') by *'die zei/zei ze'* ('she said/said she'). The lady's reported speech itself is a three-verse rhyme with considerable internal parallelism: (a) I haven't seen a white man in years; (b) (if I wanted to see one) I had to go to the road; (c) now I don't have to go anymore (he came to me). The parallelisms mark differences between main-subordinate lines and marking of the punchline:

(a)  IK (main) – BLANKE ZIEN (rhyme)
     EN (subordinate) – BLANKE ZIEN (rhyme)
(b)  IK (main)
     EN (subordinate) – ZIEN (rhyme)
(c)  NU (punchline) No formal rhyme but 'semantic rhyme': 'now I have seen him'

Especially in Scene IV, the complex poetic patterning (three verses with a clear refrain of three rhyming repetitions) produces a stylistic intensification of the narrative – Hymes would use the term 'full performance' for this – and supports the stylistic and frame shift into a doubly layered reported speech: 'I tell what Kalupeshi said the old lady said'.

## Notes

(1)  Many of the ideas in this essay became clearer during a series of long talks I had with Dell and Virginia Hymes in late September 2004, and I am very grateful to them for their hospitality and generosity in time and attention. Ethnopoetics has over the years also been a consistent topic of discussion with Stef Slembrouck, whose influence is also gratefully acknowledged. Intensive work with Speranza Ndege (University of Nairobi) while she was completing her PhD with me in late 2002 forced me to focus on many of the technical and theoretical aspects of ethnopoetics, and compelled me to adopt more nuanced views on many issues. Speranza's work resulted in a magnificent dissertation (Ndege, 2002), which provided (rare) evidence for Hymes' claims about the occurrence of numbered patterns in stories.
(2)  I heard students once refer to it as *In Vain I Tried to Kill You.*
(3)  According to Hymes, modern linguistics has consistently overlooked the problem of functional relativity, often wrongly taking functional stability and formal variability as the central assumption of analysis. This point is forcefully developed in EL; see also Hymes (1980: Chapter 1).
(4)  Hymes emphatically dismisses connections between this 'practical structuralism' and 'structuralism' as 'what has been made of linguistic analysis in anthropology, semiotics, and the like' (NK: 123). It is easy to be misled by terminology here, and Hymes is

not always the most helpful writer in this respect (witness famously cryptic lines such as 'In aim, the method is structural, but in execution, it must also be philological'; Hymes, 1966: 131). Hymes has maintained throughout his career a complex relationship with structuralism (see e.g. Hymes, 1983).

(5) The 'practical structuralism' shines through in statements such as this one: 'One must work out a 'grammar' of the local world of discourse and work out the internal relations of a text in relation to that grammar before proceeding to analytic comparison and interpretation in terms of relationships found elsewhere' (NK: 126).

(6) There has been some debate on the criteria for identifying lines, and Hymes addresses comments and proposals by other scholars – Labov, Gee, Tedlock and others – in IV, NK and EL. Along with Hymes, Dennis Tedlock is often seen as the 'founder' of ethnopoetic analysis; see e.g. Tedlock (1983).

(7) This problem of textual conversion – entextualization – is a language-ideological matter in which particular metalinguistic grids are being imposed on the text, recreating it as *a particular form* of text, culturally recognizable within the repertoire of those who edit it. See Silverstein and Urban (1996a) and Bauman and Briggs (1990) for extensive discussions.

(8) With respect to this situatedness, Hymes, especially in IV, devotes a lot of attention to the issue of dictation in the field: 'Perhaps the most obvious influence on what we know of the traditions of nonliterate groups has been the constraint of dictation, and dictation slow enough to be written down; the effect on sentence length and the internal organization of texts has been increasingly revealed by research with tape recorder' (IV: 86). He also observes that the structure of narratives in fieldwork often develops according to the informants' appraisals of the developing competence of the researcher, stories becoming more complex after long periods of fieldwork and repeated narrations.

(9) To my knowledge, very little published research of this sort exists. Partly in collaboration with Katrijn Maryns, I have investigated African asylum seekers' stories using ethnopoetics (Blommaert, 2001b; Maryns, 2004; Maryns & Blommaert, 2001).

(10) For more detailed comments and suggestions on ethnopoetic technique, I refer the reader to Blommaert (2000), a working paper originally written for the benefit of students involved in the fieldwork project. Blommaert and Slembrouck (2000) provide an extensive discussion of a range of methodological issues related to ethnopoetic analysis and data representation.

# 5 Grassroots Historiography and the Problem of Voice: Tshibumba's *Histoire du Zaïre*

## Introduction: Voice and History

There is a huge problem with the way in which documents – written as well as oral texts, inscriptions, pictures, paintings – are used as bearers of historical information. This problem, or rather a complex set of problems, is well known and has been addressed by generations of historians under the label of historical criticism. Often, the focus was, and is, on 'truth', on the way in which distinctions can be made between 'facts' and 'not-facts' in documents, the ways in which forgeries can be identified, the way in which 'truthful accounts' of historical events can be deduced from documents.[1]

As an outsider to the art of historiography, there are several things that strike me. I will outline three features, for they will guide the discussion in what follows. First, I feel that a distinction should be made between 'old' and 'historical'. Often, documents are called 'historical documents', whereas in fact, prior to historical-methodological inspection, they are merely 'old'. They *become* historical because of scholarly, disciplined and methodical interpretation. This distinction between what a document *is* and what it *becomes* will be central to the discussion here. Second, many historians have advocated the use of linguistic techniques as part of the necessary toolkit of historical criticism. Marc Bloch (whom I deeply admire) is a case in point (Bloch, 1953: 126ff). But Bloch as well as others give too much credit to the historical sensitivity of linguistics, I fear. Toward the end of this paper I will try to specify *which particular kind* of linguistics can suit a historical project (see also Blommaert, 1999b). Third, the issue of truth versus fiction/interpretation/forgery is obviously one that does not stand the test of postmodern critiques of positivism and truth. I will argue that, rather than truth, *voice* should be central to the historical inquiry into documents. Consequently, and connected to the previous point, we need an analysis that starts investigating documents long before they were produced, and needs to address conditions of productions, interactional functions, entextualization patterns and so forth. We also need to address issues of genre, seen as orthopractically organized ways of dealing with received (or locally constructed) models of text and communication.[2]

In order to make these points, I will discuss a handwritten document from Congo. It is a document entitled *Histoire du Zaïre*, written by Tshibumba Kanda Matulu in 1980. Tshibumba is one of the best-known Congolese popular painters, and the political, historical and cultural significance of his work was demonstrated by Johannes Fabian in *Remembering the Present* (Fabian, 1996). In this book, Fabian presented a collection of over 100 paintings on the history of the Congo. The paintings were commissioned by Fabian and were the result of long conversations on history between Fabian and Tshibumba. Apart from the pictures, Fabian also presented transcripts of the explanations provided by Tshibumba when he brought the paintings to Fabian's house in Lubumbashi, Shaba. So we have here two versions of the history of Congo, one painted, one orally narrated. The document I will discuss here is a third version: a written one. There is an interesting yet puzzling relationship between the three 'documents'. Each of the three deploys different communicative codes (one graphic and pictural, one oral-narrative, one written-narrative). Fabian has successfully investigated the first two modes of articulation; I will focus on the written-narrative mode. I believe it offers us, apart from clarity on what seems to be the third part of a historiographic oeuvre, insights into the political economy of language and voice in places such as Shaba (Congo, now Katanga). So my main question will be: what makes (or could make) Tshibumba's written history a 'memorable' text, one that can be used as a genuine *historiography*, not just a 'historical document'?

## Grassroots Literacy

Thsibumba's text is 73 pages long, written in a cheap copybook (a *cahier de brouillon*), handwritten and monolingual, in French. But having said this, all sorts of qualifications are in order.

The document shares all kinds of characteristics previously encountered in a variety of handwritten documents from that region, and grouped under the label of 'grassroots literacy' (Blommaert, 1999c, 2008). Grassroots literacy is sub-elite literacy and needs to be situated not in categorical 'literate–illiterate' terms but rather in terms of a gradient of literacy, ranging from 'fully literate' (multimodal and polygeneric, elite-language-variety literacy) to 'fully illiterate'. Features of grassroots literacy include: (a) instability in orthography – lower case and capitals are used interchangeably and unsystematically, punctuation is minimal and/or erratic, there is limited control over basic writing conventions such as organizing lines on a page, hyphenating, marking morpheme or word boundaries and so forth; (b) the use of sub-standard language varieties in writing, often bearing strong traces of oral language proficiency 'put on paper'; (c) problems with generic work: there are distant images of genres such as autobiography, letters or historiography, often articulated in forms of embellishment and structure (chapters with chapter titles, illustrations, etc.); and (d) that it is produced in conditions which can be summarized as 'poor literacy environments' – people who write have no access to what can be called the 'infrastructure of literacy', an 'archive' of previous writings, particular social or material conditions favorable to literacy production and consumption. Consequently, their exposure to literacy is very low, and their level of literacy production is even lower.

All of these features occur in Tshibumba's text. Even though the text is in monolingual French, when seen from the viewpoint of elite varieties of French it is replete with orthographic, grammatical and lexical errors. And even though Tshibumba's handwriting appears to be comparatively stable and well controlled – probably the steady hand of the artist – closer inspection reveals enormous problems with the basic writing skills, similar to those encountered in other sub-elite documents from Shaba and elsewhere (Blommaert, 1999c, 2008). Fabian (1996: 236) mentions that Tshibumba had read some (history) books and newspapers, and that he was an avid consumer of comic strips. But judging from his writing in the text as well as his epigraphic writing on his paintings (Fabian, 1996: 235ff), it is safe to assume that his insertion in literacy economies was rather restricted. Figure 5.1 is a copy of page 2 of the text. Note the frequency of corrections and the errors in French (e.g. *'Est pourquoi pas'*, *'Il est à dire'*, *'ou nous vivont'*).

Grassroots literacy creates a problem of voice. Even though writers such as Tshibumba attempt to produce something that can be identified as a 'serious', elaborate text, often generically marked as history or '(historical) account', and produced with an enormous investment of energy, time and resources, the texts match so few criteria of elite literacy that they most often fail to be noticed or recognized in terms of what they claim to be. Fabian again broke ground in demonstrating the various 'filters' standing

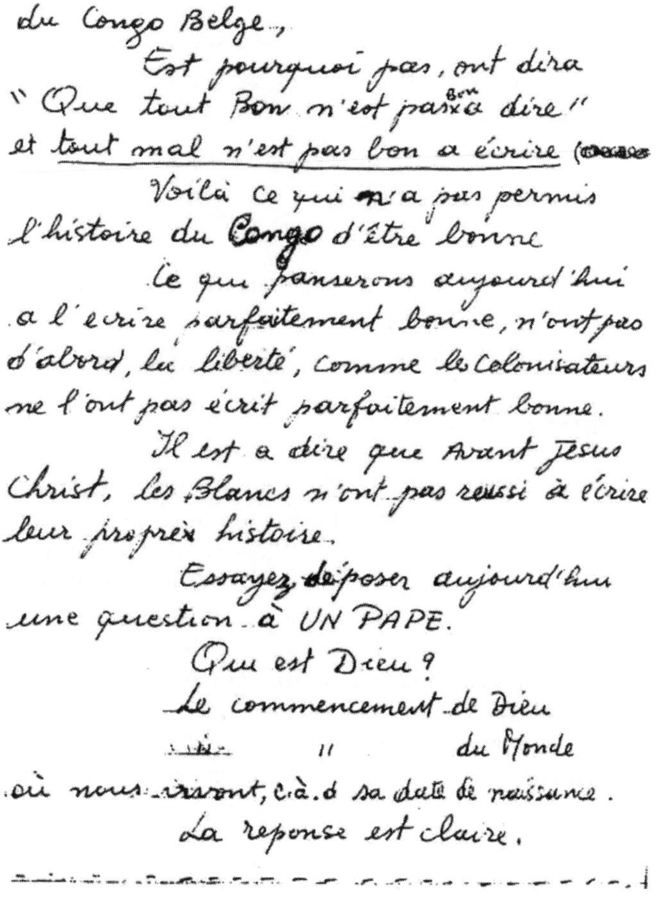

du Congo Belge.,
    Est pourquoi pas, ont dira
" Que tout Bon n'est passa dire"
et tout mal n'est pas bon a écrire (...)
    Voilà ce qui m'a pas permis
l'histoire du Congo d'être bonne
    Ce qui panserons aujourd'hui
a l'écrire parfaitement bonne, n'ont pas
d'abord, la liberté, comme les Colonisateurs
ne l'ont pas écrit parfaitement bonne.
    Il est a dire que Avant Jesus
Christ, les Blancs n'ont pas réussi à écrire
leur propres histoire.
    Essayez de poser aujourd'hui
une question à UN PAPE.
    Qui est Dieu?
    Le commencement de Dieu
    ...    "        du Monde
où nous ..., c.à.d sa date de naissance.
    La reponse est claire,

**Figure 5.1** Page 2 of Tshibumba's text

between a grassroots-literate subject and historical interpretation in the case of a printed, grassroots literacy 'history of Elisabethville' (now Lubumbashi) written in the 1960s by a former houseboy (Fabian, 1990a). Investigating a collection of three version of an autobiography written by a man from Shaba over a period of seven years, I arrived at the conclusion that the process of writing itself is probably the only instrument of remembering for a sub-elite Congolese such as the man I was investigating. I argued that a seemingly straightforward concept such as 'my life', as well as its connections to a particular subjectivity in which the Ego locates him/ herself in historical processes, all seem to be controlled by particular

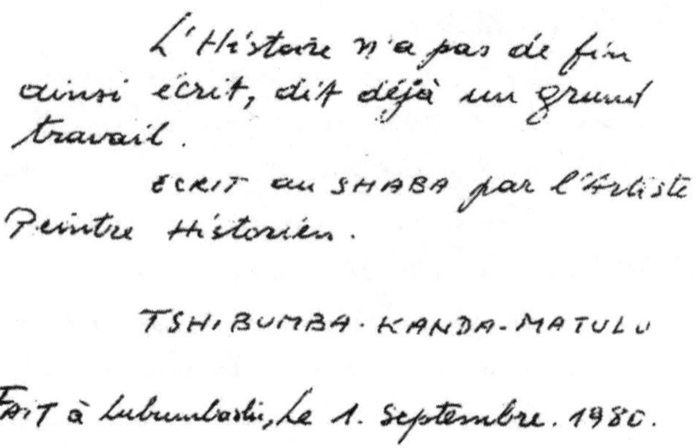

*[handwritten text]*

L'Histoire n'a pas de fin
ainsi écrit, dit déjà un grand
travail.
        ECRIT au SHABA par l'Artiste
Peintre Historien.

        TSHIBUMBA · KANDA-MATULU

Fait à Lubumbashi, Le 1. Septembre. 1980.

**Figure 5.2** Page 69 of Tshibumba's text

economies of literacy. A 'life' is not accessible to anyone. By the absence of literate archives about one's own life and about the way in which one's world developed throughout this life, 'history' is a highly problematic generic target, and documents containing such writings will rarely be recognized as significant bearers of 'historical information'.

But here we are facing someone who explicitly claims to write *history*. Even more, he identifies himself as a *historian*, both in talking to Fabian and in his written text. On page 69, he concludes his history with: '*ECRIT au SHABA par l'Artiste/Peintre Historien/TSHIBUMBA-KANDA-MATULU/FAIT à Lubumbashi, Le 1. Septembre. 1980*' (see Figure 5.2). In terms of his own generic and identity imaginings, we are confronting a historiographer. How?

### The Main Architecture of the Story

Let us take a look at the main architecture of Tshibumba's *Histoire du Zaïre*. The document is 73 pages long, but three main parts can be distinguished: (a) an introduction (pp. 1–6); (b) the main narrative (pp. 7–70); and (c) a postscript (pp. 71–73). In the initial parts of the text, Tshibumba uses chapter titles to mark periods in his historical account, but from p. 36 onwards chapter titles disappear (a feature of stylistic instability also encountered in other documents: Blommaert, 2001c, 2008; see also Fabian, 1990a for a discussion of chapter titles in the *Vocabulaire d'Elisabethville*. Page 10 contains two chapter titles, 'Royaume de Mongo' and 'Royaume des Bampende', but both chapters are blank. Page 6 is blank, marking the transition from introduction to main narrative. Page 70 is again a blank page, marking the transition from main narrative to postscript. Thematically and in terms of periodization, 11 units can be distinguished.

(1)  An introductory part containing a *preamble* and a set of *methodological reflections* on African history (pp. 1–5). Tshibumba discusses the ways in which European historiography has misrepresented African history, giving examples of the Bible, the assassination of Lumumba and Hitler. Zairian history should be written by Zairians, he claims, and the absence of history from Zairian culture is a problem.

(2)  A section on the *precolonial* period (pp. 7–15), initiated by a title '*Nos ancêtres*' ('our ancestors'). The whole of this part is structured in separate chapters on precolonial kingdoms: the Congo kingdom, the Baluba, Bakuba, Mongo (left blank), Bampende (left blank), Baluba Shankadi and Lunda.

(3)  A section on the period of the *explorers* (pp. 15–24). This whole period is structurally captured in one chapter entitled '*Dans le Sud du Katanga*' ('in Southern Katanga'). It starts from the important economic role of the Katanga kingdom, something that attracted Livingstone. Livingstone disappears, and this arouses the interest of the Belgian King Leopold I, who calls upon Stanley. Stanley finds Livingstone, and Leopold organizes the Berlin Conference. There, a campaign against the Arab slave trade is launched, and Africa is liberated from slave traders. Then, Tshibumba returns to the Katanga kingdom led first by King Katanga, then by Msiri (who came to power after having assassinated Katanga's son). Msiri meets Bodson and kills him. Msiri in turn is killed, and something mysterious happens to his head: it is probably taken to Europe. Tshibumba concludes this section with '*Et voilà l'Afrique et complétement libre aux Occidentaux*' ('Thus, Africa is completely free to the Westerners').

(4)  The next section treats the *colonization prior to the independence struggle* (pp. 24–30). This section is introduced by the chapter title: '*L'arrivée des Blancs Colonisateurs*' ('The arrival of the whites-colonizers'). After the Berlin Conference, Leopold I acquires the Congo and the establishment of the Congo Free State is proclaimed at Vivi on July 11, 1885 by the King's representative nicknamed Mbula-Matari. Tshibumba provides a sketch of the flag of the Free State (p. 25). After the death of Leopold I, the Free State is transformed into the Belgian Congo led by a Governor-General. In 1901,

a railway is built connecting the South-African railway with that of Katanga: the Compagnie du Chemin de Fer du Katanga. In 1906, groups of white South Africans come to Congo. In the same year, the Union Minière du Haut-Katanga (UMHK) sets up a major plant in Elisabethville (later Lubumbashi), and the Katanga region gradually becomes industrialized. There is migrant labor from other places, and Catholicism becomes firmly established as a religion. The Bishop of Elisabethville is the second most important figure, after the Governor. Tshibumba mentions Kimbangu, the 1941 strike of the UMHK workers[3] (according to Tshibumba, the governor and bishop of Elisabethville lured the strikers into the soccer stadium, where they were assassinated), as well as the Batetela revolt in Lodja (Kasai). In Leopoldville (later Kinshasa), the first Congolese political party, ABAKO, is founded. In 1955, the young Belgian King Baudoin visits the Congo and speaks out against racism, to the dismay of the whites.

(5)   *The independence struggle* (pp. 30–35). On page 30, Tshibumba mentions the first rumors of independence, situated after the local elections of 1957. In 1958, Lumumba attends a pan-African conference in Ghana. In early 1959, there are mutinies in Leopoldville. Kasavubu is arrested, followed by Lumumba. Belgium organizes a Round Table conference on the independence of Congo. Tshibumba provides names of the delegates. Lumumba is released and joins the Round Table. There are different opinions on independence at the Round Table, but on June 30, 1960, King Baudoin declares the Congo independent. Tshibumba provides a sketch of the flag of the new republic. There are no chapter titles in this section.

(6)   *The first republic and the Congo Crisis* (pp. 36–50). With independence, the names of all institutions change. Lumumba is the first Prime Minister, and under the chapter title '*Le Congo et ses fils*' ('the Congo and its sons'), the members of the new government are mentioned. Kalonji proclaims the secession of the Kasai, and a conflict between Luba and Lulua ensues. Kalonji proclaims himself king, resides in Bakwanga (later Mbuji-Mayi, Kasai) and makes his people dig diamonds. Tshibumba provides a sketch of the flag of Kalonji's kingdom. In the Kasaï, violent ethnic struggle erupts. In Leopoldville, there are problems between Kasavubu and Lumumba. Lumumba orders all whites out of Katanga within 24 hours, causing an exodus, and Tshombe proclaims the independence of Katanga on July 11, 1961. A sketch of the new Katangese flag is provided. Tshombe meets internal opposition from Baluba and Tshokwe in the north of Katanga. Tshombe organizes violent pogroms against people from

the north. Lumumba is deposed by Kasavubu and flees to Kisangani, but is captured and brought to Elisabethville. He is subsequently killed by the French mercenary Bob Denard. A new Congolese government is formed, and UN troops invade Katanga. In the north of the Congo, a new rebellion erupts. UN secretary-general Hammarskjoeld dies in a plane crash. Katanga is defeated in 1962, and Tshombe escapes to Europe. The Northern rebellion is crushed by a military intervention by US and Belgian troops in Kisangani. Tshombe is invited to form a government of national unity with Joseph Mobutu as Defense Secretary. In 1965, Tshombe is deposed by Kasavubu. Kimba forms a new government and introduces a new national flag.

(7) On November 24, 1965, a putch is organized by Joseph Mobutu, and the *second republic* is launched (pp. 51–55). Mobutu organizes a new government. A new rebellion organized by Mulele erupts, but is crushed by Mobutu. Mercenaries working for Tshombe organize another revolt in Kivu. As Tshombe prepares himself to join his forces, his plane is hijacked. Tshombe dies soon afterwards in Algiers. Other rebellions are crushed as well.

(8) The *Third Republic* (pp. 55–59) is started by the creation of Mobutu's *'parti-état'* MPR (Mouvement Populaire de la Révolution) in 1967. The name of the country changes, the currency changes, *authenticité* causes all people to change their names, there is a new flag, and all place names are Zairianized as well. The structure of government changes profoundly. A conflict erupts between the Church and the State, and the Cardinal has to leave in exile. Industries are nationalized.

(9) Next, *the Shaba wars* are discussed at length (pp. 60–65). The first Shaba-crisis starts in March 1977 with the invasion of former Katangese Gendarmes (members of the army of the independent Katanga republic under Tshombe), supported by the Soviets and Cubans and aimed at ousting Mobutu. Mobutu calls for aid from other countries. The 80-day war ends in victory for Mobutu. In November 1977, Mobutu's first wife dies, and Mobutu is re-elected as president. In May 1978, the mining town of Kolwezi is attacked by Katangese Gendarmes, starting the second Shaba crisis. France and Belgium as well as a number of other countries come to Mobutu's assistance. The local leader Nguz-a-Karl-i-Bond is arrested. Mobutu resides in Shaba for six months, during which the Gecamines workers organize a strike.

(10) The final part of the main narrative covers *recent events*, all dating from around 1980 (pp. 66–69). A student revolt erupts in Kinshasa

and in May 1980 Zaire is visited by Pope John Paul VI. In late 1979, the Zairian currency is changed. Mobutu visits Lubumbashi in the company of his second wife, whom he married in May 1980. The narrative ends with a coda (p. 69, see Figure 5.2): *'L'histoire n'a pas de fin/ ainsi écrit, dit déjà un grand/travail./Ecrit au Shaba par l'Artiste/ Peintre Historien/Tshibumba-Kanda-Matulu/Fait à Lubumbashi, le 1. Septembre 1980'* ('History has no end/thus written/already speaks a great/work/written in Shaba by the artist/painter historian/ Tshibumba-Kanda-Matulu/done at Lubumbashi, September 1, 1980').

(11)  After a blank page (p. 70), Tshibumba engages in a brief set of *reflections on tribalism* (pp. 71–73). Tshibumba sees tribalism at work at various levels in Zaire, causing many problems. Especially in the Shaba Wars, tribalism was rampant. Tshibumba concludes with a MPR slogan: *'Sans un Guide comme Mobutu, pas de ZAÏRE UNIT et son ARMEE'* ('Without a guide such as Mobutu, no unified Zaire and its army').

## Placing Oneself: Tshibumba's Historical Perspective

### Universalist ambitions

Tshibumba writes his *Histoire* in a neutral, declarative style, emphasizing factuality. There are hardly any judgmental or evaluative statements in his text (with the exception of the introductory part, to be discussed here). His story is never a first-person-singular story. Where he appears in person in the text, he appears as a historian, not as a witness. Just like in his paintings, Tshibumba articulates an identity through articulating a perceived genre: he is a historian because he writes, paints and narrates history.

The explicit identifications of himself as an 'artiste–peintre–historien' are one lead into this, of course. Another lead is the first part of his text, in which he presents a number of reflections on African history. Tshibumba starts this section by situating the text:[4]

| *L'histoire du Zaïre* | *The history of Zaire* |
|---|---|
| Ecrit par un ZAÏROIS aux années 1980 | Written by a ZAIREAN in the years 1980 |
| et cela au ZAÏRE dans la Region du SHABA | and this in ZAIRE in the region of SHABA |
| à LUbUMBASHI. (TSHIBUMBA. K.M.) | in LUbUMBASHI (Tshibumba K.M.) |

Next, he produces the main argument: Zairian history should be written by Zairians. As an authority, he – anachronistically – quotes Lumumba in this respect:

| | |
|---|---|
| Tous pays a son histoire, je crois que chaque chose a son histoire aussi, Lumumba, Emery Patrice l'a dit: 'L'histoire du ZAÏRE sera écrite par un ZAÏROIS'. | Every country has its history, I believe that everything has its history as well, Lumumba, Emery Patrice has said it: 'The history of ZAIRE will be written by a ZAIREAN'. |

But there is an obstacle: Africans do not know how to write. Consequently, African history is written by Europeans, and later by Africans with specific interests in mind. This, to Tshibumba, is a problem and a threat:

| | |
|---|---|
| Mais cela est une erreur très grave pour l'avenir de ce grand pays, un poison pour nos futurs historiens pourquoi pas, pour nos enfants. | But this is a very serious mistake for the future of this great country, a poison for our future historians why not, for our children. |

Tshibumba then embarks on a discussion of 'errors' in history: the fact that Adam and Eve are presented as white, not as black, and the story of Noah's son Cham:

| | |
|---|---|
| Voilà ce qui prouve déjà que l'histoire en Afrique était fort falcifiée pensée et même truquée. | See what already proves that the history in Africa was strongly falsified thought and even forged |

These problems persist after the Africans have acquired literacy. Even then, history is dominated by 'ASSISTANTS des MERCENAIRES même des MISSIONAIRES' ('assistants mercenaries even missionaries') who had 'too much complicated' the history of Zaire. Examples of this are the multiple existing versions of the assassination of Lumumba, and in Europe, the differing opinions on Hitler's death. Tshibumba then situates his own effort:

| | |
|---|---|
| Moi aussi qui ai écrit cette histoire du Congolais j'aimerais tracer mes lignes historiques sans préciser les date et des mois xx xxx xxxxxx par fautes | Me too who has written this history of the Congolese I'd like to trace my historical patterns without specifying the dates and the months xx xxx xxxxx because of failures |

| | |
|---|---|
| des mémoires pour n'est pas semer | of memory not to create |
| des confusions et pour prouver que nos | confusions and to demonstrate that our |
| ancêtre dans leur existence ne savaient | ancestors in their existence didn't know |
| pas lire ni écrire, mais sauf chez les | how to read and write, but except for the |
| Bampende et les Bakuba qui nous ont | Bampende and the Bakuba who left us |
| laissé quelques objets d'Arts, tel que des MASQUES, des STATUES et CANES. | some objects of Art, such as MASKS STATUES and STICKS. |
| Et divers, mais qui ne parles a aucun | And others, but who speak |
| point l'histoire du Zaïre. | nowhere the history of Zaire. |

So Tshibumba intends to *clarify* and to avoid creating even more confusion on the history of Zaire. He also wants to fill a blank: hitherto, Africans have left no documents on history, with the exception of some groups whose sculptures can be seen as informing history. Tshibumba underscores the importance of *writing* in the larger problem: Africans have been voiceless when it came to articulating their own history. Consequently, their history was within the realm of the whites; the main reason for this is illiteracy, and the main result is confusion. The remedy is a *written historiography*.

Neutrality, factuality, literacy: we have here a generic triad which appears to define Tshibumba's endeavor. The work he embarks on involves *particular* discourses, semiotic styles and ways of narrating. Two elements can be added to this.

The first element is an orientation to the past. History, as a neutral, unbiased and literate discourse, needs to be a story of past events. We can see this from the brief postscript, where Tshibumba explicitly thematizes 'history' versus 'the future':

| | |
|---|---|
| Ce que l'Historien ne parler pas cette fois-ci de l'Histoire mais de l'Avenir et de ce qui existe actuellem ent | What the historian does not speak this time of History but of the Future and of that which exist nowadays |

This postscript is produced on a different footing: *'l'Historien, peu nous proposer quelques lignes de:'* ('The Historian can offer us some lines on:'). This is no longer the factual declarative mode of narration which dominates the '*Histoire*', but a more speculative, putative set of reflections on what will or may happen in the Congo. The past can be told objectively, the future is a conjecture by the historian.

The second element that should be added is language (or code) choice. Whereas Tshibumba told his history to Fabian in the local variety of Swahili, he writes it in French. Interestingly, almost all of the epigraphic inscriptions produced on his paintings are in French too, and Fabian offers an explanation for this. Tshibumba's aim is to educate his people (as an artist–painter–historian), consequently, 'French, the language of school-books, would express his didactic intentions' (Fabian, 1996: 240). It may well be that Tshibumba inserts code choice in the perceived generic conventions he distinguishes for 'history': history should be a 'serious' text, written with a tight structure, linearly, in a neutral and detached tone, factually, and in a *monoglot* code. Similar generic perceptions could be found in the autobiographies discussed in Blommaert (1999b): the author there too opted for a monoglot code, unmixed Shaba Swahili, with a shift into monoglot French toward the end of the document, a shift marking the transition from an autobiographical narrative to a letter to the addressee. In the case of Julien, the author of the autobiographies, there was an explicit request from the addressee, a Belgian lady, to write 'in his mother tongue', Swahili.[5] In the case of Tshibumba, French may be the code choice normally associated with serious, factual genres such as history: it is undoubtedly a prestige code applicable to prestige genres.

So Tshibumba has clearly marked the space in which he will move: his history is framed in an objectivist epistemology and couched in discourse styles emphasizing factuality, detachment and seriousness, including a choice of French as the code. He has chosen an elite order of discourse for his history.

### The locus of history: Katanga/Shaba

But at the same time, there is a lot of subaltern sedimentation in his text, most clearly observable from the localist perspective in his text. Tshibumba does not 'move around' in his history: he writes it from Katanga/Shaba, from the place where he lives. He also articulates an interest in the fate of his ethnic group, the Baluba, a group located largely in the Shaba and Kasai regions.

The summary of the story given above already indicates this. Tshibumba writes more and more detailed stories on events in Katanga/Shaba and the neighboring province of Kasai. In his survey of the pre-colonial period, he provides some information on the Kongo kingdom (Lower Congo) and the Baluba (Kasai and Katanga) and Bakuba king-doms (Kasai). Then two chapters on kingdoms from other parts of the country are initiated but left blank: one on the Mongo (Equatorial region) and one on the Bampende (Bandundu region). Finally, he addresses two more Kasai–Katanga kingdoms, that of the Baluba–Shankadi and that of the Lunda. In the section on the explorers, a lot of space is given to Msiri, the king of Katanga. This section is entitled '*Dans le sud du Katanga*'. Similarly, when the early colonization period is treated, Tshibumba moves quickly from the proclamation of the Free State to immigration by white South Africans in Katanga, the creation of the UMHK and industrialization in Katanga and the role of the Bishop of Elisabethville. He mentions the workers' strike at the UMHK in 1941 and the way in which this strike was crushed by the Bishop and the Governor of Katanga. In the section on the First Republic and the Congo Crisis, Tshibumba spends a lot of attention on Kalonji's Baluba kingdom in the Kasai (and provides a sketch of the flag in the margins of the text) and to ethnic struggles caused by this secession. Evidently, the Katangese secession under Tshombe is also discussed and a sketch of the new Katangese flag is given. The Shaba Wars are discussed at great length, and the story ends with a visit to Katanga by Mobutu. Finally, in the postscript, Tshibumba (speculatively, see above) discusses 'tribalism', focusing strongly on the situation in Katanga.

So Katanga prevails; this is the window through which Tshibumba perceives his country. He narrates the history of the country as it occurred to a man in Katanga/Shaba. This perspective only changes when Mobutu enters the story. The discussions of the Second and Third Republics are not written 'from Shaba', but are presented from a 'national' point of view. This raises the issue of sources in Tshibumba's history, and to this we will return in the following sub-section.

Before that, a brief comparative note is in order. Fabian (1996: 240) says about Tshibumba that 'his conception of the history of Zaire, indeed his political position, was decidedly national, not regional'. To Fabian, this also informed Tshibumba's choice of French as the language for his epigraphs, and it was informed by Tshibumba's didactic and educational ambitions. Looking at the collection of paintings in the collection discussed by Fabian, his interpretation is plausible: although a lot of attention goes to Katangese or Kasai topics (Msiri, Kalonji, air raids on Lubumbashi, ethnic struggles, Tshombe, massacres in Katanga), there is more that speaks to 'Zaire' as a unit of reflection and imagination. But bear in mind the figures: of the 101 paintings in the collections, 40 are either situated in Katanga (e.g. the meeting of Stanley and Livingstone is set in Katanga, and emphasis is given to the fact that Lumumba's assassination took place in Katanga) or treat 'Katangese' topics such as Tshombe. And of the remaining 61 paintings, 12 treat Mobutu, the MPR or Mobutist political principles. Most of these Mobutist paintings are not anecdotal but abstract: they show a monument, Mobutist emblems or general developments such as the Zairianization of the economy. So, whereas Tshibumba's personal ambitions may have been situated at a 'national' level – speaking to the people of Zaire – the way in which he actually performs this bespeaks deep situatedness as a Katangese subject. Again, this raises the issue of sources.

## Sources

A number of sources can be distinguished in Tshibumba's history. First, of course, there is *Tshibumba's own historical experience*. We have seen that this experience is strongly 'placed': it is bound to Katanga, and Katanga functions as an epistemic and affective filter on history. In general, one can say that Tshibumba's own life is the organizing principle for the way in which he gets informed. But the sources are not completely idiosyncratic. As mentioned above, there is a shift in general footing and framing as soon as Tshibumba embarks on the Mobutu period in his history – a phenomenon noticeable both in the written history as well as in the sequence of paintings presented to Fabian. In some paintings, Tshibumba only represents symbols of Mobutism and *'authenticité'*: slogans, emblems, political principles. Similarly, when writing on the Mobutist period, a degree of distance and reverence can be distinguished, and Tshibumba's last sentence in the text is a Mobutist slogan: *'Sans un Guide comme/ MOBUTU, pas de ZAIRE UNIT et/son ARMEE'*. So a second identifiable source in the history is *official Mobutist propaganda*, probably performed by MPR sections in Tshibumba's environment. And it is illustrative of the hegemony organized by MPR over many years that this kind of vision of Zaire penetrated Tshibumba's perspective on history.

Two more sources need to be identified. There is some influence of *official Belgian colonial history*, notably in the way in which Tshibumba discusses the Bakongo Kingdom, the early period of exploration, the campaign against Arab slave traders, the Berlin Conference and so on.[6] Tshibumba was about 27 years old in 1973–1974, when Fabian met him (Fabian, 1996: ix), so he must have been born around 1946–1947. He must have gone to school in the heyday of the Belgian colonization, the 1950s, and the impact of official Belgian schoolbook history is unmistakable. The other, final, source is what could be called *Congolese mass media:* a rather diffuse set of images, tropes and event accounts derived from an apparently widespread body of messages and information disseminated in the Congo during the early years of independence. This source would inform most of the stories on the Congo Crisis, including the political events involving leading figures such as Kasavubu, Lumumba, Tshombe, Ileo, Kimba, Adula and others, as well as the rebellions of the mid-1960s.

These sources, with the exception of the first experiential source, define Tshibumba as a *recipient* of information, someone who is part of large, systemic trajectories of information in a society. At the same time, they offer us a glimpse of this economy of information, which seems to dominate the environment in which Tshibumba works. It is an economy heavily dominated by specific voices at specific times: the colonial school authorities in one period, Congolese official history and the media at another, Mobutist propaganda at yet another. The sources are thus anchored autobiographically, with one single source dominating each phase of his life and – consequently – his version of history. Interwoven through all this is Tshibumba's own experience as a Katangese subject with a keen interest in all these matters. And of course, more important than anything else, there is the act of writing (after having performed acts of painting and narrating) that creates a story out of rough and partial building blocks. This construction works brings us back to Fabian.

## History born out of ethnography

Tshibumba does not produce his history out of the blue. In his book, Fabian emphasizes the fact that the history of Congo emerged out of a series of events: the paintings, but even more a meeting between an artist with great interest in telling the story of his country and an ethnographer interested in it (Fabian, 1996: 220). The identity of *historien* is thus brought about in ethnographic interactions, and the outcome is an inter-actional product, co-constructed by Tshibumba and Fabian, and orga-nized around the sequential ordering of paintings and comments, expatiations and narratives triggered by questions about the paintings and their sequential ordering. It is all about practices and discursive events – being a historian is, in this case, definitely 'doing being a historian' in the Sacksian sense.

Consequently, when we turn to the written text, one cannot avoid the enormous degree of intertextuality (or 'inter-practicity') inscribed in it. It is a re-telling, re-ordering of what emerged in conversations with Fabian in 1973–1974, six to seven years after the fact, in 1980. As outlined above, the similarities in general outlook and framing are overwhelming, and the text as well as the paintings and narratives still belong to an action com-plex organized around, and oriented toward, an inquisitive and genuinely interested ethnographer.

But there is more to it, and the problems are not solved by invoking coherence between the history painted and narrated, and the history written some years later. The triple object raises numerous questions and allows us to discover one or two new things. The main question is: why did Tshibumba feel compelled – or simply want or desire – to produce a formal, written version of the account he produced six or seven years ago? The question is hard to answer, but some clues may be gathered from what we discussed earlier. *Genre* may be an important lead, and *remembering* another.

Let us start with genre. Above, I emphasized the fact that the document emanates a series of generic aspirations toward serious, epistemologically objective text organized around stories of the past. I also emphasized how Tshibumba identifies himself as a historian, explicitly in the form of repeated self-qualification as well as in his attempt to provide notes on epistemology and methodology. My suggestion is that the repeated acts of performance as a historian are identity work, culminating in a textual artifact that would most clearly articulate this identity: a written, generically regimented text, constructed on the basis of available and accessible textual-generic resources and oriented toward an imagined (or distant) genre of historiography. It is the written text that establishes Tshibumba as a historian producing structured knowledge. In an economy of communication where few people have access to elite genres of literacy (something which, in Tshibumba's case, can be established on the basis of features of his orthography, both in the handwritten text and in epigraphs on his paintings), the attempt to produce such a genre also establishes him as an intellectual. Adding to his pictorial and epigraphic world, Tshibumba now places himself in a world of literate intellectual production.

This involves both continuity and a break with the two previous versions. This time, owing to the generic work performed by Tshibumba, he emerges as a monological author, not someone who interactionally co-constructs an account but someone who autonomously constructs a prestigious, quotable and archivable text-artifact. It is obviously coherent with his historical work performed years ago with Fabian, but moving into the literacy domain is a different stage in the identity work performed by Tshibumba. It is a shift in medium, but the medium is socially evaluated and politically loaded: using it shifts Tshibumba into a different position, and the knowledge he now produces is knowledge produced from a different vantage point in society.

There is a second aspect to this, the aspect of remembering, and we notice it through a very small window in the text. One of the remarkable anachronisms in the text is the use of 'Leopold I' where 'Leopold II' would be expected. Tshibumba commits this error in the section on the exploration and the early colonization, and he commits it systematically. This is remarkable because of the fact that Leopold II must have been a rather well-known figure to most Congolese of his generation, being the central hero in the Belgian story of conquest, pacification and civilization in Congo. It is also remarkable because, in his conversations with Fabian, the error does not occur. He systematically uses, correctly, Leopold II as the architect of colonialism in Congo (see e.g. Fabian, 1996: 224). Such errors may indicate the absence of an archive for remembering. Tshibumba probably had no notes nor drafts of his history (apart from epigraphs on his paintings – which he sold); he constructed it while writing, and the act of writing thus seems to be the most crucial instrument of remembering. So apart from the identity work, there may also be a desire to remember, and to remember correctly, in an environment where documentation is a rare commodity. Similar features of attempts toward precise, 'final' remembering occurred in the autobiographies by Julien analyzed in Blommaert (2001c, 2008). They are paradoxical because both in the case of Julien and in that of Tshibumba, the *product* of remembering – the original text – was sent off to an addressee and no copies were presumably kept.

Merge this with the earlier comments on identity work, and the idea that texts are there to be quotable and archivable needs to be twisted a little: they are quotable and archivable *for someone else*, not for the author. The record constructed in writing is not a record for one's own use: it is again a record that can be inserted in interactions with and by an audience, written literally *for* that audience. In this respect, Fabian comments on the *Vocabulaire d'Elisabethille*:

> Clearly, the *Vocabulaire* situates itself in a strain of popular thought which conceives of 'history' as the activation of intellect, as practical reflection on the present predicaments of life, rather than as an archival return to the past for its own sake. (Fabian, 1990a: 118)

More specifically, Fabian concludes that 'the Vocabulaire is not a memory but a reminder' (Fabian, 1990a: 188). These comments probably need to be qualified, for there are significant differences between the *Vocabulaire d'Elisabethville* and Tshibumba's *Histoire du Zaïre*. Tshibumba's *Histoire* is an act of remembering, a crucial act in this respect. The resulting text-artifact, however, is not seen as a lasting repository for one's own memory. As soon as remembering results in a text, the text becomes a reminder for someone else.

## Conclusions

Tshibumba writes history as a historian, in a neutral tone and objectivist epistemology, emphasizing factuality and unbiasedness, and meaning to instruct and to educate. But he does so from within a specific place, a place marked by inaccessible resources to accomplish this generic goal. There are constraints stemming from his location, spatially as well as socially, in economies of information, semiosis and language. But these constraints are overruled, when it comes to identifying the attempt toward a particular kind of textuality (one that also allows a particular kind of identity work), by the manipulation of textual-generic conventions. Tshibumba is a historian because he writes in a particular, generically regimented way. This generic regimentation is what allows him to assume the stance of the historian, because using this genre involves an enormous shift in status and image of his actions. This is a case of orthopraxy (Scott, 1990: 117), in which Tshibumba adopts (real or perceived) 'model' practices without necessarily adopting their established, conventional 'load'.

The reason is that all of this is done within categories and criteria that are local, i.e. the meanings, status and impact derived from the production of such a generically regimented text are part of local economies of signs and symbolic capital. These economies have epistemic dimensions: they define what can be allowable as 'historical knowledge', and using them inserts texts in generically controlled epistemic fields. In Tshibumba's case, we have seen how written textuality generates hierarchical relocations of knowledge: it organizes knowledge and memory in such a way that it becomes history, and it results in a text-artifact that can be used for the benefit of someone else's memory. But in order to attain this function, a complex set of linguistic, generic, stylistic resources needs to be mobilized and deployed, all of which belong to local value-scales (and thus involve an important relocation of linguistic resources into new referential and indexical frames). Even non-standard French can pass as an elite code when it is written in a society where both French and writing are rare and unevenly distributed commodities. Tshibumba is aware of these value scales: we have seen above that Tshibumba identifies the absence of African writing as the key to understanding why African history has so often been misrepresented. He thus displays an acute awareness of the relationship between writing, authority and power. Putting the story previously painted and orally narrated into particular forms of writing is what makes him into a historian: he orthopractically aligns the story so as to fit models of text which to him would qualify it as 'historiography'.

It is an awareness of such intricate, nuanced and delicate relations between signs and economies in which they acquire value and meaning that allows us to construct 'voice' for Tshibumba as a historian. A blank, linguistic or propositional reading of the text does not produce anything that comes close to vindicating the document as a source for historical research. We need an ethnographic approach in which signs are seen as relatively fixed, hierarchized (or at least stratified) resources with attributable functions derived from the economies, not from the single signs. This is a linguistics that is not linguistic, but one that addresses language as something into which people make investments. And only through the application of such a linguistics can texts become historical documents. If not, they are merely old, for it is voice, its genesis, structure and the constraints under which it operates that inform us about history.

We can make texts historical as soon as we are able to identify the voice they articulate. Carlo Ginzburg demonstrated this with respect to a 17th-century miller from Friuli (Ginzburg, 1990). It can be productively applied to subjects from Africa, Latin America or other disenfranchised parts of the world where regimes of language work in different ways from ours, and where knowledge, truth and historical experience consequently take on different shapes.

## Acknowledgments

Research for this paper was facilitated by a personal research grant from the National Science Foundation-Flanders. Thanks are due to Bogumil Jewsiwiecki, who passed me a copy of Tshibumba's text. The interest I have in this kind of work was triggered by Johannes Fabian and Dell Hymes, whose intellectual influence is gratefully acknowledged. Judy Irvine commented perceptively and generously on the version presented at the AAA session in November 2001. Trevor Stack also sent me useful comments on that version. My friends and colleagues in the FWO research group on 'language, power and identity' – Monica Heller, Jim Collins, Ben Rampton, Stef Slembrouck and Jef Verschueren – between 1999 and 2003 considerably sharpened my attention to issues of inequality and distribution patterns in language. Their impact deserves grateful acknowledgment as well. A more elaborate analysis of Tshibumba's (and Julien's) texts can be found in Blommaert (2008).

## Notes

(1)    See for instance the Catholic Encyclopaedia on the Internet, probably not a very good example (http://www.newadvent.org/cathen/04503a.htm). The lemma 'historical criticism' reads: 'Historical criticism is the art of distinguishing the true from the false

concerning facts of the past'. I am familiar with critical traditions such as New Historicism, which offer far more nuanced views on text and truth. But the point to be made here is the connection between text-ideologies and notions of 'truth' or 'historical validity'.

(2)  Some inspiration for this was found in Caplan (1997), a work in which a delicate treatment of oral narrative, written documentation and ethnographic conversation is offered. A similar, very stimulating work on relations between stories and history is Collins (1998).

(3)  The Union Minière du Haut Katanga was a Belgian mining company later nationalized by Mobutu and renamed Gecamines. The UMHK was the major industrial power in the Shaba/Katanga mining areas, and its plant dominated the city of Lubumbashi to the extent that it became emblematic of the place and central to historical narratives such as that of the *Vocabulaire d'Elisabethville*. It also figures in a good number of Tshibumba's paintings.

(4)  In giving these examples, I will be using a transcription format in which as many graphic characteristics of the handwritten text as possible have been maintained: superscript insertions, corrections, strikeouts and so forth. A maximum of such features are also maintained in the English translation following each example.

(5)  Which was not his mother tongue at all. More likely, Julien was a native speaker of a Luba language, and Shaba Swahili was the language he used as an employee in a multilingual urban environment in Lubumbashi.

(6)  The Bakongo Kingdom was a well-established trope in official schoolbook history, as it instantiated conversions to Christianity in a period far preceding that of colonialism and could thus be seen as a model for establishing a 'civilized' – Christian – society in Congo.

# 6 Historical Bodies and Historical Space

## Introduction

In this chapter, I will offer some building blocks for an ethnographic theory of linguistic landscapes. The core of this theoretical argument is to see space as a historically configured phenomenon and as an actor, as something that operates as a material force on human behavior performed in space. Space is not neutral, in other words, and if it is our intention to bring Linguistic Landscape Studies (LLS) to maturity, we need to provide a sharply delineated vision on how space is semiotized, and how it semiotizes what goes on within its orbit. In this chapter, I will begin by sketching our main obstacle in this exercise: the deeply anchored synchronic view that dominates sociolinguistics and other disciplines. This obstacle, however, can be cleared in a remarkably simple way, using some tools developed in the work of Ron and Suzie Scollon.

Theoretically, sophisticated ethnography is rare, and it takes an effort to discover it, because sometimes it is found in work that does not announce or present itself as 'typical' ethnography (the fieldwork-based monograph is still the 'typical' ethnographic product). The work of Ron and Suzie Scollon is a case in point. Much of their major works do not *look* like ethnography. There are no lengthy introductions about the fieldwork which was conducted, for instance, and the main drive of their work is to contribute to semiotics and discourse analysis. Yet they systematically insisted on the ethnographic basis of their work (e.g. Scollon & Scollon, 2009). And this paper will argue that their work contains very useful, even momentous, interventions in ethnographic theory and method. If we talk about sophisticated ethnography, the work of the Scollons certainly qualifies for inclusion into that category.

I will focus in particular on two efforts by the Scollons: *Nexus Analysis* (Scollon & Scollon, 2004) and *Discourses in Place* (Scollon & Scollon, 2003); and I will try to show that both works contain and articulate a theoretical overture toward history – an overture I find of major importance for ethnographic theory and method. The works do that, respectively, by means of a theorization of embodiment in the notion of 'the historical body', and by a theorization of space as agentive and non-neutral. Taken together, these two interventions offer us key ingredients necessary for transcending the perpetual risk of localism and anecdotism in ethnography, by allowing ethnography to move from the uniquely situated events it describes to structural and systemic regularities in interpretation. This has implications for ethnography, to be sure, but also for a broader field of studies of human conduct, including linguistics and sociolinguistics. Before moving on to discuss the two interventions by the Scollons, I first need to formulate the problem more precisely.

## The Problem of Synchrony

The main methodological problem of ethnography, identified close to three decades ago by Johannes Fabian (1983), can be summarized as follows. Ethnography, typically, depends on data drawn from a bounded set of human encounters in real space and time. The ethnographer and his/ her 'informant' interact, like all humans, in a contextually specific space-time which (as decades of research in pragmatics have taught us) defines the outcome of such interactions. The outcome is, typically, an epistemically genred collection of texts: recordings, field notes and later a published paper or a monograph. Ethnographers walk away from the field with a collection of such texts, and these texts bear witness to the contextual conditions under which they were constructed. Concretely, phonetic descriptions of a language can differ when the informant misses both front teeth from when the informant has a fully intact set of them. They will also differ when the ethnographer had access to a sophisticated digital recording device for collecting the data, from when he or she had to rely solely on their ear and competence in the use of the phonetic alphabet. Or a narrative account of a robbery will differ depending on whether the narrator was the victim, the perpetrator or a witness of the robbery. And of course it will differ when the ethnographer him- or herself was involved in such roles in the robbery. The point is that ethnography draws its data from real-world moments of intersubjective exchange in which the ethnographer and the informant are both sensitive to the contextual conditions of this exchange (see also Bourdieu, 2004; Blommaert, 2005b).

The problem is, however, that as soon as the ethnographer tries to present his or her findings as 'science' – as soon as the 'data' enter the genre-machines of academic writing, in other words – this fundamental contextual sharedness is erased and replaced by a discursively constructed distance between the ethnographer and his or her 'object'. The sharedness of time and space, of language and of event structure gives way to a unidirectional, textual relationship in which the ethnographer is no longer an *interlocutor* alongside the informant, but a detached, 'objective' voice who does not talk with the interlocutor but *about* him or her. This problem is particularly acute when the ethnographer tries to generalize, i.e. use his or her data to make claims of general validity, of the type 'the Bamileke are matrilinear'. Fabian observes how in such textual moves, the timeless present tense is preferred over a discourse that represents this knowledge as situational and context-dependent. He notes that 'the present tense "freezes" a society at the time of observation' (Fabian, 1983: 81) and detaches ethnographic knowledge from the dialogical and context-sensitive frame in which it was constructed. The shared timespace in which it emerged is erased and replaced by a timeless present – something that Fabian calls the 'denial of coevalness' and identifies as a major epistemological problem hampering any ethnographic claim to general validity and generalization (see also Bourdieu, 2004).

This introduction of the timeless present is, of course, a widespread practice in the textual politics of scientific generalization and abstraction. It is central to what is known as 'synchronic' analysis in structural linguistics, mainstream sociolinguistics and discourse analysis, structuralist and functionalist anthropology and so forth. And in all of these disciplines, we encounter the same fundamental epistemological problem: as soon as scholars try to address structural or systemic features of a society, they have to shift from real time into abstract time, they have to extract features of dynamic lived experience and place them at a timeless, static plane of general validity. Whatever makes data social and cultural – their situatedness in social and cultural processes and histories – disappears and is replaced by 'laws' and 'rules' that appear to have a validity which is not contextually sensitive.

We are familiar with this move in structural linguistics, where notably the development of modern phonology in the early 20th century made 'synchrony' into the level at which scientific generalization of linguistic facts needed to be made. Michael Silverstein concisely summarizes this move as follows:

> Late in the 19th century, linguistics as a field transformed itself from a science focused on language change, the generalizations based on comparative and historical Indo-European, Semitic, Finno-Ugric, etc. At the center of such change was 'phonetic law', and in seeking the causes for the

'exceptionlessness' of phonetic changes, scholars went both to the phonetics laboratory and to the dialectological and 'exotic language' field.
The important results of such study, certainly achieved by the 1920s,
were: the postulation (or 'discovery') of the phonemic principle of
abstract, immanent classes of sound realized variably in actual phonetic
articulation and audition; and the *synchronicization* of linguistic theory
as the theory of phonological structure involving structured relationships
among the abstract sounds or phonological segments of any language, a
syntagmatic and paradigmatic structure of categories of sound.
(Silverstein, 2009: 14–15)

In this new Modern linguistics, sound *change* was replaced by sound
*replacement*. For people such as Bloomfield, this discovery of 'elementary
particles' (phonemes) and of synchrony as the level of linguistic abstraction was cause to claim fully scientific status for linguistics (Silverstein,
2009: 15). Science, for him and many others in the heyday of structuralism, was the art of generalization, of identifying the immobile, non-
dynamic, non-contextual, non-stochastic facts of language and social life.
And this was done, precisely, by the elision of real time and real space
from the purview of analysis. Analysis was synchronic, and to the extent
that it was diachronic, the diachronicity of it rested on a sequenced juxta-
position and comparison of solidly synchronic states of affairs (Meeuwis &
Brisard, 1993). Such diachronicity, in short, was not (and can never be)
*historical*. To go by the words of Edwin Ardener commenting on the
Neogrammarian approach,

> The grandeur of the Neogrammarian model for historical linguistics lit-
> erally left nothing more to be said. This grandeur lay in its perfect genera-
> tiveness. It did not, however, generate history. (Ardener, 1971: 227)

History is time filled with social and cultural actions; it is not just chronology on which events have been plotted. A lot of historical linguistics is in
that sense chronological linguistics, not historical at all. Time in itself
does not inform us about social systems, about patterns and structures of
human organization. What can, historically, be seen as systemic or structural features (i.e. features that define a particular social system in a particular period) becomes in this chronological and synchronic paradigm
converted into permanencies and hence into essences. Synchronicity therefore inevitably contains the seeds of essentialism.

The way to escape this trap is, one could argue, relatively simple:
reintroduce history as a real category of analysis. The simplicity is decep-
tive of course, for what is required is a toolkit of concepts that are

*intrinsically* historical; that is, concepts whose very nature and direction point toward connections between the past and the present in terms of *social* activities – concepts, in short, that define and explain synchronic social events in terms of their histories of becoming as social events. This is where we need to turn to the Scollons.

## Historical Bodies and Historical Space

Our branches of scholarship already have a number of such intrinsically historical concepts. Terms such as intertextuality, interdiscursivity and entextualization, especially in their rich Bakhtinian interpretation, explain the textual present in relation to textual histories – not just histories of textual 'stuff', but also histories of use, abuse and evaluation of textual materials (e.g. Bauman & Briggs, 1990; Blommaert, 2005b; Fairclough, 1992; Silverstein, 2005a; Silverstein & Urban, 1996a; see Johnstone, 2008: Chapter 5 for a survey and discussion). Whenever we use a term such as 'bitch' in relation to a female subject, we are not only introducing a semantic history into this usage of the term – the transformation of the meaning of 'female dog' to 'unpleasant woman' – but also a pragmatic and metapragmatic, indexical history of the term – the fact that this term is used as an insult and should, consequently, not generally be used in public and formal performances. The extension to include a pragmatic and metapragmatic dimension to intertextual processes introduces a whole gamut of contextual factors into the analysis of intertextual processes. It is not just about borrowing and re-using 'texts' in the traditional sense of the term, it is about reshaping, reordering, reframing the text from one social world of usage into another one.

*Nexus Analysis* started from a reflection on intertextuality. For the Scollons, human semiotic action could only be observed at the moment of occurrence, but needed to be analyzed in terms of 'cycles of discourse' (Scollon & Scollon, 2004: Chapter 2) – a term which Ron Scollon later replaced by 'discourse itineraries' (Scollon, 2008). Such itineraries are trajectories of 'resemiotization', something which in turn relied on the Scollons' fundamental insight that discourse was always mediated (Scollon, 2001) – it was never just 'text', but always human social action in a real world full of real people, objects and technologies. Consequently, intertextuality needs to be broadly understood, for 'the relationship of text to text, language to language, is not a direct relationship but is always mediated by the actions of social actors as well as through material objects in the world' (Scollon, 2008: 233). And whenever we use words, that use 'encapsulates or resemiotizes an extended historical itinerary of action, practice, narrative, authorization, certification, metonymization, objectivization and technologization or reification' (Scollon, 2008: 233). Changes in any of these processes and practices are changes to the discourse itself; even if the discourse itself remains apparently stable and unaltered, the material, social and cultural conditions under which it is produced and under which it emerges can change and affect what the discourse is and does. Discourse analysis, for the Scollons, revolves around the task 'to map such itineraries of relationships among text, action, and the material world through what we call a "nexus analysis"' (Scollon, 2008: 233).

Such an analysis naturally shares a lot with Bakhtinian notions of intertextuality; at the same time it broadens the scope of the analysis by focusing on the interplay of the social and the material work in relation to discourse. And while intertextuality in the work of Fairclough and others still mainly addresses purely textual objects, the objects defined by the Scollons – nexuses – display far more complexity. A nexus is an intersection in real time and space of three different 'aggregates of discourse':

> the *discourses in place*, some social arrangement by which people come together in social groups (a meeting, a conversation, a chance contact, a queue) – the *interaction order*, and the life experiences of the individual social actors – the *historical body*. (Scollon & Scollon, 2004: 19)

Discourse, as social action, emerges out of the nexus of these three forces, and an analysis of discourse consequently needs to take all three into consideration. To many, of course, this move is enough to recategorize the Scollons as semioticians rather than as discourse analysts. For the Scollons themselves, the ambition was to develop

> a more general ethnographic theory and methodology which can be used to analyze the relationships between discourse and technology but also place this analysis in the broader context of the social, political and cultural issues of any particular time. (Scollon & Scollon, 2004: 7)

Observe here how this ethnographic-theoretical ambition takes the methodological shape of *historical* analysis. So when the Scollons talk about an ethnographically situated object – human action and practice – this object is historically grounded and generated, and the features of the synchronic object must be understood as outcomes of this historical process of becoming. The three aggregates of discourse are all historical dimensions of any synchronic social action, and their historicity lies in the fact that all three refer to histories of 'iterative' human action crystallizing into normative social patterns of conduct, expectation and evaluation – *traditions* in the anthropological sense of the term. Synchronic events, thus, display the traces of (and can only be understood by referring to) normative-traditional complexes of social action, resulting (in a very Bourdieuan sense) in habituated, 'normal' or 'normalized' codes for conduct. And these codes, then, are situated in three different areas: individual experience, skills and capacities (the historical body); social space (discourses in place); and patterned, ordered, genred interaction (the interaction order).

The notion of 'interaction order' is attributed to Goffman (Scollon & Scollon, 2004: 22). Yet the actual meaning of that term and its use in *Nexus Analysis* is an amendment to Goffman's 'interaction order'. In order to see that we need to look at the two other notions: historical bodies and historical space.

We have seen above that the Scollons defined the historical body as 'the life experiences of the individual social actors'; somewhat more explicitly, they also described it as people's 'life experiences, their goals and purposes, and their unconscious ways of behaving and thinking' (Scollon & Scollon, 2004: 46). Whenever people enter into social action, they bring along their own skills, experiences and competences, and this 'baggage', so to speak, conditions and constrains what they can do in social action. Historical bodies have been formed in particular social spaces and they represent, to use an older notion, the 'communicative competence' of people in such social spaces.

Thus a teacher has grown accustomed to the school system, the actual school building where s/he works, his/her colleagues, the curriculum, the teaching materials and infrastructure, the ways of professionally organizing his/her work, academic discourse, the students. Various processes intersected in this: there is formal learning, there is informal learning, particular patterns are acquired while others are just encountered, certain skills are permanent while others are transitory, and so on. The end result of this, however, is that the teacher can enter a classroom and perform adequately – s/he knows exactly where the classroom is, what kinds of activities are expected there, and how to perform these activities adequately. The historical body of the teacher has been formed in such a way that s/he will be perceived as a teacher by others, and that most of the actual practices s/he performs can be habitual and routine. Precisely the habitual and routine character of these practices makes them – at a higher level of social structure – 'professional' (see Pachler *et al.*, 2008 for illustrations).

There is a long tradition of speaking about such things in relation to the mind; the Scollons, however, locate them in the body. What is actually perceived, and acted upon semiotically by other people, is a body in a particular space. This body talks, and behind the talking one can suspect thinking, but it also moves, manipulates objects, displays particular stances (aggression, tenderness, care, seriousness, etc.). It is the Scollons' preference for material aspects of discourse that makes them choose the body rather than the mind as the locus for such individual experiences.

But by doing so they open up a whole range of issues for the social study of language: issues of learning and acquisition in the semiotic field, questions about the way we appear to know what we know about signs and meanings. Until now, such questions have dominantly been answered by reference to the mind as well. The questions raised by a notion such as the historical body, however, shift the debate away from the mind and into the field of embodied knowledge. The gradual process by means of which teachers, for instance, acquire the habitual and routine practices and the knowledge to perform them adequately, cannot just be seen as a process of 'learning' in the traditional sense of the term. It is rather a process of *enskilment*: the step-by-step development, in an apprentice mode, of cultural knowledge through skillful activities (Gieser, 2008; also Ingold, 2000; Jackson, 1989). Shared kinesthetic experiences with social activities (and talking would be one of them) lead to shared understandings of such activities, and 'meaning or knowledge is discovered in the very process of imitating another person's movements' (Gieser, 2008: 300).

Consider now how the Scollons describe a sequence of actions in which a teacher hands a paper to the student. First, the teacher must approach the student with the paper, and the student needs to understand the proximity of the teacher, and his/her holding the paper in a particular way, as the beginning of a 'handing-the-paper' sequence. Both participants need to know these bodily routines of physical proximity, direction of movement and manipulation of an object. Then,

> the paper itself is handed through a long and practiced set of micro-movements that are adjusted to the weight of the object and the timing of the movements of their hands toward each other. Any very small failure of this timing and these movements and the object falls. This can easily lead to the embarrassment of the student or the teacher having to reach down to the floor to regain control of the paper. (Scollon & Scollon, 2004: 64)

Observe how this moment of complex physical-kinesic handling of the paper is *semiotic*: if it is done wrongly, embarrassment may ensue – there may be giggling from the class, blushing from the student and/or the teacher, muttered mutual apologies and so forth. The 'practiced set of micro-movements', therefore, is replete with semiotic signs and signals, and carries social risks and rewards (making it, of course, a normative set: things have to be done in a particular way). It is embodied cultural knowledge – movements and positions of the body that convey cultural information and have acquired the shape of routine skills. Such movements have been 'practiced', they have a measure of immediate recognizability and they induce particular frames of action and understanding for all the partici-pants. Whenever the Scollons discuss the ways in which students get used to keyboard-and-screen handling in a virtual learning environment, or seating arrangement and attention organization in traditional ('panoptic') classrooms, they emphasize the minute details of bodily practices – as acquired, enskilled forms of social conduct in a learning environment.

Through the notion of the historical body, thus, we see how a connec-tion is made between semiotics and embodiment. Participants in social action bring their real bodies into play, but their bodies are semiotically enskilled: their movements and positions are central to the production of meaning, and are organized around normative patterns of conduct. And they do this, as we have seen, in a real spatial arena too. They do this, in actual fact, in close interaction with a historical space; so let us consider that historical space now.

As *Discourses in Place* (Scollon & Scollon, 2003) makes abundantly clear, space is never a neutral canvass for the Scollons. The book is, in fact, one of the very rare profound and sophisticated problematizations of space in the field of sociolinguistics, and while the notion of 'discourses in place' re-emerges in *Nexus Analysis*, as we have seen, the treatment of space in *Discourses in Place* reads like a mature contribution to linguistic landscaping. While a lot of work of LLS hardly questions the space in which linguistic signs appear, *Discourses in Place* develops a whole theory of signs in space ('geosemiotics'), revolving around notions such as 'emplacement' – the actual semiotic process that results from the specific location of signs in the material world. A 'no smoking' sign has this restrictive meaning only in the space where the sign is placed. So, while the sign itself has a latent meaning, its meaning only becomes an actual social and semiotic fact when it is emplaced in a particular space. It is then that the sign becomes consequential: someone smoking in the vicinity of that sign can now be seen as a transgressor, someone who violates a rule clearly inscribed in that space. Emplacement, thus, adds a dimension of spatial scope to semiotic processes: it points toward the elementary fact that communication always takes place in a spatial arena, and that this spatial arena imposes its own rules, possibilities and restrictions on com-munication. Space, in that sense, is an *actor* in sociolinguistic processes, not a human actor but a social actor nevertheless (see also Blommaert *et al.*, 2005; more on this in the next chapter).

It is very often a *normative* actor in sociolinguistic processes, and this is where history enters the picture. There are expectations – normative expectations – about relationships between signs and particular spaces. One expects certain signs in certain places: shop signs and publicity billboards in a shopping street, for instance, or train timetables in a railway station. We do not expect such timetables in a café or a restaurant. When signs are 'in place', so to speak, habitual interpretations of such signs can be made, because the signs fit almost ecologically into their spatial surroundings. When they are 'out of place', or 'transgressive' in the terminology of Scollon and Scollon (2003: 147), we need to perform additional interpretation work because a different kind of social signal has been given. In a shopping street, shop signs are in place, while graffiti is out of place. The former belong there, the latter does not, and its presence raises questions of ownership of the place, of legitimate use of the place, of the presence of 'deviant' groups of users in that place, and so on. So, we attach to particular places a whole array of objects, phenomena and activities, and we do that in a normative sense, that is, we do it in a way that shapes our expectations of 'normalcy' in such places. We expect the people sitting in a university lecturing hall to be students, and we expect their behavior to be that of students as well; we can have very flexible expectations with regard to what they wear and how they look, but we would have more restrictive expectations about the objects they bring into the lecturing hall (a student entering the hall with a shotgun would, for instance, be highly unexpected and, consequently, alarming). We also expect them to use certain types of speech and literacy resources during the lecture – and when all of that is in place, we feel that the lecture proceeded 'normally'.

It is *the connection between space and normative expectations*, between space and 'order', that makes space historical, for the normative expectations we attach to spaces have their feet in the history of social and spatial arrangements in any society. The fact that we have these clear and widely shared expectations about university lecturing rooms is not a synchronic phenomenon: it is something that belongs to the history of institutions. And getting acquainted with such histories is part of the processes of enskillment we discussed earlier. We have been enskilled in recognizing the nature of particular places, and we are able to act appropriately – that is 'normally' – in such places. We now enter a lecturing hall, and we know exactly what to do and how to do it; we are instantly tuned into the patterns of normative expectations that belong to that place – for instance, silence from the students as soon as the lecturing starts – and we react accordingly when transgressive signs are being produced (as when a student's mobile phone goes off, or someone walks into the hall with a shotgun). An 'interaction order' falls into place, literally, as soon as we have entered that place and the place has been mutually recognized as such-and-such a place. The historical bodies and the historical space now operate in terms of the same order.

The historical body is, thus, narrowly connected to historical spaces: we get enskilled in the use of social and physical space, and our bodies fall into shape (or out of shape) each time we enter or leave a certain space. This, I believe, is the core of the Scollons' insistence on language in the material world: the material world is a spatial world, a real material environment full of objects, technologies and signs, upon which we act semiotically. Human semiotic behavior, thus, is behavior in real space, in relation and with reference to real space. The nexus of the historical body and of discourses in place is a historical, normative nexus, in which both dialectically generate the conditions for communication, its potential and its restrictions. The third element of the nexus triad, the 'interaction order', in that sense becomes something rather far removed from Goffman's initial formulations. The interaction order is *an effect* of the dialectics between the historical body and historical space. It is the actual order of communicative conduct that ensues from enskilled bodies in a space inscribed with particular conditions for communication. It has very little existence outside of it, and the three elements of the triad now form one ethnographic object of inquiry.

## The Zebra Crossing

As an illustration of the way in which space is densely packed with several different discourses, and so forms a 'semiotic aggregate', Scollon and Scollon (2003: 180–189) analyze a very mundane thing: crossing the street in five cities. In each of the cities, such places where pedestrians can cross are littered with signs, some for the traffic, some for the pedestrians and some for both; some directly related to the regulation of crossing the street and halting the traffic, some (e.g. shop signs) unrelated to it. Pedestrians must make sense of these multiple discourses, and such sense-making processes are part of the habitual routine practice of crossing a street. With the remarks made above in mind, I would now like to return to the example of crossing a street, focusing specifically on how the nexus triad should be seen as a historically shaped complex organizing everyday practices. I shall focus on one particular moment, documented in Figure 6.1, and explain how we can see such a moment as a moment of social semiotics.

**Figure 6.1** To cross a street

We see someone on a zebra crossing in what looks like a relatively busy shopping street. The person (incidentally, this author) moves forward on the zebra crossing; he looks to the left and his left hand is raised in a gesture signaling 'stop', 'careful' or 'thanks'. We notice also that a bus has just passed the zebra crossing, and from Blommaert's gesture we can infer that another vehicle is approaching the zebra crossing.

The zebra crossing is on the corner of the street in Antwerp, Belgium, where Blommaert lives, and it has a history. It was only recently put there by the municipality after protracted campaigning by the neighborhood. As mentioned earlier, this is a shopping street with rather dense traffic; there is a primary school on the street, and every day hundreds of children had to cross this street without the protection of a zebra crossing. It used to be a hazardous place to cross the street, and the zebra crossing significantly improved traffic safety for pedestrians. In the terminology of the Scollons, the zebra crossing would be a 'municipal regulatory discourse' (Scollon & Scollon, 2003: 181–185); the fact is that the sheer existence of this zebra crossing makes a huge semiotic difference, one that is inscribed in Blommaert's gesture while crossing the street. How?

The zebra crossing flags a particular set of rights and obligations in that particular place; it creates, so to speak, a historical micro-space with a particular order. A pedestrian on a zebra crossing has right of way, and it is mandatory for cars and other vehicles to halt in front of the zebra crossing. If a pedestrian crosses the street elsewhere, where there is no zebra crossing, she or he has no such rights and car drivers have no such obligations. Consequently, while car drivers will almost always and instantly halt their car when someone crosses a zebra crossing, they may hoot their horn, flash their headlights or even start scolding and shouting at pedestrians crossing elsewhere. The zebra crossing is thus a semiotic space, a 'discourse in place' that imposes, within the small confines of that space, a particular interaction order – one into which all possible participants have been effectively enskilled. Car drivers know immediately that they should halt in front of a zebra crossing; they will scan the road ahead for such signs and will react almost instinctively when they see a pedestrian on a zebra crossing. Pedestrians, in turn, will walk toward the zebra crossing if they intend to cross the street. They know how to recognize it, and they know that they should cross the street there if they intend to do it safely. The actual crossing, then, is another instance of enskillment, in which the pedestrian first looks left and right, ensuring that no danger is ahead, then moves across while keeping eye contact with approaching cars and, if necessary, communicating with them by means of gestures. Crossing a street is an act of ordered and localized communication, in which bodies interact in an orderly fashion with regulatory signs and with other participants in that space. There are dimensions of institutionality here as well as dimensions of a more general kind of social order: people responding and adjusting to 'normal' and orderly ways of doing things.

This moment is a nexus of practice, and we see the three elements of the aggregate interacting: there is the enskilled historical body which has been adjusted to or enskilled in the orderly use of a particular historical micro-space (the zebra crossing), resulting in a particular interaction order. The interaction order emerges and becomes activated as a compelling normative frame for all participants as soon as the enskilled body engages with the historical space – as soon as Blommaert, a seasoned street-crosser, walks into a space which is institutionally defined in terms of formal rights and obligations, the zebra crossing. His engagement with that space moves his body into an environment in which certain acts of communication are mandatory, expected or desired, others transgressive. He is, for instance, expected not to unnecessarily delay the crossing; car drivers would as a rule not be overly amused if he would start doing Michael Jackson's moonwalk on a zebra crossing in a busy street such as this one; the hooting and shouting would start at once, no matter how entertaining the performance may be.

The fact is that Blommaert knows this and so do the drivers. All of us have acquired the codes valid in such micro-spaces, and all of us are capable of shifting in and out of such codes when we enter and leave such spaces. The next space will impose different codes, and again we will be familiar with them. Blommaert is, for instance familiar with the shops behind him; he knows how to behave adequately there and he can shift in and out of the interaction orders valid in them in no time. As we move through daily routines, the nexuses of practice follow each other swiftly, in a matter of seconds, often with dramatic differences between them, but rarely causing dramatic problems for those who engage in them. In fact, we all possess a tremendously complex array of such enskilled knowledge, capable of navigating us through spaces that are experienced as entirely mundane and unproblematic, while they are, in fact, extraordinarily complex. We experience this complexity only, as a rule, when we leave our familiar environments and find ourselves in places where, for instance, car drivers do *not* have the obligation to stop (or the habit of stopping) in front of zebra crossings. Many a broken rib or leg testifies to that sudden experience of unexpected complexity.[1]

Mainstream notions of communicative competence, with their emphasis on formal learning and acquisition and their focus on cognition, are not sufficient to cover this vast field of flexible skills we possess and deploy in our interaction with our environments. It is to the credit of the Scollons that they understood this and offered clear and stimulating suggestions for overcoming this problem. They were particularly successful in blending the small and the large dimension of human social practice: the ways in which each act of communication is at once exceptional and typical, that it always consists of completely new forms of patterning and organization, while it derives its communicability from sharedness and recognizability of patterns. And they understood quite clearly that the way to blend these different dimensions is by introducing historical lineages to individual practices, by suggesting that uniqueness always has a pedigree, an intertext or interdiscourse which needs to be understood in the broadest possible way – that is, in relation to the totality of features of practice, including the bodily, spatial and material ones.

Their ethnography, consequently, avoids the problem of synchrony. Every aspect of the synchronically observable practice – the nexus – is historically loaded, so to speak, it drags with it its histories of use, abuse and evaluation. Thus, whenever we ethnographically investigate a synchronic social act, we have to see it as the repository of a process of genesis, development, transformation. If we see it like this, we will see it in its sociocultural fullness, because we can then begin to understand the shared, conventional aspects of it, and see it as a moment of social and cultural transmission. In that move, the Scollons focused our attention on two things we are not much used to in the field of language: on bodies as

repositories of histories of experience, and on space as historically organized, ordered and patterned, thus becoming a genuine actor in semiotic
processes.

## Note

(1)   The compelling nature of our expectations of such order can be illustrated by the
following anecdote. Some time ago I was in Dubrovnik, Croatia, waiting for a bus to
take me back to my hotel. The bus stop was very crowded: school was out and dozens
of students were waiting for the same bus. When the bus arrived, a scene erupted
which I found not entirely unfamiliar: a titanic life-and-death battle developed at
once between the dozens of people scrambling to get on the bus. At a given moment,
I found myself shoulder to shoulder with a lady, a tourist clearly, and British in addition, for she kept muttering 'there is a queue, there is a queue', while she attempted,
politely, to board the bus.

# 7 Semiotic and Spatial Scope: Toward a Materialist Semiotics

## Introduction

In this paper I intend to join a project that ties together much of Gunther Kress' work, and can also be found, among others, in the 'Geosemiotics' developed by Scollon and Scollon (2003). This project is the construction of a materialist theory of signs: a study of signs that sees signs not as primarily mental and abstract phenomena reflected in 'real' moments of enactment, but as material forces subject to and reflective of conditions of production and patterns of distribution, and as constructive of social reality, as real social agents having real effects in social life. Kress consistently calls this a *social* semiotics (e.g. Kress, 2009), but it is good to remember that, methodologically, this social semiotics is a materialist approach to signs. Such a materialism reacts, of course, against the Saussurean paradigm, in which the sign was defined as '*une entité psychique*' with two faces: the signifier and the signified (De Saussure, 1960: 99). The study of signs – semiotics – could so become a study of *abstract* signs; retrieving their meaning could become a matter of digging into their deeper structures of meaning *systems*; and semiotics could become a highly formal enterprise (for an example, see Eco, 1979).

Much of the problem resides in the way in which 'system' is imagined here. In classical structuralist approaches, a system is necessarily timeless and context-less – it is the deeper level that generates the 'real' phenomena operating in a concrete context. Systems, or 'structures', consequently display an uneasy relationship to history: the structuralist 'synchrony' was necessarily 'achronic' because it did not claim to have any empirical existence. After all, an empirical 'synchrony' in linguistics, for example, would come down to 'the recording of all the words spoken at the same time by thousands of speaking subjects' – an enterprise which Greimas, for instance, qualifies as 'rather pointless' (Greimas, 1990: 95), and which from a structuralist viewpoint would also not be worth one's while.

'System', however, can also be imagined as a *historical* given, as something that brings historical coherence (and hence, understandability) to isolated facts by means of patterns – cultural patterns such as e.g. 'classicism', historical ones such as e.g. 'absolutism', economic ones such as e.g. 'capitalism' and so on. Foucault's work addressed and decoded such systems – regimes of power/knowledge – and much of Bourdieu's work can be read as an analysis of the class system in France. Such patterns define systems, they are systemic, but they are not abstract. They have a real ('synchronic') existence in a plethora of individually insignificant but observable material features, and such features make sense when they are seen in their totality. This is the core methodological point in ethnography, and incidentally also the point Bourdieu always emphasized because it is what allows us to discover 'the logic of practice' (see e.g. Bourdieu, 1990). It is such a historical, material, real system that we have in mind, and the way we approach such a system is by means of ethnography.

The angle from which I approach this is from questions of public space. More in particular, my point of departure is sociolinguistic-ethnographic research in areas marked by 'super-diversity', forms of social, cultural, linguistic diversity emerging from post-Cold War migration movements into the urban centers of Western Europe (Vertovec, 2006; Blommaert & Rampton, 2011). I will draw on work done in London Chinatown (Huang, 2010) and in a popular inner-city neighborhood in Antwerp, Belgium (Blommaert, 2010). From empirical reflections on signs in public space, we will move to make a simple point, that signs rarely have a *general* meaning and mostly have a *specific* meaning. This simple empirical observation, however, draws semiotics into a different theoretical realm and propels us toward materialist and ethnographic approaches to signs. Before we get there, a few background remarks are in order.

## Public signs

Public signs both reflect and regulate the structure of the space in which they operate. Sociological, cultural, sociolinguistic and political features of that space will determine how signs look and work in that space, and signs will contribute to the organization and regulation of that space by defining addressees and selecting audiences and by imposing particular restrictions, offering invitations, articulating norms of conduct and so on to these selected audiences. Messages in the public space are never neutral; they always display connections to social structure, power and hierarchies. The reason for that is that public space itself is an area (and instrument) of regulation and control, of surveillance and power: 'spatial anchoring is an economic-political form that demands detailed study' (Foucault, 2001 [1977]: 195; see also Lefebvre, 2000). It is an institutional object, regulated (and usually 'owned') by official authorities whose role will very often be clearest in the restrictions they impose on the use of space (prohibitions on smoking, loitering, littering, speed limits, warnings, and so on). Communication in the public space, consequently, is communication in a field of power; the question is 'how does space organize regimes of language?' (Blommaert et al., 2005: 198). This question assumes that regimes can be 'polycentric' but that they nevertheless function as regimes, i.e. as authoritative patterns of normative conduct and expectations to which one should orient.

Two recent branches of scholarship have taken signs in public space as their object: linguistic landscape studies (henceforth LL) and geosemiotics (henceforth GS), the approach developed by Scollon and Scollon (2003) to language in the material world. While LL has over the past years become part of the mainstream of sociolinguistics, GS remains a somewhat idiosyncratic approach. Let us zoom in on LL.

Studies on LL are mainly devoted to the public visibility of multilingual phenomena within bi/tri-lingual countries and cities. An increasing amount of work focuses on highly globalized and internationalized cities such as Beijing (Pan Lin, 2009) and Tokyo (Backhaus, 2007). According to Backhaus (2007: 12), 'the lack of a summarizing term' could be why, in spite of precursors going back to the 1970s, LL has only become a topic in sociolinguistic studies in recent years. In these more recent formulations, 'Linguistic Landscape is concerned with languages being used on signs (hence, languages in written form) in public space' (Gorter, 2006: 11; cf. also Barni & Extra, 2008; Ben-Rafael et al., 2006; Landry & Bourhis, 1997; Shohamy & Gorter, 2009; see Juffermans, 2010, for a survey and discussion). This formulation, of course, begs all sorts of substantial methodological questions, and underdeveloped methodologies continue to haunt LL.

In order to clarify that remark, we turn to one prominent example of LL, Backhaus' (2007) study of Tokyo. Backhaus' study is overwhelmingly quantitative: it lists the languages publicly observed in areas in Tokyo, juxtaposes them and ranks them on the basis of frequency and density of distribution. Backhaus (2007: 60) pointed out that LL cannot develop without a clear quantitative corpus, and he refers critically to GS in this respect. Backhaus, however, fails to see the fundamental difference between GS and his LL: the fact that, according to GS, a better comprehension of the sociocultural meaning of language material requires ethnographic understanding rather than numbers, and that signs are necessarily addressed as *multimodal* objects rather than as *linguistic* ones. Backhaus' study was focusing on numbers and on general linguistic description around the numbers – concretely, counting the languages we can identify on public signs. Now, signs can be a lot more interesting than that. Signs in social space tell us a lot about the users of the space, how users interact with signs, how users influence and are influenced by them; so they start telling stories about the cultural, historical, political and social backgrounds of a certain space – the 'system' in the sense outlined earlier. Quantitative LL studies, as the very first step, draw attention to the existence and presence of languages in a particular space and can answer questions such as 'how many languages are used in space X'? But the argument does not cut very deep, and what we get is a superficial, 'horizontal' and distributional image of multilingualism. The fact that these languages are ingredients of multimodal signs, and that these signs occur in non-random ways in public space, is left aside, and this is where we need to begin our own search.

## Scope and Demarcation

We will start with a picture from London Chinatown (Figure 7.1). This is of course a mundane sign: a no entry sign at the entrance of a parking garage in London Chinatown. We see 'text' (the Chinese writing, saying 'entrance prohibited'), as well as a conventionalized iconographic shape widely construed as 'no entry'. Text co-occurs here with the visual shape of the sign, and from this co-occurrence, we can infer that one has to do with the other: the text supports, emphasizes or repeats the information contained in the non-textual, visual sign, and vice versa. What interests us here is their co-occurrence and the way in which such co-occurrences actually function. Let us run through some issues that emerge at this point.

(1) Even if words, colors and shapes co-occur and interact here, the different elements operate in different ways. Kress and Van Leeuwen (1996), as we know, defined such co-occurrences as multimodal signs and showed that the different 'modalities' (words versus shapes, colors, etc.) have different 'affordances'. One can do different things with different modalities, and constructing a multimodal sign revolves around combining the affordances of the different modalities. Thus, while the visual shape of the sign is quite generally understood (the sign can be found across the world with the same meaning), the Chinese text is not understandable for all (even if the co-occurrence with the sign may offer plausible hypotheses about the meaning of the

**Figure 7.1** Traffic sign, London Chinatown

text). Thus, the different modalities appear to have a different *semiotic scope*: they both *select different audiences*. While everyone is the addressee of the visual sign, not everyone is an addressee for the Chinese text.

(2) The sign is also put in a specific location (the entrance to the parking garage), and its meaning is specific to that physical location (the 'no entry' message only applies to the parking garage). Scollon and Scollon (2003) provide the term 'emplacement' for this: signs occur in a *specific* space, and their emplacement defines their effects. A no smoking sign inside a pub means that smoking is prohibited *inside*, not *outside* the pub. Signs, consequently, not only have a semiotic scope but also a *spatial scope*: they operate in particular, identified spaces, and define such spaces.

(3) If we combine semiotic scope and spatial scope, we understand that one of the major functions of public signs is *demarcation*. Signs cut up a space into micro-spaces where particular rules and codes operate in relation to specific audiences. As we saw in the example here, there can be overlap and conflict. In the 'no entry' sign, we saw on the one hand

the almost universal semiotic scope of the visual road sign combined with a much narrower one articulated through the Chinese writing. Both forms of demarcation co-operated with a third one, spatial scope, which restricted the effect of the sign to a particular micro-space (the entrance to the parking garage). But this is where we see that public signs are cultural as well as social (and even political) objects. The different modalities that enter into the signs and make it into its multimodal outcome need to be seen in these terms: as affordances that have a cultural, social and political dimension.

(4) They also have a *historical* dimension. Space is very often a *normative* actor in sociolinguistic processes, and this is where history enters the picture (cf. Blommaert & Huang, 2010). There are normative expectations about relationships between signs and particular spaces. One expects certain signs in certain places: shop signs and publicity billboards in a shopping street, for instance, or train timetables in a railway station. We do not expect such timetables in a restaurant. When signs are 'in place', so to speak, habitual interpretations of such signs can be made; when they are 'out of place', or 'transgressive' in the terminology of Scollon and Scollon (2003: 147), we need to perform additional interpretation work because a different social signal has been given. So we attach to particular places a whole array of objects, phenomena and activities, and we do that in a normative sense, that is, we do it in a way that shapes our expectations of 'normalcy' in such places. It is the connection between space and normativity that makes space historical, for the normative expectations we attach to spaces have their feet in the history of social and spatial arrangements in any society.

(5) Closely connected to this is the notion of *visual repertoire*. We all perceive and interpret signs on the basis of skills and competences we have gathered in life. Such skills and competences are cultural and social, and they revolve around the capacity to decode and act on the explicit and implicit codes used and deployed in signs. They strongly depend, consequently, on one's social position in a particular space. Someone belonging to the established diaspora in London Chinatown (with e.g. origins in Hong Kong) may be able to read most of the public signs that are visible there, since she or he can read (at least some forms of) Chinese script as well as Latin script. Someone entering Chinatown with an Eastern-European background, in contrast, and literacy competences restricted to Cyrillic alphabet, will not be able to make much sense of most of the signs there, with the exception perhaps of 'universal' aspects of signs such as the road sign in our example. The visual repertoires of both people are strongly different; the

way in which they engage with and can operate in relation to signs is thus very different as well. In superdiverse spaces, such differences between visual repertoires account for much of what goes on in the way of understanding and misunderstanding.

Let us now turn to another image, taken from inner city Antwerp (Figure 7.2). This handwritten sign was posted in the window of what used to be a florist shop. The sign is written in a mixture of traditional and simplified Chinese script, and it announces: 'apartment to let: first class furnishing, water and electricity included, 350 Yuan per month' (followed by a phone number).

In terms of what we discussed above, we can see the following. The spatial scope is relatively clear: this sign operates within the space of the former shop. We can assume that activities connected to the sign would also be connected to this particular place: either the apartment is in this building, or those who rent it out live there. The semiotic scope is rather clear too, even if certain questions arise here. Every sign tells a story about who produced it, and about who is selected to consume it. In that sense, *every sign points backwards to its origins, and forward to its addressees.* It is obvious that this sign selects 'Chinese' audiences and organizes an interaction between 'Chinese' interlocutors. Those who rent out the apartment are in all likelihood 'Chinese' immigrants, and the people to whom they intend to let the apartment are 'Chinese' as well. The scare

**Figure 7.2** Handwritten Chinese sign, Antwerp

quotes around 'Chinese', however, suggest that this notion warrants qualification. We saw that the sign is written in a mixture of traditional
Mandarin script (used in, e.g. Taiwan, Hong Kong and most of the traditional Chinese diaspora), and simplified script (used in the People's
Republic). The mixture suggests 'incomplete' or emergent competence in
either scripts: either the author is familiar with traditional script but does
his/her best to accommodate potential customers from the People's
Republic (the largest contingent of Chinese immigrants nowadays) or vice
versa. (The fact that 'Yuan' is used as identifying currency, rather than
'Euro', may lend support to this hypothesis.) In any event, the resources
deployed in this sign suggest a heterogeneous, unstable and transient community of diaspora 'Chinese'. An attempt to describe the semiotic scope
of this sign leads us, thus, into sociolinguistic aspects of signs, and from
there to wider sociopolitical and historical developments often hardly visible to the casual language-counting observer.

The neighborhood is in fact predominantly Turkish and Belgian, both
groups being the most visible (and audible) ones there. Since the late
1990s, however, it has witnessed an influx of transient groups of immigrants from Eastern Europe, the Balkans, Asia and Africa. Chinese immigrants have been largely invisible in this neighborhood; there are two
Chinese – or to be more precise, Cantonese – restaurants that have been
there for a lont time, but Chinese people are not part of the regular 'street-
scape' of the neighborhood. The handwritten sign in Figure 7.2 was in fact
the first piece of handwritten Chinese text I had observed in this neighborhood in many years. If we adopted a quantitative LL approach to it, it
would not be a significant item.

It is significant if we take our approach though. The sign demarcates a
space: a very small space, just one flat. But by doing that, it adds one more
claim to ownership and legitimate presence and belonging to the semiotic
landscape of the neighborhood, because here is a Chinese actor interacting
with potential other Chinese actors – here is, in other words, the suggestion, the possibility, of an existing social network. This network, we repeat,
is largely invisible when we deploy everyday forms of observation. It is also
statistically insignificant; but the presence of this sign suggests a process of
transition in which a hitherto invisible community enters the public space
and communicates there. Part of the public space is now theirs too; they are
also recognizable in the superdiverse neighborhood where they live. The
Chinese interlocutors have carved out a small space for themselves, a place
they own and claim exclusive access to.

The insight that signs demarcate space allows us now to make a qualitative statement about the public space. Obviously, when we compare the

two signs above, we see that 'public' means different things in both cases. The semiotic scope of the road sign is wider than that of the 'apartment for rent' sign, and is in that sense *more public* – it addresses more potential interlocutors and excludes fewer. 'Public' space is therefore manifestly layered and segmented; that is, space is not just a horizontal, distributional given, but also a vertical, stratified one. It is never uniform because the signs in public space demarcate areas and audiences, some of which are vast while others are microscopic. Road signs would typically have a vast scope; a scribbled post-it on a door saying 'John, I'll be back in five minutes' would represent the other extreme of the scale, a very 'private' notice in public space addressing just one specific interlocutor.

Such different signs coexist in public space, and we must realize that they do very different things in that space. It is important to realize this, because when we encounter a forest of signs, we understand that this abundance of signs does not reflect a chaotic, disordered pattern, but reflects a *specific* and complex form of order. Even if signs crisscross, overlap and contradict each other, this does not mean that we are facing what may seem a random display of semiotic resources. We may be facing different interacting (and sometimes conflicting) social orders, as when different groups compete over rights of ownership of a place and contest or overwrite each other's signs (a frequent feature of graffiti). We can also be facing historical layering of signs, where older signs have become amended or erased by newer ones. *We see politically and socioculturally dynamic and polycentric space.* The density of signage raises questions about social order, agency and social structure, because each of the signs will have a particular scope and operate within that scope: they order, request, ask, demand or inform people within that spatial zone.

We can also make another qualitative statement at this point. The demarcating effect of signs in public space also defines *identities*. When potential addressees are being selected by a sign they become potential legitimate users of the demarcated space. Such categorizations of legitimate usage, naturally, are social and political categories; they fuel the dynamics of power in public space and they are core ingredients of social and political conflicts – as when the police act against groups of young immigrants congregating in shopping malls after closing time. The shopping mall is made for 'shoppers' between 8 am and 6 pm; as long as one displays shopping behavior there and then, one is a legitimate user of that space. After 6 pm, however, it can become a skaters' paradise or a haven for homeless people looking for shelter for the night. Ownership and legitimate use of such spaces change during the course of the day, and conflicts often ensue from denials of or contests about such changes – as when the shopping mall management refuse to turn their space over to skaters and homeless people after 6 pm, and send in the police to remove them from the grounds.

The upshot of this, however, is that when we walk through a street, *our identities can and do change every few steps* – from someone who is included in a communication network to someone who is excluded from it and back; and through this, from someone who belongs to a particular network or community to someone who does not belong, and back. We do not consciously feel such immediate changes in identity because we do not choose them. The signs select them for us and pin them upon us; we may experience them, though, when we suddenly feel 'out of place' when entering a shop or a bar in which we are not members of the 'normal' community of users. It is when people stare at us upon entering, or when we find that the people in that space are amazed, scared, disturbed or irritated by our presence there, that we realize that space has done something to us. Many if not most real spaces operate on a 'members only' basis. And this, of course, is a *systemic* observation.

## Conclusions

The central insight I have applied in this paper is trivial. It is the fact that most signs have a specific meaning, not a general one. The meanings and effects of signs, in actual social life, are not unlimited or unrestricted; they are specific to the space in which they are emplaced and to the addressees they select. This trivial insight propels us into a different realm of analysis, though. It is not enough that the road sign in Figure 7.1 means 'no entry' in general. It is a real sign, planted in a real space, and it has a function there: it makes that specific space into a social and political object, an object of control, surveillance, power. Why? Because it is not just *a* sign, an unspecified sign, it is *this particular* sign, a sign planted at the entrance of a parking garage in London Chinatown. A social or materialist semiotics starts from this fact: that this is not just any sign, but a specific one, and that we can only understand it when we dissect the specifics of its appearance and function. This social or materialist semiotics, thus, adopts an ethnographic point of departure: that social and cultural phenomena are situated, and that to understand them means that we have to understand their situatedness. Other exercises are, to adopt Greimas' words again, rather pointless.

# 8 Pierre Bourdieu and Language in Society

## Introduction

It is no overstatement to say that Pierre Bourdieu is one the most influential social-scientific thinkers of the end of the 20th century and the beginning of the 21st. Terms designed by him – 'habitus', 'field', 'symbolic violence' and so forth – have become part of the core vocabulary of anthropology, sociology, sociolinguistics, discourse analysis, cultural studies and media studies, to name just a few disciplines. Ignorance of his work is widely construed as a major intellectual flaw because 'French Theory', the complex of Anglosaxon scholarly interpretations of the work of Derrida, Ricoeur, Bourdieu and Foucault (Cusset, 2008), is an important part of the canon of social sciences and humanities. The mediating effect of Anglosaxon uptake and interpretation is substantial: the history of translations of works by the French *Mandarins* can be shown to have an impact on how such work was read, understood and incorporated in general and specific theoretical projects worldwide. In Bourdieu's case, Gorski (2013) notes that the sequence of English translations of Bourdieu's books did not chronologically mirror their sequence in Bourdieu's own development and that some of his work remains untranslated. Such factors can explain the lack of attention to Bourdieu's ethnographic and historical ambitions in much secondary work. I shall have occasion to return to this issue below.

Given Bourdieu's status, I have the comfort of assuming that most readers will be at least superficially acquainted with the baseline of his work in the field of language (especially his *Language and Symbolic Power*, 1991), and focus on some perhaps less widely understood aspects of it that are of direct relevance to contemporary theorizing in the field of language in society. Three aspects, in particular, merit elaborate discussion: (a) Bourdieu's theoretical investment in a post-orthodox 'new left' Marxism and his deep interest in the ethnographic stance developed in

American symbolic interactionism; (b) his view of research methodology, in particular his ethnographic bias and the way in which that bias led to a continuous 'loop' of ethnography and quantification; and (c) the way in which, throughout his oeuvre, Bourdieu sought to develop 'nexus concepts' such as habitus, where 'micro-' and 'macro-' features coincide. All three aspects, I hope, can be seen as useful for addressing the phenomenology of contemporary social change and the role of language therein.

## New Left Foundations and Symbolic-interactionist Interests

The big questions addressed in Bourdieu's work are clear, and Bourdieu himself was generous in spelling them out in prefaces to his major works, often as a story of cohesion between different parts of his oeuvre (see e.g. the prefaces to *Distinction*, 1984, and *The Logic of Practice*, 1990). These questions demand some measure of erudition and insight into the intellectual history of the 20th century, because as we shall see, Bourdieu sweeps up large chunks of theory and methodology reflection from various different branches of social sciences and humanities before he positions his own efforts. A great many of his theoretical and methodological concerns were aimed at answering the Marxian question that has kept much of 20th-century intellectual history going: that of the relationship between 'social being and social consciousness' – does 'subjective' consciousness shape the 'objective' world or is the 'objective' world determining consciousness? Do humans shape the social conditions in which they live and the interests they draw from them, or are they shaped by them? Engagement with these issues, certainly after the Second World War and the appearance in print of Gramsci's *Prison Notebooks*, defined (and defines) the so-called New Left as a 'humanist' Marxism that questions the simple mechanics of basis and superstructure of an earlier orthodoxy and searches for spaces of human agency and intellectual creativity as 'objective' forces of history.

Much of what Bourdieu was concerned with in his oeuvre revolves around this: how exactly do we describe what Marx called 'socialized humanity' – individuals and communities that are deeply formed by the historical and social environments in which they develop, the social structures they are part of and which they – here comes 'habitus' – have incorporated in such a way that it shapes their bodies, attitudes, thoughts and everyday behavior? How do we describe the patterns by means of which such forms of socialization emerge, operate, get reinforced or changed? And how do we, then, handle 'objectivity' and 'subjectivity' in scientific practice?

The answers to these questions required, for Bourdieu, an entire reconstruction of himself as a scientist and of the science he practiced. Showing the nature of the socialized subject, as described above, involved a challenge to scientific 'objectivity' as then described and prescribed in Lévi-Straussian structuralism. As an anthropologist trained in this distinguished French tradition, Bourdieu had learned to turn the observed subject of anthropology into an 'object' of structuralist analysis by rendering the researcher (and his instruments) invisible. Lévi-Straussian anthropologists were never 'really there' in research other than as an unchallengeable epistemic superior, a position that Bourdieu found untenable in actual fieldwork (see Bourdieu, 1990: 14, 2000: 23–25; Blommaert, 2005a offers a discussion). Instead, an *ethnographic* stance grounded in the practice of fieldwork in Algeria, on local economic issues, pushed him toward fundamentally different insights:

> It was … because I found myself in a situation where I could directly observe the disarray or the distress of economic agents devoid of the dispositions tacitly demanded by an economic order that for us is entirely familiar … that I was able to conceive the idea of statistically analyzing the conditions of possibility of those historically constituted dispositions. (Bourdieu, 2000: 18)

Bourdieu had, thus, ethnographically encountered a *contrast* between 'historically constituted dispositions', one set determining how rural Algerians uncomfortably handled a capitalist economic system and another set determining his own habituated ways of going about economic aspects of life (cf. Blommaert, 2005a; Reay, 2004; Wacquant, 2004). Two 'habituses' (we would now say) had clashed in fieldwork interactions between an anthropologist and his 'subject', since both occupied very different historically constituted 'positions' in the 'field' of economic behavior – the French intellectual had the habitus of a sophisticated *habitué* of such practices, the Algerian farmer that of a novice lacking many of the resources and skills long rendered 'normal' in the French intellectual's way of life.

Very little of Bourdieu's work can be understood unless we grasp this vital epistemological and methodological moment where Bourdieu breaks away from structuralism and moves toward what was to become 'reflexive sociology'. The move is grounded in ethnography, the realization of the fact that knowledge emerges not from one 'objective' partner interacting with a 'subjective' one, but from *intersubjective* engagement negotiating the 'objective' historically constituted positions from which each party acts and produces meaning (cf. also Fabian, 1983). 'Subjects' can be 'objectively' studied by recognizing their fundamental subjectivity, in itself grounded in and generated by objective social-historical conditions. These historically constituted positions, we can see, shape the 'socialized subject' Bourdieu wanted to describe: history in society has put all of us in a specific position toward specific things and toward other people. This position can change as we live our lives, but its initial conditions are what they are – a point of departure which is never neutral but always covered with specific interests, preferences, habitual patterns of action, speech and understanding. It is in *La Misère du Monde* (Bourdieu, 1993) that this is clearest: through a large interview project in the working-class suburbs, he shows 'the tragedy of the confrontation, without concession or possible compromise, of viewpoints that are incompatible because they are all grounded in social reason' (Bourdieu, 1993: 13, my translation).

This ethnographic and intersubjective streak in Bourdieu's work is rarely identified as crucial in understanding his work (but see Hanks, 2005). It not only helps us understand the large intellectual project he undertook; it also helps us understand his deep and active interest in the work of American symbolic-interactionist sociologists such as Goffman, Garfinkel and Cicourel. The interest is not hard to justify, given the insistence of symbolic interactionists on observing everyday lived experience in its 'natural environment' in order to 'catch the process of interpretation from the standpoint of the acting person', where this standpoint is defined as interactional, i.e. in terms of responses to and anticipations of the moves of others in social interaction (McCall & Becker, 1990: 2–3, drawing on Blumer, 1969). The insistence of symbolic interactionists (especially those raised in the tradition of the Chicago School of Sociology) on meticulous fieldwork and participant observation was another point of attraction for Bourdieu, since such fieldwork inevitably provoked an explicit (reflexive) questioning of the researcher's role and showed the epistemic potential of such role-play in fieldwork in which the ethnographer was present, visible and salient as an actor in the process of knowledge construction.

Bourdieu emphasized these merits of symbolic interactionism in several of his writings, most notably in the obituary he wrote for Erving Goffman and the introduction to the last publishing effort he made in his lifetime: a French edition of several of Aaron Cicourel's classic essays on interaction in medical practice (Bourdieu, 1982; Bourdieu & Winkin, 2002).[1] In particular, developments such as ethnomethodology and, later, cognitive sociology (Cicourel, 1972) received accolades from Bourdieu, who saw clear parallels between ethnomethodological concerns and his own focus on 'logic of practice': the ways in which people interacting in social settings co-construct the realities they inhabit by means of habituated and socially ratified modes of thought and action adjusted to specific social fields. The difference he had with symbolic interactionism was made explicit in the opening pages of *Language and Symbolic Power*:

> although it is legitimate to treat social relations – even relations of domination – as symbolic interactions ... one must not forget that the relations of communication *par excellence* – linguistic exchanges – are also relations of symbolic power in which the power relations between speakers or their respective groups are actualized. (Bourdieu, 1991: 37)

In this book – Bourdieu's most influential intervention on language – he subscribes to the fundamentally dynamic, practice-based and 'emic' approach to communication developed by the likes of Goffman, Cicourel and Garfinkel, but he couches it into a broader historical frame (making his approach effectively Bakhtinian, one could say) and designs his analysis of language in society through the theoretical vocabulary developed in *The Logic of Practice* (Bourdieu, 1990). Thus, social interaction articulates sociohistorically configured 'positions' from whence people speak; these positions are defined by a 'market' of symbolic capital in which resources are circulated and unevenly distributed, ensuring, for instance, that a 'high' Parisian accent will be perceived as superior vis-à-vis a 'low' upcountry accent. The play of different positions in social arenas is the play of symbolic violence, or 'misrecognition' and 'recognition' of linguistic-communicative resources not because of their 'linguistic' features but of the sociohistorical load, they carry within a given social field. Thus, in any social field, distinctions will emerge between 'legitimate' language (the 'norm', one could say) and deviant forms of language. The target of Bourdieu's critical efforts in *Language and Symbolic Power* is classical structuralism – Saussure, this time, with a polemical gesture toward Chomsky – and the instrument he uses for his critique is a blend of symbolic-interactionist ontology with his own unique historicizing methodology.

## The Bourdieuan Methodological Loop

This blending of an ethnographically inflected ontology with a tendency to aim for larger, historically configured patterns of social structure, all of this often pitted against classical structuralist assumptions, yielded a remarkable research procedure in much of Bourdieu's work.[2] Let us take a closer look at his methodological toolkit.

Bourdieu started from an acute awareness of 'framing' in research. We all enter our research sites under particular sociohistorical conditions and they have an effect on what we see and perceive and understand. Bourdieu was aware of this during his 1960s fieldwork in Algeria. The country had just passed through a traumatic war of liberation, and the impact on his fieldwork was considerable – former enemies had to collaborate in research. In order to escape this bias, Bourdieu explored two measures. First, he emphasized the importance of revisiting the same object over and over again, of comparison (his work in Algeria was followed by 'native ethnography' in the Béarn) and expansion (including more materials than just those collected during fieldwork). Second, as we know, he turned to the kind of structuralism then advocated by Lévi-Strauss, in order to find a vantage point which allowed scientific objectivity. In doing this, like Lévi-Strauss, he intended to move from ethnography to ethnology – a search for transcontextual (or a-contextual) 'driving principles' in the social system observed, by focusing on correlations, contrasts and forms of systemic coherence. This ethnological tendency explains Bourdieu's search for higher-level validity – his difference from symbolic interactionism.

Whereas the first set of measures was maintained throughout Bourdieu's oeuvre, the second set – the appeal to structuralism – was abandoned. The main reason, I repeat, was ethnographic experience. Bourdieu had encountered paradoxes, contradictions and flexible potential in the field, rather than the strict, transparent and mechanic schemes of structuralism. Furthermore, and as we have seen above, he had experienced *experience*, so to speak: the fact that the distance advocated in ethnology is, in actual fieldwork conditions, overgrown with sharedness of meaning, joint understandings of 'the logic of the game' and so on. In other words, Bourdieu had ethnographically experienced that the ethnological claim to distance generates another, and a potentially more dangerous form of ethnocentrism than the intrinsic ethnocentrism of his own observer's – but participating and co-constructing – role in ethnography (a point also extensively belabored in critical ethnography, e.g. Fabian, 1983). Bourdieu worried about the specific role of the observer, and this role is not substantially different whether one investigates faraway Algeria or his home region in the Béarn. We have seen that he allowed himself to be deeply inspired by Goffman, Cicourel and other ethnographers in this respect. And this led to his rejection of Lévi-Straussian ethnology as 'methodologically provoked anamnesis' (Bourdieu, 2000: 24) which suggests closure and total strangeness – absence of shared understanding – between observer and observed. From that point onwards, 'dispositions' occur, and Bourdieu theorizes how he himself became part of the object – the objectification of subjectivity. This is also the point where he makes the shift from anthropology (or ethnology, see above) to sociology: a science in which precisely the objectification of subjectivity is central, and a science that can aspire to eventually develop a subject.

Bourdieu used extensive surveys as the backbone of some of his most impressive work. *Distinction*, for instance, presents its readers with the results of a large-scale series of survey studies in which aspects of subjective experiences of class structure were investigated. He had, however, grave reservations about 'naïve' statistical research – a point for which he found ample motivation in Cicourel's (1964) classic critique of quantitative approaches in sociology (e.g. Bourdieu & Winkin, 2002: 19). *Distinction*, that survey-driven study, is, remarkably, presented by Bourdieu as 'a sort of ethnography of France' (Bourdieu, 1986: xi), and as we shall see in the next chapter, such statements were never frivolous.[3]

We have seen above where his tendency to aim for a 'grammar' – a generalization – came from: from structuralist ethnology. But generalization (the 'grammar' mentioned in the quote above), for him, should be *empirical*, not abstract, and reflecting the on-the-ground realities detected in ethnography. And such generalizations would be built by statistical work entirely grounded in ethnographic observation – the questions would be ethnography-based – and framed in an ethnographic epistemology, that is, an awareness that outcomes of statistical generalization needed to be fed back to the empirical on-the-ground realities from which they emerged, and that they needed to speak to the 'lived experience' of everyday social engagements. Echoes of Cicourel's (1964) famous statements on ecological validity are evident.

This created a loop: ethnography–statistics–ethnography–statistics and so forth. And this loop explains the other major feature of Bourdieu's approach mentioned earlier: he would return throughout his career to the same field sites for ethnographic follow-up work. This move *historicized* his work: the loop in which ethnographic material was tested statistically and then brought into a new ethnographic round of inquiry removed the synchronic bias of Lévi-Straussian structuralism and made Bourdieu's object *dynamic*. His methodology, consequently, was one that addressed *change* rather than stasis. The acute historical awareness in Bourdieu's work is the second point, along with his ethnographic epistemology, that shines through in almost every major theoretical statement made by him. Consider his definition of habitus (Bourdieu, 1990: 54):

> the structures characterizing a determinate class of conditions of existence produce the structures of the habitus, which in their turn are the basis of the perception and appreciation of all subsequent experiences.

The habitus, product of history, produces individual and collective practices – more history – in accordance with the schemes generated by history.

The ethnographic grounding of Bourdieu's approach removed the 'snapshot' (i.e. synchronic) quality from survey methodology and replaced it with a dynamic and change-oriented one.[4] Note once more that the dynamic theory, lodged in his central theoretical concepts, is generated by ethnography. Bourdieu moves from ethnographic generalization – his theory – to statistical generalization. The latter he qualifies as 'corroboration': statistical analysis enables him to grant his theory not just ecological validity but also representativeness. His level of generalization is no longer, *contra* Lévi-Strauss, an ethnology grounded in universalist abstractions; it is an empirical (ethnographic) generalization, and this enables him to call *Distinction* with its many statistical data an 'ethnography of France'.

## Nexus Concepts and Language Ideology: Habitus

The preceding discussion already shows that simple and widespread scalar metaphors such as 'micro versus macro' are hard to apply to Bourdieu's work. It is not as if statistics 'just' enables an extrapolation to a scale-level we usually call 'macro', *in contrast with* ethnographic observation which would be 'micro'. Reading Bourdieu in these superficial and schematic micro-macro terms is invariably disappointing and risks missing the entire point.

A concept such as habitus is an attempt at 'macro' generalization at the level of what we would call 'micro' practices – let us call it a 'nexus concept' in which different scale-levels of social behavior are shown to be dialectically connected. Habitus shows itself in *every* social activity – we always embody the sociohistorical realities that formed us as individuals who take specific (non-random) positions in a social field, with degrees of access to the material and symbolic capital that characterizes these positions, and the relationships of dominance or subordination they involve with others. The fact that these positions are being renegotiated over and over again in social encounters, that they can be negated or challenged (as shown in e.g. Goffman, 1971), and that they are dynamic and do change over time does not detract from the essential *reproductive* quality of social structures and the habituated characteristics they attribute to everyday social practice. While *Reproduction* (Bourdieu & Passeron, 1970) emphasizes this reproductive systemic quality, *Homo Academicus* (Bourdieu, 1988) shows its potential for development and change over time: profound economic and political changes in the foundations in society also involve reshuffling the symbolic markets in society. They recreate its 'culture', one could say, as an intrinsic part of these deep changes.

*Language and Symbolic Power* can be seen as Bourdieu's most advanced argument in favor of this view, but note that in studies such as *Academic Discourse* (Bourdieu *et al.*, 1994 [1965]), *Homo Academicus* and *Reproduction*, developments in the discursive field were crucial evidence for the central thesis of symbolic capital reproduction and circulation: language usage is an extraordinarily sensitive indicator of actual social ('macro') relationships and their dynamics, and such 'macro' features occur across the entire field of language in society.[5] The analysis is, as suggested earlier, Bakhtinian: Bourdieu sees words, expressions and discourses as filled with historically configured symbolic power features, in such a way that any aspect of speech can be seen as what Bakhtin called 'voice' – an index of social positions within a given social *status quo* (Bakhtin, 1981; cf. Blommaert, 2015a). Thus, the country folk from the Béarn will, when talking to the 'sophisticated' Parisian, 'lose voice', feeling insecure about pronunciation and lexical choice, leading to hypercorrection and self-stereotyping, out of an awareness that the Parisian's French occupies a different, superior symbolic position in the public order projected onto language usage.

A very similar argument (influenced more by Bakhtin than by Bourdieu) was made in Asif Agha's major study on *Language and Social Relations* (Agha, 2007; cf. also Blommaert, 2005a; Collins & Blot, 2003; Hanks, 2005; Kroskrity, 2000). Agha surveys linguistic-anthropological work on language ideologies, emphasizing the concept of 'register' as an ordered set of indexical (i.e. language-ideological) form–function–effect mappings (Silverstein, 2003). 'Order' here stands for the non-random character of such orders of indexicality: it is the skillful deployment of specific 'enregistered' forms of speech in particular social arenas that sets the tone and key of interactions and indexically projects identities onto the speakers. An identity such as 'wine connoisseur', for instance, demands the careful and sustained deployment of specific jargons, genres and modes of talk about wine – a *discourse* indexing someone as 'wine connoisseur' (Silverstein, 2006a). Violations of such orders come with a penalty: one is identified as 'awkward', a 'wannabe', a 'dilettante' or just a 'weirdo'. The order is socially *compelling* since 'recognition as (identity X)' is a socially regimented effect that demands *recognizability* within a frame of intersubjectivity. While, of course, various degrees of deviance can and do occur without heavy penalties, the deployment of specific registers imposes a stereotypical 'frame' on interactions, the effects of which are relatively stable – registers are part of the stuff that constructs the benchmarks of social order (cf. also Rampton, 2006).

Observe the obvious connection between Agha's view of register and that venerable object of sociology that has been a central concern since Simmel and Durkheim: social *norms*, what it takes to be seen as socially 'normal'. Registers are conventional and therefore 'normative' of course, and in Agha's view, they are arrangements of behavioral features that, within given social arenas and social groups, *count as understandable language*. The echo of symbolic interactionism is evident here – norms are 'emic' and emerge out of intersubjective social interaction – and so is the parallel between this view and Bourdieu's notion of 'legitimate' language – something that emerges out of the dynamic of recognition and misrecognition. And observe how a notion such as language-ideological 'register' becomes, like habitus, a nexus concept in which the small stuff of everyday interaction is intrinsically colored, patterned and regimented by the 'big' stuff of culture, social structure and history (cf. Scollon & Scollon, 2004; Silverstein, 2004). While recognizability – the crucial feature of register – is always uniquely and variably enacted in situated moments of interaction, it derives its effects from prior existence *as* an order of indexicality in which the deployment of certain features stereotypically points toward particular social categories and relationships (cf. Blommaert, 2015a). Register and processes of enregisterment, therefore, can be seen as the empirical aspects of habitus formation and development. The social order is incorporated, reproduced and amended, practically, in enregisterment.

This insight, I would argue, turns Bourdieu's social-theoretical legacy even more into an ethnographic invitation, in which longitudinal and slow processes of social structuration can be read, followed and appraised, so to speak, through the lens of register development and change in actual moments of social interaction. 'Micro'-ethnographies of social interaction can be shown to *directly* (not by prior or posterior assumption) relate to 'macro'-social and political relationships in non-random ways, and patterns of shifting from one register into another (Goffman's 'footing changes', Agha, 2005) can be understood as effects of the complexity of social environments in which people dwell, and as proof of the social versatility required from real people in real societies (cf. Collins, 2014; Rampton, 2014; Silverstein, 2004). Sociolinguistically, this methodological line suggests important potential for revisiting 'macro'-features of language in society such as language policies, now possibly seen as one set of norms amidst several other socially recognizable ones, leading to language behavior which appears, from a formal language policy viewpoint, as a violation of rules but proves to be, upon closer inspection, perfectly 'normal' in view of the polycentric normative environment that characterizes real and highly diverse social arenas (Blommaert, 2005b, 2014; Blommaert & Rampton, 2011). At the same time, this view suggests a profound critique of classical notions of 'structure' as *stable* and replaces them with a view of social life as governed and patterned by means of complex interplays of multiple and dynamic structures demanding a capacity to change and shift rather than a capacity for adherence to (fixed, singular and dominant) 'rules'.

## Conclusion: Bourdieu as Inspiration

Bourdieu's work is canonical – his books are almost without exception classics. Whereas a degree of reverence in reading them is expected (and perhaps desirable), the classic status of such work invites continuous re-reading, updating and reappraisal in view of recent insights. Real classics, in that sense, are works that continue to be relevant not as a fixed codex but as a flexible source of inspiration, allowing exploratory confrontation with new relevant data, methodologies and theoretical concepts.

What contemporary scholars of language and society can take from Bourdieu's work is the fundamental insight that language can be approached from the viewpoint of society, as an extraordinarily sensitive index of social relationships, processes and developments. I have pointed above to the ways in which Bourdieu used discursive data as key evidence for *change* in the social system – the central plot of *Homo Academicus* is the shift in the social and cultural composition of French academic infrastructures. Ethnographic and discursive data did what mainstream statistics could not achieve: they identified the effective locus of change in actual, situated non-random social behavior, and his usage of statistics was in that sense a technique of confirmation and double-checking of what ethnographic and discourse-analytic data had established (yielding, in the process, additional ethnographic questions). He stood, in this respect, shoulder by shoulder with his American friends and colleagues, Goffman, Cicourel and Garfinkel. And he took their efforts further into the direction of 'macro'-social generalization by means of nexus concepts such as habitus, providing a theory of Marxian 'socialized humanity' as a matter of actual practice, governed and regulated by historically configured (but dynamic) dispositions that circumscribed the possibilities and limitations of social practices within specific fields.

This achievement is formidable, even if in many respects incomplete and unfinished, and even if drawing these fundamental insights from Bourdieu's work demands hard reading, not just of *Language and Symbolic Power* but of large parts of the entire oeuvre. He did, indeed, establish sociology on a different footing, providing a fundamental set of images of man and society deeply different from those advocated by Durkheim, Weber, Parsons or Lévi-Strauss. Bringing recent advances in sociolinguistic and discourse-analytical analysis and theorizing within the framework of these images of man and society is both a challenge and an opportunity that is hard to dismiss for creative and innovative scholarship on language in society.

## Notes

(1)   The patterns of referencing in Bourdieu's work are also telling. While his universe of referencing is clearly dominated by the likes of Lévi-Strauss, Durkheim, Weber and other major scholars from the French structuralist canon, references to Goffman, Garfinkel and Cicourel are hard to overlook in Bourdieu's work.

(2)   The following paragraphs are adapted from Blommaert (2005a) and Blommaert and Van de Vijver (2013). I refer the reader to the latter source for a more elaborate discussion of the potential of the Bourdieuan methodological loop.

(3)   Bourdieu was usually generous when it came to informing his readers about the types of data he used in his research, and reading the appendices to works such as *Homo Academicus* is worth the trouble for those who wish to explore the highly unorthodox ways in which he built his arguments, seen from a conventional sociological stance. Bourdieu uses large quantities of popular published data – newspaper articles, 'rankings' and 'pop polls', gossip stories and so forth – as well as lengthy interviews in preparing the grounds for statistical extrapolation, and some seriously good discourse analysis precedes that quantitative stage of work. See Hanks (2005) for comments on this point.

(4)   The 'schemes' mentioned by Bourdieu fit into the category of notions such as 'genre', 'register', etc. In fact, it is on the basis of such notions, all referring to the partly systemic (structured) nature of human conduct, that ethnographic generalizations are made.

(5)   Hanks (2005) offers an insightful review of Bourdieu's focus on language practices in support of his larger conceptual efforts, notably in the development of the concepts of habitus and field.

# 9 Combining Surveys and Ethnographies in the Study of Rapid Social Change

## Introduction

This short research note is intended to stimulate debates across disciplinary and methodological-traditional boundaries. Such debates, we believe, are necessary for several reasons, of which two can be highlighted. First, exploring compatibilities and synergies across and beyond the layers of disciplinary structure that determine academic work is at the heart of scientific practice: it is the search for innovation and optimization of research tools and insights. Second, such exercises are always, perpetually, needed because our objects of research refuse to sit still. As scholars of humans in society and culture, our research instruments demand perpetual reality checking, because humans in society and culture are unpleasant enough to change perpetually, and methods for understanding social and cultural processes that were adequate yesterday are not guaranteed to be adequate tomorrow.

Certainly, in an age of globalization, superdiversity and complex online–offline dynamics in social and cultural life, several major adjustments are required to a scholarly apparatus rather more at ease with clear-cut categories, linear processes and transparent propositional meanings. This contemporary world is characterized by very rapid social change, some of it superficial but other aspects of it fundamental. Such changes occur across the total spectrum of human activity, collective as well as individual. They involve intense demographic changes: changes in the economic structures of society; in social structures of community, belonging, power and entitlement; in political structures responding to these other changes; to cognitive, psychological and identity changes; to linguistic and semiotic changes; to changes in the relationships between urban and rural areas, regions, nation-states and larger geopolitical units in the world. Such changes were anticipated almost two decades ago by e.g. Castells (1996) and Appadurai (1996). But it is now that the full scope, scale and weight of these changes become apparent and inescapable.

These rapid processes of change defy the synchronic, sedentary, linear and static bias of sciences based on structuralist assumptions about the social and cultural world. They also challenge the structuralist assumption that generalizations need to be context-free abstractions. And they question the most fundamental presuppositions deployed in disciplines about how the world is and how humans fit into that. *Complexity, mobility* and *dynamics* are key defining features of the present world, and they need to be converted into useful research instruments. This job is far from being done at present.

In what follows we will attempt to sketch a broad methodological platform on which two very different methodological frameworks will be joined: ethnography and survey research. It is part of the tradition we mentioned just now that many would see these two approaches as the extreme poles of a continuum of scientific methodology. The former one would be the archetypal 'qualitative' kind of research, focused on inter-subjective small-scale interpretive work. The latter would be the archetypal 'quantitative' approach based on an analytical distancing of researcher and object, standardized procedures and statistical factual outcomes. The non-compatibility of both is often, and widely, taken for granted, and practitioners of both would often be seen as hard-nosed methodological fundamentalists with severely limited patience for the arguments of the other side. While profoundly committed to our respective disciplines, we believe that this old ritual of mock hostility prevents certain interesting and creative things from happening on both sides, and we believe that exploring differences and similarities between these frameworks can be highly productive in light of the challenges described earlier. We share an object, and this object is changing fast. Consequently, all of us permanently risk getting out of touch with that object.

The notion that we share an object is fundamental. It is the shared nature of the object that should make us realize that the views of that object from within our disciplines are necessarily partial. Different views represent different sides and features of the object, *but it is the same object*. And an object as complex as humans in society and culture surely tolerates multiple and very different views which, together, might perhaps bring us closer to a comprehensive picture.[1] Interestingly, this exercise has precedents, and a lot of what we will say contains echoes of work done decades ago but largely neglected nowadays.

## The Issue: What do we Know?

If social and cultural environments are marked by complexity, mobility and dynamics, it means that very little can be presupposed with respect to the features of such environments. We can believe that a 'neighborhood' hosts a sedentary population – the neighbors – only to discover that an important part of the population there is actually nomadic, using the neighborhood as a transit zone to other destinations (e.g. Blommaert, 2013). We can believe that two refugees from Iraq share a significant amount of features, enough to treat them similarly, only to discover that one is a highly educated person who prepared his escape from Iraq in some detail and can rely on a support network in the diaspora, while the other person is the victim of brutal and exploitative human trafficking leaving her with no support whatsoever, and with a very different set of challenges from the first one. We can believe that a pupil is learning disabled because he cannot memorize the inflections of the French verb *avoir*, only to discover that that same pupil knows all the players of FC Barcelona by heart, as well as huge amounts of relevant data about them. We can believe that a 'friend' on Facebook is a 14-year-old girl, only to find out that this friend is a 28-year-old man.

Such problems of presuppositions not holding true confront a broad variety of actors, from immigration officers to schoolteachers, urban planners, medical personnel, policy makers and – note – researchers. Superdiverse environments are best seen as complex systems in which several different forces generate crisscrossing, overlapping and conflicting processes, in which the statistical average or numerical majority is not the engine behind power and control, in which small 'deviations' or 'exceptions' – the 'error margin' of large-scale research – often represent the onset of massive future change, and in which well-known activities and characteristics may result in non-linear, unexpected effects. Complex systems have stochastic characteristics: they move in directions of which the general vector can sometimes be identified, but of which the precise outcomes cannot be predicted (cf. Prigogine & Stengers, 1984; see Blommaert, 2013, for a discussion).

This generates problems. If a researcher cannot rely on accurate and robust baseline knowledge of the social and cultural environment she or he investigates, epistemological and methodological problems quickly occur at all levels. Designing a reliable population sample for survey research, for instance, is hard when the baseline knowledge of the population is questionable. Research on social media usage in China, where because of strict internet policing very many users hide behind aliases and phony profiles, is a case in point. If we do not know how many 'real' people are there, whether these people are male or female, young or old, highly educated or not, and so on – how then can we construct a reliable and representative sample? We can always make a sample, surely, but what is that sample actually representative of?

Informed readers have detected by now that the foregoing point leads us to a well-known issue in social-scientific and humanities research: the problem of ecological validity in survey work. The problem was powerfully sketched and stated half a century ago by Aaron Cicourel (1964). A more recent and clear formulation by Cicourel is the following:

> The ecological validity problem can be stated as follows: To what extent is the content of questions asked commensurate with the socially distributed knowledge possessed by the respondents? Do the questions asked address topics, beliefs, attitudes and opinions the respondents routinely discuss in everyday life during social interaction with others? Further, to what extent can we assume that given the absence of ethnographic information about different communities, we can ignore the extent to which the wording and content of the questions are comprehended similarly by the entire sample? Are the questions, therefore, different from or are they in correspondence or congruent with observing the way respondents express themselves in their daily life encounters with others? (Cicourel *et al.*, 2004: 8)

What Cicourel flags as a major issue here is that, when we abstain from involving ourselves in ethnographic research that establishes the specific universes of meaning and interpretation that individual people use in handling survey questions, we can only compensate for that absence of ethnographically gathered knowledge by using a very large, and *valid*, range of presuppositions about the sharedness of such universes among our respondents. This can perhaps be reasonably feasible when we investigate groups of people whom we know share a lot of social and cultural material, and use this sharedness as our focus of investigation (think of small religious communities or soccer teams). It is, however, extremely hard to sustain when we engage in research involving very different groups of people. The more diverse the populations we investigate, the lower our certainty is about the characteristics of these populations. Simple-sounding terms such as 'labor', or 'satisfied', used in identical questions to a very diverse sample of respondents, may consequently be understood in ways so deeply different that it renders the outcomes effectively incommensurable. Pierre Bourdieu – a close friend and associate of Cicourel – made a similar point when he observed that opinion research presupposes the fact that everyone *has* an opinion on the topic of research, whereas for many respondents the confrontation with a survey question is actually the first time they have ever been invited to think about a particular topic (Bourdieu, 1994 [1972]). And both were undoubtedly inspired by Herbert Blumer's remarks, made in 1947, that 'current public opinion polling has not succeeded in isolating public opinion as a generic object of study' (Blumer, 2000 [1947]: 148). In other words, the 'public' qualification of opinions is not *a priori* an ecologically valid statement, for we do not know in advance whether the opinions we intend to describe are effectively present, shared and generalizable as 'public' prior to our inquiry. *We cannot presuppose this.* What we can do, however, is first to establish ethnographically whether or not our object displays an adequate degree of social and cultural fit in the communities we shall investigate, and how this object is locally treated, thought about, discussed and/or acted upon by our respondents.

We will shortly move to consider attempts at doing precisely this. At present, it suffices to observe that the rapid change we currently witness in society and culture raises the issue of ecological validity from the dead and brings it back with a vengeance. The complexity now characterizing social systems precludes quick assumptions about semantic and praxeological sharedness and stability among nearly any population we intend to investigate. So what do we know? Not much in advance.

## Ordered Indexicalities

Cicourel's critique of ecological validity quickly zoomed in on the methodology of interviewing. Let us recall what he had to say on this issue:

> The serious problem associated with self-contained interviews and surveys without ethnography is that we sample bodies but not their everyday behavioral environments. We lack systematic observation of respondents' daily life activities and the condition under which attitudes, opinions, beliefs, and folk knowledge emerge and are displayed. ...

> Conducting interviews with closed- or fixed-choice questions or sending respondents questionnaires to fill out fixed-choice survey questions has often been an end in and of itself. There has been little or no interest in conducting systematic observation of the ecological settings in which respondents lived or played or worked, including their discourse practices. It is customary to interview a small sample of respondents before constructing a sample survey. The general idea was to explore questions in some detail before settling on a particular set of them for the larger survey. The small subset of a sample (the 'pretest') was intended to satisfy

validity issues, but respondents, even if interviewed at home, often answered questions with guarded enthusiasm. The quality of surveys, therefore, could be partially improved by using tape recorders. Random recordings would provide a sense of how the language used in the pretest oriented respondents to the study's goals and the extent to which they resulted in modifications of the final questions employed. Tape recording a random subset of the final questionnaire sample could enable the research analyst to compare the way interviewers and respondents carried out the task. (Cicourel *et al.*, 2004: 8–9)

The problem, in its simplest form, is this: how can we be sure that the same question (containing the same lexicogrammatical and semantico-pragmatic pattern) has the same meaning for all the respondents we ask the question to? Cicourel himself, referring to the 'paraphrase problem', puts it as follows: 'Is the format and content of a question commensurate with the way the information is organized in memory that would enable the respondent to answer?' (Cicourel *et al.*, 2004: 10). Cicourel's answer is negative, unless we ethnographically investigate this question, and for that to happen, we need to pay specific attention to the interactional structure of the research interview. The seemingly routinized and uniform question–answer sequences performed by survey researchers with their respondents hide a potentially debilitating interpretational diversity – this point has been made above.

But why? Cicourel formulated his concerns in the 1960s, more or less simultaneously with the birth and growth of sociolinguistics and linguistic anthropology, to which he himself substantially contributed. And from within sociolinguistics and linguistic anthropology, the details of the problem of the research interview gradually became clear: human interaction turned out to be governed by what is now called 'indexicality' – delicate connections between talk and sociocultural context that are highly meaningful. The kind of meanings generated by indexicality broadly contain what is in more common parlance known as 'connotation': implicit but crucial structures of inference that are able to create entirely different meaning effects for the same lexicogrammatical and semantico-pragmatic patterns. Put simply, the same sentence can have an entirely different meaning uptake, depending on who, when, where and how it was formulated. Context is not just an influence and not just a dominant factor in the creation of meaning, it is a *determining* factor. The lexicogrammatical and semantico-pragmatic patterns in communication are directed by a *metapragmatic* pattern, which has its feet firmly in the sociocultural conditions – macro as well as micro and nano – under which such patterns are produced (see Agha, 2007; Blommaert, 2005b, 2006a; Blommaert & Rampton, 2011; Gumperz, 1982;

Hymes, 1972; Rampton, 1995; Silverstein, 1992, 2006b). In Cicourel's own formulation:

> Indexical expressions imply either ambiguity or unstated elements of meaning. Their local comprehension, therefore, involves the interaction of prior or present compression of information. For example, phonology, syntax, semantics, pragmatics, prosody, mundane knowledge, and the perception of the social setting within which such expressions occur can all influence their meaning. Interview and survey questions invariably involve indexical expressions. The paraphrase problem, therefore, could include aspects of an expression's indexical properties. The notion of indexical expressions as used by ethnomethodologists assumes explicit reference to the respondent's local understanding of an expression, but to my knowledge does not refer explicitly to the organization of their memory of past experiences that might be relevant for understanding how a respondent might formulate or choose a fixed choice or open-ended answer to a question. (Cicourel *et al.*, 2004: 10)

Cicourel's student Charles Briggs synthesized and systematized the various issues raised by indexicality in research interviews in his classic *Learning How to Ask* (1986), still an indispensable book for anyone using interviews in research. Briggs' caution, strongly emphasized also by Cicourel, was that attempts to bring context 'under control' by, for instance, using white room environments for respondents, do not remove the problem because a white room is a context as much as any other context (quite an unnatural context as well), and various respondents can respond in very different ways to that context. Variability is *not a function of the context itself*, it is a function of *how individuals interact with contexts*. Using an identical context, thus, can lead to important insights in how individuals absorb and act upon such contexts, but it does not create a context in which meanings are no longer subject to variable indexical inferences.[2]

Several decades of systematic work on indexicality have led to an awareness that communication – *any* communication – contains a level of interpretational uncertainty because the indexical orientations displayed in communication are, in principle, not *a priori* detectable. Suggestions as to interpretational stability derived from the observation that identical utterances produce identical propositional meanings are dismissed because utterances contain vastly more than just propositional meanings. And if these non-propositional, indexical meaning effects are not taken into account, any suggestion about interpretational stability is an expression of the researchers' wishful thinking but methodologically entirely unsustainable. Little firm belief can be given to research findings not based on this critical insight.

This insight naturally has the potential of removing any possibility of investigating large collectives of respondents. Indeed, in sociolinguistics and related branches of science, it gave rise to a rich tradition of micro-analysis of uniquely situated utterances or stretches thereof – much of contemporary discourse analysis instantiates this approach (see Blommaert, 2005b, for a discussion). If meaning is uncertain even at the level of the individual utterance, how can it be certain at the level of groups?

The answer to this is *indexical order* (Agha, 2007; Blommaert, 2005b; Silverstein, 2003). Indexicals appear not to be randomly generated – indexicality, thus, is not the cause of chaos in meaning. They occur in forms of order: dynamic and highly changeable forms of order, yes, but always order. The reason for this is relatively simple: we can only produce meanings, 'make sense' of what people including ourselves say, when there is a degree of *recognizability* in the signs we use, and this recognizability rests on conventionalization and ordering of indexicals into relatively per-during fields and patterns we call 'code', 'register', 'genre', 'intertextuality' and so forth (see Agha, 2007, for a survey).[3] Such forms of indexical order explain the fact that widely divergent groups of speakers – for instance, a highly international group of academics at a conference, using wildly different varieties of English – can still understand each other quite well. While every instance of communication is entirely unique, it still requires a level of recognizability, and hence collective sharedness, to become real communication. Recent work has shown that even in highly unstable and rapidly changing sociolinguistic environments, *ad-hoc* norms – agreements on the recognizability of communicative signs – emerge continuously and operate effectively in what, at first sight, may appear as a chaotic language context. This process of rapid norm development is called 'enregister-ment': people continuously create communicative orders, communicative norms, even in entirely unstable environments (e.g. Agha, 2007; Blommaert, 2012; Creese & Blackledge, 2010; Möller & Jörgensen, 2011; Rampton, 2006; Silverstein, 2003).

This means that there *is* a level of collectiveness to indexicals, that the 'paraphrase problem' can be brought, at least to some extent, under control, and that some degree of ecological validity may be achieved. It also means, however, that this can only happen if adequate investigation of such forms of order precedes the use of order as an assumption in research. Indexical order, in sum, cannot be taken as a given; one needs to go out and find out before it can be thus established. Ethnographic exploration of orders of indexicality are indispensible in any form of research that uses human interaction, *in any form*, in its research methods.

## Combining Ethnography and Statistics: Bourdieu

Let us keep this in mind now, and turn to attempts to combine ethnography and survey work in coherent research designs. Let us also recall the fundamentally different orientation between both methodological traditions. Ethnography is concerned with validity and does not attempt to generalize over populations – it is not concerned with representativeness, in other words. Statistical survey work is aimed exactly at representativeness and less at validity. When it comes to generalization, ethnography provides *qualitative* generalizations, i.e. *theoretical hypotheses* based on the systemic aspects of uniquely situated cases. Statistical approaches provide *quantitative* generalizations, i.e. calculated calibrations that speak to the entire population, *respective to a theory*. Both are valid forms of generalization – it is important to underscore this in a scientific universe in which increasingly only the second type of generalization looks respectable. A theoretical generalization is different in type from a qualitative generalization. The former is, as we know, dominated by the criteria of validity, the latter by criteria of representativeness. Misunderstandings over the notion of 'theory' tend to cause the confusion about generalizations: representativeness does not in itself constitute theory, it constitutes *proof* of theory. The line of production, so to speak, of theory itself is of a different order. Theory demands validity; its proof demands representativeness.

Pierre Bourdieu surely had a very sharp understanding of this. A point rarely picked up by his critics and followers, but perennially underscored in his own work, is the *ethnographic epistemology* that underpinned his work (Blommaert, 2005a; Reay, 2004; Wacquant, 2004). Crucial theoretical concepts from his work – think of *Habitus, Logic of Practice* and *Field* – are ethnographically grounded. That is, they are heuristic (and thus generalizable) notions derived from intense intersubjective engagement with respondents in real social environments (what Bourdieu always termed as the meeting of different Habituses). As we have seen in the previous chapter, Bourdieu used surveys as a crucial instrument in much of his work. *Distinction*, for instance, presents results of a large-scale series of survey studies on 'subjective' experiences of class structure, while it is introduced as 'a sort of ethnography of France' (Bourdieu, 1986: xi). In an article inaugurating the journal *Ethnography*, he specified this connection between ethnography and statistical analysis:

nothing had prepared me to understand the economy, especially my own, as a *system of embodied beliefs*, I had to learn, step by step, through ethnographic observation later corroborated by statistical analysis, the practical logic of the precapitalist economy, at the same time as I was trying as best as I could to figure out its grammar. (Bourdieu, 2000: 24)

It is important at this point to understand that Bourdieu started his academic life as an anthropologist – a science then dominated in France by Claude Lévi-Strauss' version of structuralism. This structuralism, with its clear and abstract categorization patterns and lines of abstract generalization necessarily severing connections with experienced and empirical reality, clashed with Bourdieu's ethnographic experiences, in which he found confusion, contradiction and tension rather than the harmony of Lévi-Straussian 'ethnology'. Generalization (the 'grammar' mentioned in the quote above), for him, should be *empirical*, not abstract, and reflecting the on-the-ground realities detected in ethnography. And such generalizations would be built by statistical work entirely grounded in ethnographic observation – the questions would be ethnography-based – and framed in an ethnographic epistemology, that is, an awareness that outcomes of statistical generalization needed to be fed back to the empirical on-the-ground realities from which they emerged. The methodological loop in Bourdieu's work, described in the previous chapter, was born.

## Toward an Applicable Instrument

Recall that Cicourel always insisted that he had nothing against statistics, and even found it a very important analytical tool, provided the statistics was applied to a field of which the validity had been tested. This validity resides in the commensurability of what is tested in surveys with what in local real conditions is experienced and articulated, how locally the world is constructed, so to speak. The solution offered by Bourdieu – a methodological loop in which ethnography and statistical survey work are continuously sequentially used to confirm or amend the findings – provides validity and enables representativeness. We thus get a two-pronged reality check, in which valid findings can be generalized toward representativeness, and in which this representativeness is in turn checked as to its validity in the field. The strengths and weaknesses of both approaches have now been blended into one approach, methodologically diverse but epistemologically unified, and tied together by a single object of which the various dimensions are recognized.[4]

Using this model as a template for further development and using the benefit of a vastly more refined understanding of ordered indexicals – i.e. of (temporarily) conventionalized links between forms and interpretations in specific contexts – enables new and more reliable forms of interviewing and questioning, so that we can start thinking of a concrete research instrument targeted at investigations of processes of rapid social and cultural change. The uncertainty and complexity characterizing such processes demands an approach which

(1) invites and privileges longitudinal, or at least repeated inquiry;
(2) necessitates a continuous reality check of any insight and finding;
(3) applies both to validity and representativeness, given the intensely dynamic nature of the object;
(4) uses ethnographic findings as (realistically) ecologically situated and (hypothetically) systemically meaningful features of a social system; and
(5) uses statistical insights as pertaining to the scope and level of saturation of such features, thus credentialing the systemic nature of the findings.

Such an approach could be useful to determine the *vector of change* in complex and dynamic social systems. To be more precise, the dialectic between locally grounded findings, their scope and level of saturation might begin to tell us something about the way in which social and cultural change starts, develops and culminates over time within a given population. We know that in stochastic systems, change can begin in what is usually seen as 'exceptions' and 'deviations'. Such features are statistically insignificant, yet they can grow into the major transforming force in a system. Repeated statistical analysis can establish such patterns of developing change, elucidating its directions and scope, while repeated ethnographic inspection can establish the specific ways in which transformations in scope and level of saturation trigger qualitative changes in the feature.

To give a trivial example, changes in popular-cultural, say musical, trends start outside or in the margins of the music industry. Few people will know the music and the artists, and those who know them might see them as a revolutionary innovation in the field of music. When this 'new' music becomes popular, however, the revolutionary and innovative character of it will rub off, as artists and their music become mainstream. The growth in (statistically verifiable) scope here goes hand in hand with an (ethnographically verifiable) change in the place of this music in social and cultural contexts, a change in what it means in real life. The totality of this phenomenon cannot be comprehended by using just one angle – we need both.

This trivial example instantiates an elementary kind of social and cultural process, which is however occurring with astonishing speed and scope in contemporary societies – think of the explosive growth of online social media and gaming communities, the viral nature of seemingly innocuous memes on the internet, or the rapid demographic transitions in superdiverse neighborhoods.

We are well underway to such an approach. In the last five years we have built up much experience in analyzing fairly unstructured interviews so as to discover the discourse (language registers) individuals from various ethnic groups in South Africa use to describe themselves and others. These studies have yielded significant insights by combining a high ecological validity with statistical procedures in the analysis. We are currently using diary methods, again in South Africa, to get better insight into those with whom actors in a diverse environment interact on a daily basis and what the topics of their interaction with members of the various groups are (e.g. Cheung *et al.*, 2011; Valchev *et al.*, 2013). The analyses of these data will allow us to develop 'identity landscapes', which refer to the multiple identities people and highly diverse environments have, and link these identities to their context of occurrence. Such studies can be easily extended to other environments, and combined with 'deep' ethnographies aimed at, for instance, linguistic landscape description. By repeating such open-ended questions across time periods, we will be able to unobtrusively gauge the shifting social context of immigrants and mainstream members. We will better understand whether there are differences in the groups with whom each interact. Understanding the open-ended answers of panel members requires much ethnographic knowledge of the respective groups. This knowledge is used in a close analysis of the responses, ethnographically described and analyzed using quantitative procedures (usually after tabulation and the use of statistical procedures for contingency tables). This combination of approaches has run smoothly in the teams we deployed until now. We can develop it further.

One final remark is in order. The analytic instrument we have in mind obviously involves teamwork, in which teams combining different methodological angles are formed around specific unified research objects. While it would be good if such teams were composed of people equally skilled in all the techniques deployed in the team, academic realists realize that this is not possible. It may not even be necessary to train people fully in both approaches, for what is needed is a *sensitivity* for different approaches and how they arrive at insights. We do not *per se* need ethnographers who are entirely versed in advanced statistical analysis. We need (to paraphrase Hymes) ethnographers who can *read* and *understand* statistical analysis, and vice versa with people trained in survey research.[5]

As mentioned earlier, the crucial operational point is to establish an object of research that can be recognized as relevant to both. It is the presence of a shared object that establishes the ground for dialogue in such heterogeneous teams. While this is not difficult work, it is often left aside, and with disastrous effects on communicability of findings and analytical punch. Intrinsically shared objects are abundant out there. What is needed is to get them in, discuss the different aspects that make up the complex nature of the objects, and draw an approach aimed at disentangling that complexity. Rapid social and cultural change is perhaps the most crucial feature of the social environments in which all of us dwell, and the most urgent thing to decode, understand and get used to. Analytically, it creates challenges, but the challenge is not just a euphemism for 'problem': it is also an invitation to think outside the box.

## Notes

(1)  Other sciences appear to have captured this. Establishing a diagnosis in a cardiology unit, for instance, involves extraordinarily divergent methodologies, including ('ethnographic') clinical inspection of outward features of the patient, anamnesis (i.e. talk), blood pressure measuring, blood testing, electro-cardiography, magnetoscopy and scanning, physical stamina testing, and so forth. The object – the patient's heart – holds it all together.

(2)  We can add a second warning here, formulated by Hymes (1966). Hymes points out that people very often are able to explicitly reproduce only specific, and severely limited, amounts of cultural material. Consequently, *asking* is not the best way to find out what there is to be found out: observation is indispensible.

(3)  The 'ethnomethods' of Garfinkelian and Goffmannian ethnomethodology, to which Cicourel importantly contributed, also looked for locally ordered forms of making sense in everyday behavior. Cicourel later distanced himself from ethnomethodology and conversation analysis on grounds that it neglected the cognitive and psychological aspects of everyday practices.

(4)  The preciseness of this formulation is essential and deviates from many descriptions of what is commonly called 'mixed methods'. Methods are, in effect, not mixed but sequentially ordered; the epistemological direction is important, as well as the description of the object.

(5)  This also counts for *publishing*. A frequently expressed anxiety is that work within 'mixed methods' creates problems in publishing, and given the tremendous pressure to publish, and publish in monodisciplinary key journals, this anxiety is understandable. There is, however, no compelling reason why *some* of the outcomes of joint work could not be routed toward monodisciplinary outlets while others are targeted at different audiences. In addition, innovative work done in-between disciplines invariably has innovative effects on the core disciplines, which is why cross-over work often acquires theoretical significance and relevance in specific disciplines.

# 10 Data Sharing as Entextualization Practice

## Introduction

This paper will attempt to discuss some issues related to the way in which certain forms of discourse analysis – a broad term here, referring to the various ways in which social-scientific disciplines represent and analyze stretches of text – make, define, construct and/or represent data. The cover term I would like to use for the whole complex of data-related activities is 'data formulation'. Data formulation often proceeds almost automatically, on the basis of received wisdom and as part of our perception of professional behavior. It is a custom rather than a method.[1]

The target of my comments, and the starting point of a broader and more general inquiry into 'data', will be one specific practice, shared mainly among scholars in conversation analysis and commonly called 'data sharing': the circulation of more or less decontextualized corpora of 'prepared' (i.e. transcribed, sometimes annotated and/or translated) data among members of the scholarly peer group, thus making the data accessible for analysis by scholars other than the one(s) who recorded or elicited the data and put them in a conventional format for data representation (transcription). The suggestion, commonly used in data sharing, is that as long as data are correctly transcribed on the basis of a shared set of transcription conventions, these data 'tell their own story' and can be analyzed successfully by other scholars. This practice and its epistemological and methodological assumptions (or indeed its theoretical decisions) are, I believe, problematical, and I will attempt to explain why.

This reflection was prompted – apart from an incident in my own professional practice, to be discussed below – by participation in a workshop on Discourse Analysis in Amsterdam, March 1997, which used data sharing as one of its main structuring tools. All of the participants to this workshop were sent three transcripts of recorded fieldwork interviews on interethnic relations in New Zealand, gracefully made accessible by

Margaret Wetherell. The decontextualization feature, characteristic (to varying degrees) of data sharing, was made explicit by the workshop organizers in their accompanying letter (December 10, 1996, italics added):

> Some people may wish to have more background information on the interviews. However, we consider it a challenge to study *these data as they are*. Professor Margaret Wetherell, *who may know more about the interviews*, may fill us in during the workshop if necessary.

This quote from the organizers' letter already reveals much of the problematic I want to discuss in the next sections. 'Data as they are' are one category of phenomena, and they consist of the kind of artifact that was sent to all the practicipants: well-transcribed fragments of spoken discourse. Additional information (e.g. elucidating the reasons *why* these interviews would fit into a wider societal problematic of multi-ethnicity in New Zealand) are qualified as *background information*. In the case of this workshop, no background information was be given: we shall discuss the data *as they are*. Yet the source of background information – the fieldworker, Professor Wetherell – may 'fill us in if necessary'.

We find, in this short quote, a cluster of categories which belong to our professional vision (to use Goodwin's 1994 term) and which distinguish potential sets of phenomena that could serve as objects of our analytical practice from others that fall, strictly speaking, outside the scope of our analysis. The former set of phenomena are the 'data', the latter are 'background information', which is not necessarily informative in itself. Background information can be called in 'if necessary', i.e. when it is required in view of answering the question – I quote again – 'of what needs to be taken into account when one wishes to say something intelligible about ethnicity issues in discourse and research interviewing'.

Before embarking on the discussion, I want to stipulate that my interest in this sort of questions related to professional practices in our own field has to be situated into a wider framework, in which I attempt to question the ways in which various branches of contemporary language studies deal with so-called 'macro-influences' on their data: historical, cultural, sociological – indeed – 'backgrounds', which stand in a meaning-giving relationship to textual objects usually selected as the target of analysis. This means that the end point of this exercise (which may seem, in itself, a Latour-like sociology of science) should be theoretical and methodological, viz. a better understanding of text–context distinctions and the way in which we treat them in our analyses. The bit of background we have on the data at hand, viz. the fact that they should be situated in a societal problematic of interethnic relations in New Zealand, might make the reflections I shall make potentially relevant.

## Not all Data are Sharable: An Incident

A while ago, a colleague of mine and I did research on communication problems between (mainly Turkish) immigrant women and Belgian welfare workers in shelters for women who were victims of domestic abuse (Bulcaen & Blommaert, 1997). The research project was sponsored by the government, and it was supervised by the local authorities of the city in which we did our fieldwork. Data were collected by Chris Bulcaen in four shelters during an 11-month period, and comprised the usual ethnographic data categories: over 100 hours of (audio)recorded material including intake interviews, feedback interviews, team sessions, meetings between professionals, everyday conversations inside the refugees and so on; a huge amount of observation notes sometimes accompanying recordings, sometimes instead of recordings where the presence of a tape recorder was either undesired or impossible; and thousands of copies of professional notes, case reports, information leaflets, letters, forms and so on, documenting the procedures in which the individual narratives of the women were gradually transformed into professional *dossiers*.

The fieldwork situation was rich and complex and it involved various feedback sessions and team meetings with members from the professional staff in these four centers, as well as the supervision and training of two immigrant female co-workers, who participated in the professional practices in the centers (assisting the treatment of immigrant women) and served as privileged informants for us. At the same time, the whole fieldwork period was accompanied by a layer of 'political' activities about our project. It was clear, right from the start, that our sponsors had their own agenda with respect to what they would do with our results. The different Boards of Trustees of the four shelters were also apprehensive about what would come out of the research project, and they repeatedly stressed the highly sensitive and confidential nature of what we were investigating. For these reasons, they had earlier declined our request to use video equipment for recording purposes.

In the spring of 1996, I was invited for a guest lecture in an 'intercultural communication' course at a college in The Netherlands. I had prepared slides with one or two fragments of transcribed material from our fieldwork, but since the overhead projector was out of order, my slides were copied as handouts and distributed among the students. I had mentioned the confidential nature of the data during my talk. Sometime later, the colleague who had invited me for the guest lecture called me and informed me that she had used my data during a talk at a conference on intercultural communication. She suggested that we should write a joint paper.

But it was not all that simple. One practical obstacle was the fact that the data from this project were legally the property of its sponsors, not of us. The research contract stipulated that we should request permission to use data in publications, and given the highly personal and deeply emotional nature of some of the recorded material, this was certainly a point we had to honor. In other words, these data were legally (and in fact ethically) *not sharable.* A more fundamental obstacle, however, was that we felt that our colleague could in no way understand the full depth of what was going on in the transcripts: the complex forms of interaction involving peculiar forms of troubles talk, administrative talk, psychosocial counseling, but also intimidation, distancing and so on; the interaction of personal-emotive, professional and bureaucratic voices; the clash of jargons and cultural schemata observable in many professional–client interactions; the wider context of cultural stereotyping, the structure of welfare work for immigrants, the intertextuality between various cases and professional discourses; the transformation of a narrative into written notes, case reports, team meeting talk, summaries given to other professionals (doctors, police officers) and so on. All of these elements and their intricate interplay had only gradually become clear to us, and there was no way in which simple things could be said about any of the data we had gathered. To put it in its crudest form: we felt that out colleague could not understand the data, because she had not been involved in the fieldwork from which the data had emerged. So also from an intellectual point of view, we felt that the data were not sharable.

They were sharable, in another sense and with some qualifications, of course. Evidently, the transcripts can be communicated and anyone can perform certain types of research on them: sequencing, adjacency pairs, turn taking, even accents and speed of delivery could be checked by anyone else. But we felt that, without the fieldwork context, no significant insights *into intercultural communication* could be gathered from our data. The intercultural dimension was not data-internal, in the sense that it could not be read from a transcript in the form of members' categorizations, orientations and so on. It was a pervasive characteristic of the whole 'immigrant-women-in-refuges' situation, synchronic as well as diachronic and even historical, and it had taken us months, as well as access to lots of other types of material, to discover the complex ways in which this dimension came about and related to single interactional encounters. So the data might have been sharable, but not for all purposes. In order to place the data in a framework of intercultural contact, superficial knowledge of the transcripts – a relatively small part of the totality of the ethnographic data we had collected – was simply not enough.

The reasoning we applied is typical for what we could call an ethnographic viewpoint, as opposed to a conversation-analytical viewpoint.[2] In the former, and I generalize heavily, a close connection is made between *fieldwork–data construction–analysis* in generating knowledge. In the latter, there is a degree of disconnection between fieldwork and the two other components. Data construction and analysis are not necessarily conditioned by fieldwork. An armchair conversation analyst is perfectly imaginable; an armchair ethnographer would be an oxymoron. But the connection between fieldwork and knowledge of what particular data are and represent is a crucial and indeed highly problematized ingredient of modern ethnography (see e.g. Fabian, 1983; Stocking, 1983). The fieldwork situation, the informants, the time and place at which the data were gathered, are all crucially informative elements of the data themselves. On top of that, and partly as a consequence of the situated nature of data in ethnography, informants' attitudes, opinions, knowledge, rationalizations and so on (as collected e.g. through feedback interviews, overhearing, or in metacomments during transcription and analysis in the field – see for the latter Urban, 1996) are also a central source of data (Rampton, 1996, is a fine example of the calibration of accounts and interactional data). In conversation analysis, *post-hoc* rationalizations, comments and so on would constitute a data-external and hence inadmissible element of data distortion (often qualified as 'mind-reading').

As a (random but typical) example, Dell Hymes' classic paper 'Breakthrough into performance' (1975, see also 1981: Chapter 3) can be mentioned. In this paper, Hymes discusses different versions of Chinook stories in a search for generic differentiations. In developing his argument, he compares versions he himself collected in the 1950s with versions collected by Edward Sapir in 1905. Particularly interesting (and characteristic) is the way in which Hymes introduces the versions of the stories he himself recorded. These introductions are long and circumspect, and extremely detailed. The story 'The crier', performed by an informant named Philip Kahclamet, is introduced by two full pages of information on the informant (including mentioning that he had previously worked with Walter Dyk), and the time and the setting (a café) of the elicitation event (pp. 21–23). Also, in Hymes' analysis the different stories remain closely associated with their performers. He speaks of 'Mr. Smith's version' and 'Mr. Simpson's version' of 'The story concerning Coyote' (pp. 25ff.), and not, for instance, of 'Hymes' version' versus 'Sapir's version'. So, there always remains a close agentive and intertextual link between the recorded narrative – the 'data-as-they-are', so to speak – and the fieldwork event and its participants, expressed metonymically by assigning the different versions to their original narrators. The data are not drawn out of their context of production, but remain firmly situated and embedded in it. The original, contextualized one-time event during which a narrative was told to a researcher remains the original, contextualized one-time event in Hymes' analysis performed (in the case of Mr Simpson's version) 70 years later. And Sapir's analytical work, documented in what he says about the informant, the story and its characteristics, pops up repeatedly as a source of information for Hymes too (see e.g. the discussion of one of Sapir's illuminating footnotes by Hymes, p. 46). So what Hymes does is to follow the trajectory of the 'data-as-they-are', from their origin in informant–researcher interaction through their first analysis into his own analysis, each time scrupulously indicating how the 'data-as-they-are' have been molded, even generated, by their fieldwork context.[3]

Bringing this example back to the issue of sharability of data, we see that Hymes (but again, Hymes as an exemplum of a whole tradition) practices a form of data sharing by incorporating Sapir's work on and with Mr Simpson into his own analysis. But he does not restrict this incorporation to just the data-as-they-are; along with the text of the narrative, he draws into his analysis the whole context of the text – including the whole Ducrotian polyphonic complex of text-as-told, text-as-noted, text-as-analyzed and so on, with ample attention to the producer (a tradition reproduced in an interactional event), the locutor (Mr Smith/Mr Simpson) and the enunciator of the text (Dell Hymes, Edward Sapir) – *as elements of text meaning*. The data come with their history of production, communication and analysis, or, to use terminology which gained some currency in recent years, the data consist both of *discourse* and *metadiscourse*, and both are firmly grounded in a series of interactional events such as fieldwork and analysis (including notation) without which data-as-they-are would either not have come into existence or would have no meaning at all.[4]

## Data Representation as Entextualization

Let us now return to the way in which this workshop was set up, and more specifically to some of the things mentioned in the introduction. I take the small phrase from the organizers' letter ('we consider it as a challenge to study these data as they are') in opposition to the types of information called 'background' and situated as the prerogative of

Professor Wetherell, as a definition of *what data are* for the purposes of this workshop. And what are the data? Three long transcripts of interviews, labeled each time 'New Zealand Interview' followed by a handwritten number. The 'data' for this workshop are text-artifacts, conventionalized notations of spoken discourse the features of which are transformed into written text by means of a set of standard transcription conventions. Thus, the data are 'a graphic representation of selective aspects of speaking and of one or more persons' behavior and setting concomitant with speaking' (O'Connell & Kowal, 1995: 646).

This lexical semantics of 'data' is quite important and needs to be kept in mind in the rest of our discussion: 'data' as used by ethnographers are not the same thing as 'data' used by conversation analysts. Let us therefore elaborate this point somewhat further. In the first letter from the organizers (October 29, 1996), the data are described as follows (I quote at length, italics added):

> The central issue ... concerns the different methodologies used by researchers in interpreting and analyzing *data produced by open interviews*. Especially *open interviews on controversial topics*, like prejudice, ethnocentrism, ethnic categorization and stereotyping *are difficult to interpret*. These interviews very often entail contradictory and ambiguous statements. Besides, the meaning of these statements [is] partly dependent on the interaction between interviewer and respondent.

Note (a) that data and interviews are separate entities, the interviews (i.e. the fieldwork event) being the *source* (or producer) of the data; and (b) that the *interviews* (not the data) are problematical for a number of reasons, partly connected to the structure of fieldwork interaction and partly characteristic of a subtype of fieldwork interviews, viz. interviews on controversial topics.

The distinction between 'data' (transcripts) and the source event from which they originated (the fieldwork interviews) becomes blurred in the second letter from the organizers (December 10, 1996). Here we find statements in which data, transcripts and interviews are synonyms (italics added):

> Hereby we send you three *transcripts* for the workshop. ... The main topic *of these interviews* concerns the relationships between different ethnic groups in New Zealand ... *The interviews* were held in the beginning of the eighties.

> We expect that some people will discuss all *the data*, whereas others may restrict themselves to only a small part of one *transcript*.

> Some people may wish to have more background information on *the interviews*. However, we consider it as a challenge to study these *data* as they are.

But we also find a statement in which the source–product relation is maintained:

> It is therefore worthwhile to compare different methodologies used by researchers in interpreting and analyzing the same *data produced by open interviews.*

Similarly, the cover sheet of the three transcripts synonymizes 'transcripts' and 'interviews'. The three transcripts are labeled 'New Zealand *interview #*', and the second paragraph of the introductory notes states '*This face to face interview* was collected and transcribed ...'.

So despite the recognition of a source–product relationship between the fieldwork interviews and the transcripts, the transcripts are presented for analysis *as the interviews*. In other words: the transcripts (remember 'a graphic representation', etc. above) *are* the interviews, and all the problems associated with the interviews ('difficult to interpret', 'contradictory and ambiguous statements', the relation to interview structure and so on) have been projected onto the transcripts. Therefore – to put it crudely – since the *interviews* are hard to interpret, contain ambiguous statements and rely on the interaction structure of fieldwork interviewing, the workshop participants are expected to investigate the *transcripts* of these interviews in order to find solutions for interpreting and analyzing *interviews.*[5]

Of course, this is problematical, and even battle-hardened conversation analysts will agree. Transcription is always a 'graphic representation of selective aspects' of interaction structure (O'Connell & Kowal, 1995); it is even a theory-oriented selective representation, as Drew & Hutchby (1995: 184) confirm:

> Transcripts aim to provide a detailed but accessible rendering of those features that, for C[onversation] A[nalysis] researchers, prove to be the most relevant for analyzing the methods in which participants concertedly accomplish orderly and intelligible social interaction.

Without passing judgment on the theoretical framework incorporated in this view of transcripts, the incorporation of a theoretical framework in the practice of transcription is in itself an inescapable fact. Transcripts are blueprints of what conversation analysts look for in conversations: 'an institutionalized substratum of rules and procedures by reference to which conversationalists engage in recognizable, coherent and accountable interaction' (Drew & Hutchby, 1995: 189).[6] Transcripts are therefore a form of *entextualization*, in which discourse is provided with a metadiscursive contextualization, guiding it and situating it within an interpretive frame of reference – a preferred reading, so to speak. They represent a stage in the history of discourse: the original fieldwork interaction is 'lifted out of its interactional setting' and so made into a *text*, a new and decontextualized/recontextualized discourse (Bauman & Briggs, 1990: 73; see also Silverstein & Urban, 1996b: 1).

Two qualifications are in order. First, every type of data representation is a form of entextualization. It is a characteristic of (social) science to make representations of reality in the form of textualized (i.e. decontextualized and recontextualized) artifacts. So, entextualization is not a characteristic of conversation analysis alone. Second, there are important differences in the ways in which ethnography and conversation analysis entextualize their data. In the former, aspects of context-of-production and subsequent histories of the text are, as a rule, incorporated, as could be seen in Hymes' treatment of fieldwork data. In conversation analysis, the incorporation of contextual information proceeds on the basis of a minimal definition of context, as will be seen in the next section. Consequently, the transgression of historical phases and the concomitant transformation of one discourse into another – from the fieldwork interview to the researcher's transcript – is kept *implicit* because of the synonymous relationship between 'data/transcripts' and 'interviews', whereas in the case of Hymes' ethnographic work, the historical situatedness of the data was made *explicit* and incorporated into the analytical and interpretive work.

Let me summarize my argument with respect to the workshop data so far. The data consist of a set of transcripts of fieldwork interviews, which are taken to be fully representative replicas of the interview events themselves, including all the problematic aspects of the interviews. This transformation of 'interviews' (a historically contingent and highly specifically contextualized event) into 'transcripts' (a selective and theory-oriented graphic representation of the event) de- and recontextualizes (entextualizes) the 'original' discourse into a 'new' discourse. This new discourse is our 'data', and the particular form of definition and representation of 'data' is strongly influenced by a conversation-analytical tradition of data-formulating practices.

So far, I have only treated one aspect of the organizers' definition of 'data': the 'data' themselves. The second element involved, 'background', now needs to be looked at.

## Text and Context – Data and Background

Where does all this leave 'background'? What about 'context'? I have already quoted and discussed the organizers' distinction between 'background information' and 'data-as-they-are', and I indicated that background was presented as the prerogative of the fieldworker, Professor Wetherell, who would 'fill us in ... if necessary'. So to some extent, the organizers have already answered their central question: 'what needs to be taken into account when one wishes to say something intelligible about ethnicity issues in discourse and research interviewing' (December 10, 1996 letter): by presenting us with transcripts-as-data, what needs to be taken into account is likely to be situated *inside* the transcripts, with some possibilities for (a) *'inferences* made in the analysis' (Dec. 10) and (b) *'filling in'* of some background information by the fieldworker (Dec. 10).

There are two issues which I would like to raise at this point: (a) the fact that we already know quite a bit of 'background'; and (b) the phenomenon of 'background talk' in discourse analysis.

On the *first issue* we already know a lot. We know, for instance, the *topic* of the interviews: 'the relationship between different ethnic groups in New Zealand, especially between Pakeha's and Maori's' (December 10). And we know that this topic is *'controversial'* and fits in a cluster containing 'prejudice, ethnocentrism, ethnic categorization and stereotyping' (October 29). We also know the interaction format and the participants. As for interaction format, it is the 'open interview' format; the participants are the interviewer and Pakeha respondents (December 10). We know that these respondents are male or female from their symbol identification in the transcripts. As for the identity of the interviewer, there is some doubt: the symbol identification in the transcripts reads 'Jill (female) interviewer', but the interviews are described as 'collected ... by Margaret Wetherell and Jonathan Potter'. About interviews on topics such as this one (and hence, through the move described above, about the structure of the interview transcripts given as data), we know that they are 'difficult to interpret', that they 'very often entail contradictory and ambiguous statements ... The meaning of [which is] partly dependent on the interaction between the interviewer and respondent' (October 29). The information on time and place of the interview (elements so scrupulously given by Hymes) is vague. We are informed that the interviews took place 'in the mid-1980s in New Zealand', but we are left uninformed about the potential (ir)relevance of these factors.

We also know a bit about the *research history* of these data, be it in a very partial manner. We know how the transcripts came into being and got their final shape: the interview

> was collected and transcribed by Margaret Wetherell and Jonathan Potter [but done by a female interviewer identified as 'Jill'] in the mid-1980s in New Zealand. It was retranscribed by Marjon Vos van der Born. (Transcript)

In contrast to the information, we get on the *transcripts*, but not surprising in view of the comments made earlier, we have no idea of a number of crucial issues in the research history not related to the history of the transcripts. First, the *interview situation* itself remains underdocumented, despite the potential relevance of situational factors and the pragmatics of interviewing for the outcome of interviews (see Briggs, 1986). Thus we have no answers to questions such as: (a) were the interviews *formal* interviews in terms of set-up (e.g. in university classrooms or offices, with potential 'white room effects'); (b) what was the criterion of selection of the respondents (e.g. how they related to the topic: whether they were involved in political movements or just lay people); (c) who, in fact, was 'Jill', and given the (presumably) supervising role of Potter and Wetherell, did 'Jill' script her interviews; and (d) when precisely did the interviews take place, and was there any connection between the moment of interviewing and the particular topic (e.g. whether the interviews happened at a time when interethnic issues were widely debated, for instance owing to Pakeha–Maori conflicts)? Second, we are left uninformed about the *general research targets* set for these interviews, and about their history in terms of publication, interpretation (who said what about these data in the past), discussion, circulation and so on (apart, of course, from the fact that they were circulated for this particular workshop). So *why* were these interviews recorded – for 'Jill's' MA or PhD research, for Potter and Wetherell's research on racism or as part of a 'public opinion' research project? We do not know.

Summarizing, we know a bit of (transcript-external) background on topic, participants, time and place, enough to set our eyes looking for issues of Pakeha–Maori interethnic issues in New Zealand in the mid-1980s. We also have a more or less precise idea of the history of the transcripts. But we have no *ethnographic* background to the transcripts. We are uninformed about the precise pragmatic situation of the fieldwork interaction event, and we are uninformed about the scholarly history of the data, in the sense that we do not know how and why the data were interpreted and analyzed in the past.

The *second issue* is background talk. There is a particular format for 'giving background information' to data in contexts such as this one, and aspects of it were already discussed on a previous occasion (Blommaert, 1996, 1997). A hint is already given in the way in which the organizers describe Professor Wetherell's potential role: 'filling in ... if necessary'. 'Background information', i.e. elements that are not readable in the transcripts (or texts, in the case of text analysis) and are the object of 'inferences' in analysis, is almost invariably captured in the form of authoritative, factual but rather loose talk. Discourse analysis has a distinct tendency to treat 'background information' as mere unquestionable facts, known by certain people and simply communicated to others. The background itself is, however, hardly ever the target of critical scrutiny or analysis. It just 'fills in' gaps in the analysis, 'where necessary'. Background information is very often given loosely, in the form of not-really-part-of-the-exposé, at the beginning of papers or talks, or squeezed into footnotes with local relevance in the text or argument.

Nothing is wrong with that, of course, were it not that we often provide immense amounts of highly debatable, controversial statements under the guise of simple background *facts* (e.g. statements about the nature of political regimes, about social or ethnic categories and structures, about social roles and power hierarchies, about pertinent concepts, values and attitudes of the people we discuss, and so on). Secondly, by doing this we often practice a very intriguing form of lying. We often take for granted (as background facts) things which in other domains would be seen as 'social constructions', 'discursive constructions' and so on (e.g. things such as political identifications of the type 'left/right', 'neonazi', 'antisemite', etc.). Also, when it comes to writing papers, we often pretend not to know what we in fact *needed* to know in order to be able to do fieldwork. Setting up fieldwork requires a degree of knowledge – intuitive or well-informed – of the social structure, the social roles, the institutional contexts, etc., in vigor in the community in which we work. Concretely, when we make recordings in a classroom, we usually know perfectly well who the teacher is, and who the pupils are (and so do, in fact, the teacher and the pupils themselves). Details about the discursive realization of these roles may be nice as corroborating evidence, but discursive realizations need not be presented as the only empirical evidence for the existence and/or the salience of these roles, institutional structures, power hierarchies and so on.[7] Put simply, we often pretend to know less about our data than we in fact do. But we eliminate parts of this knowledge from our professional *presentation* of data, because they would not fit into a narrowly conceived idea of 'empirical facts' and are, in the eyes of many, 'just stories' or 'commonsense' which 'we happen to know'. Thus, we make believe that our analytical apparatus reveals more than it does.

The phenomena discussed in this section all point toward a restricted use of 'text' as the main object of analysis ('data'). In contrast to ethnography, the text incorporates only minimal contextual information, especially with regard to the history of the text. 'Text' is the transcript, manufactured using conventions that should make *necessary* contextual factors visible: turn patterns, non-verbal features such as pauses, intonation contours, emphasis patterns and so on. These contextual elements should provide us, alongside *what* people say in the transcripts, with enough clues for getting a picture of the orderly and cooperative structure of talk-as-social-interaction. I believe they can, but that was not the question. The question guiding this endeavor will be discussed in the next section. Let us again compare this narrow view of 'text' and 'context' with that of Dell Hymes, discussed earlier. We see in the data presentation for this workshop how the fieldwork situation has been dissociated from the data proper. The data only have a history from the time of transcription onwards. Contrary to what Hymes did with Mr Smith's and Mr Simpson's texts, the situatedness of the discourse production in a real, temporally and spatially precisely defined communicative event has been eliminated as a potential *source of meaning* for the transcripts. In this entextualization process, all potential influences of the various phases in the history of the discourse have been eliminated as factors shaping the 'data'. What is left is a highly abstract, monological but poly-interpretable text-artifact, of which all kinds of potentially informative 'background' elements have been cut off and replaced by a series of theoretical assumptions regarding the status of transcripts as replicas of contextualized interaction events.

By no means do I wish to sound derogatory about this practice, which I associated with conversation analysis. My point is simply this: the lexical-semantic difference between 'data' in ethnography and 'data' in conversation analysis hides a more important set of differences, this time *epistemological differences*. In ethnography, fieldwork and the ensuing situatedness of the data gathered through real interaction processes between researcher and informant have an important epistemological status. The process of fieldwork cannot be separated from the *products* of fieldwork: meaningful discourse (or discourse made meaningful). To put it simply, all of the bits and pieces of 'background' picked up by an ethnographer during fieldwork *are data*, not just factual stories given at the beginning of a talk or paper to make an analysis of a transcript more interesting or comprehensible.[8] In the conversation analytical tradition, fieldwork is not given an epistemological status and conversation analytical data can be informative even though they bear no traces of their context-of-production. It is this epistemological stance that allows people in conversation analysis to practice and legitimize data sharing as a perfectly valid intellectual practice. This works well as long as one researches things that are researchable in terms of the set goals of conversation analysis. But I do believe it creates difficulties whenever macro-contextual elements – history, culture, politics, social structure and so on – are involved.

## Retrieving Interethnic Relations

The question guiding this workshop was how to analyze (successfully) interviews related to interethnic relations in New Zealand. First, a number of qualifications are in order. On the basis of what I said above, it is perfectly plausible to offer methods for analyzing (transcripts of) interviews related to interethnic relations in New Zealand. We can accept the transcript-as-data definition offered to us, and focus exclusively on discourse structure in the three transcriptions at hand. Then, we are analyzing *interviews*, more or less regardless of their topic. Given the fact that we have been provided with some essential non-textual background (New Zealand, Maori–Pakeha, 1980s, etc.) we may even say very interesting things about interviews *related to*, etc. (It would be hard, given the minimal contextualization, to see the interviews as related to something else.) But if we want to come up with insights into interethnic relations in New Zealand *through and by means of* an analysis of the transcripts, then I fear that Professor Wetherell will have to be quite active in 'filling us in'.

Let me illustrate this point by referring back to the incident on data sharing discussed earlier. As mentioned, I presented a couple of transcripts drawn from fieldwork on immigrant women in refuges, more specifically, transcripts from one intake interview between a young Turkish girl and a Belgian female welfare worker. In the transcript, a clear case of intercultural communication failure occurred: the welfare worker had pictured the girl, on the basis of some of her statements, as a 'westernized' girl. This categorization had triggered a frame of cultural features and expectations: the welfare worker expected the girl to want more independence, opportunities for personal development through studies and so on. But all of a sudden, the girl emphatically stressed her faith in Islam – a statement which was totally incongruous with the scenario of westernization dominant in the welfare worker's perception of the girl. Conversation structure showed clear indications of communicative breakdown around and after the 'Muslim' turn, and so the conclusion was clear: here was a case of *local intercultural conflict*, triggered by the use of macro-social cultural scenarios about immigrants in Belgium. But what became clear in a later phase of our research project, when we started investigating the whole trajectory of the girl's story through the various phases of professionalization, was that this local intercultural conflict did not lead to undesirable actions from the part of the welfare worker. Despite the rather gross misinterpretation of the girl's motives for leaving home and seeking refuge, and despite the reproduction of the cultural scenario through the various channels and phases of professional discoursing, a perfectly acceptable solution for the girl's problem was found through successive conversations involving various actors (professional as well as non-professional). The girl's stay in the refuge could be qualified as 'successful'. Feedback taught us that both the girl and the welfare worker had the impression that they had related well to one another. So what about intercultural conflict? Certainly, interculturality was present at various levels, a local level in the intake interview, and a more general level – that of an intercultural *relationship* – covering the whole of the girl's presence in the refuge, the totality of her interactions with Belgian professionals, and her final attitude upon leaving the refuge. At the local level there was conflict, at the more general level conflict was absent in ways that were relevant to the participants.[9] We could only come to that conclusion after having put various pieces of a puzzle together: the intake interview, the welfare worker's notes, records and transcripts of team meetings in which the girl's case was discussed, informal talks with both the girl and the welfare worker, the outtake interview, and so on. In other words, whereas the individual transcript of the intake interview might have led to a hypostasis of culture as a resource for conflicts between the girl and the welfare worker, the examination of a larger body of data involving aspects of the organizational sociology of the refuge, different textual representations of the girl's story and the procedural sequence of the treatment of her case, cancelled this interpretation, valid though it was on the basis of an analysis of the single transcript.

Can we retrieve significant insights into interethnic relations on the basis of a close scrutiny of transcripts of interviews? Maybe yes, but I have some reservations about the informativity of single cases or episodes for as wide and deep an issue as interethnic relations. Even if we come up with macro-social hypotheses, the pertinence of these hypotheses formulated on the sole basis of an examination of transcripts may not always be that clear. I do not believe that transcripts alone lead us to plausible prognoses of 'context', i.e. that we can reconstruct a world, a society and all its paraphernalia from singular instances of discourse alone. In cases such as this one, I would prefer to work the other way round: start with 'context', with 'background' so to speak, and then see how discourse samples would fit in. I would be forced to do so, if for nothing else because I simply know nothing about New Zealand.

## Data Sharing

I have been meandering through a series of reflections on definitions of data, distinctions drawn between data and background or text and context, and the potential offered by one particular definition of data (as opposed to background) for the basic question guiding this workshop. This long and winding détour was, I believe, necessary. The simple practice of data sharing – sending a uniform set of materials to every participant for individual analysis – hides a fairly important complex of methodological and epistemological issues. In our fields of study, reflections on object construction, commensurability between various objects or indeed basic methodology are relatively rare, and Cicourel rightly called our attention to this issue. An occasion such as this one may prompt us to start looking in greater detail at some of the predispositions of our work: issues of what we work on, how and why. The comments I have offered so far are not a data analysis, but they are a form of data treatment: they are to be situated in the phase preceding data analysis, at the moment of *formulating data*. Reflection on data formulation is a necessity, I think, for all those committed to interdisciplinarity and cross-disciplinary dialogue.

In my argumentation, I have sketched an opposition between two ways of defining data, generalizingly labeled 'ethnographic' versus 'conversation analytical' definitions of data. The differences were semantic and referential, to the extent that when a conversation analyst talks about 'my data', she or he talks about transcripts (and sometimes of tapes), while an ethnographer would refer to the totality of fieldwork data (recordings, notes, the Malinowskian *corpus inscriptiorum* – see Auer, 1995 for an overview). But apart from these semantic differences, which are all in all easy to accommodate, the two definitions of data also hide a different epistemological agenda: the data tell us a very different story, and knowing/analyzing/interpreting them involves different strategies, assumptions and theoretical decisions. This type of difference is hard to remedy, I believe. It is not merely a matter of 'contextualized' versus 'decontextualized' data: the 'data' themselves are formulated differently, especially with regard to what counts as 'context' in an epistemological sense, i.e. what do we need to know in order to be able to claim knowledge of the data.

I have pointed to the way in which data representation can be seen as an entextualization practice. With the data – the text – comes a meta-discursive frame which steers our interpretation of the text into specific directions. So data sharing is not a neutral – or, if I may use the term, 'pluralist' – act of 'sharing'. It is an entextualization practice in its own right, by means of which 'data' are offered not in their bare form, but accompanied by a whole set of pre-inscribed patterns of interpretations, assumptions, frames of reference, epistemological agendas. It is the politics of representation in full swing (see Bauman & Briggs, 1990: 76). And so apart from the beneficial dimension of gaining access to data previously inaccessible to other people than the researcher who made the data, data sharing also has a dimension of authority and – through the acceptance of the entextualization of the data – of peer group formation. Data sharing in the sense outlined here identifies a subgroup of scholars, bound by a consensus on what counts as 'empiry', as 'facts', as 'analysis', as 'science' and as 'evidence'.

## Notes

(1) It was Aaron Cicourel who pointed to the importance of investigations into 'data' as one of the main concerns of pragmatics in a comment made during the *Round Table on the Handbook of Pragmatics* (International Pragmatics Conference, Kobe, July 1993). I am grateful to Aaron, and to Chris Bulcaen and Michael Meeuwis for useful comments on the very first draft of this paper as well as for stimulating discussions on this topic. Sigurd d'Hondt, the late Pat Haegeman, Boris Metz and Jo Van den Hauwe (perhaps unknowingly) provided valuable insights and 'data' for this paper.

(2) Both labels are evidently idealizations, and they represent sources of influence rather than clear-cut and closed sub-disciplines of pragmatics. Conversation-analytic approaches to data have for instance also penetrated certain forms of discourse analysis (e.g. some discourse analysis within the paradigm of discursive social psychology).

(3) This is a point which was later picked up with considerable insight and force by Johannes Fabian in a number of publications. See in particular Fabian (1990b, 1991b: part 1).

(4) This is why fieldwork interaction, notation and early analyses as ways of discourse representation are a central preoccupation in ethnography focused on metadiscourse and language ideologies. See e.g. Bauman (1995), Haviland (1996b), Irvine (1995), Silverstein (1996b) and Urban (1996).

(5) This synonymizing of the analytical text-artifact with the 'real' communicative event is a common trope in the conversation-analytical literature. One often reads, in reference to analyses of *transcripts*, statements such as 'as the *conversations* show', 'in this episode of *conversation*' and so on. An awareness of the metalevel nature of transcription seems to be often obscured by a strong belief in the representativity of transcription-as-replica of the event. For a particularly problematical expression of this belief, see Schegloff (1988).

(6) The selectivity of transcription procedures also involves a set of unmotivated (or barely motivated) preferences, which we could call (following Jefferson, 1996) 'transcriptional stereotyping', such as (a) restricting transcription to audible signals and (b) preferring transcription of speech into standard orthographies of known languages. As for the former, there is a tendency to incorporate visual and non-verbal signs into transcription work; see e.g. the papers in Auer and Di Luzio (1992: part 2). As for the latter, I have always experienced problems with rendering East-African codeswitched speech into standard orthographies of either English or Swahili. Not

capturing the peculiar phonetic realizations made by speakers may give rise to illusions of bilingual competence as a prerequisite for codeswitching (see Meeuwis & Blommaert, 1997).

(7) The same may count for some work on negotiating identities in talk, epitomized for instance in Carol Myers-Scotton's work on codeswitching (Myers-Scotton, 1993).

(8) See, for instance, the scope of contextual elements treated in the papers in Silverstein and Urban (1996a) as parts of the 'natural histories of discourse'.

(9) Which casts some doubt on the conversation-analytical thesis that what people actually do in (individual instances of) interaction represents what they find salient or real (see Schegloff, 1988).

# 11 Chronotopes, Scales and Complexity in the Study of Language in Society

## Introduction

The conceptual work that I wish to document in this essay must be seen as part of a bigger effort in linguistic anthropology and adjacent sciences to arrive at more *precise* and *realistic* accounts of an object of study which, by exactly such attempts, is bound to remain unstable and subject to perpetual upgrading and reformulation. In the most general sense, the issue is one of adequate contextualization of language signs in an attempt to understand their meaning effects, but as we shall see, precisely this attempt toward adequate contextualization creates objects that are no longer linguistic in the strict disciplinary sense of the term, but more generally semiotic, complex objects.

The particular axis of contextualization I shall discuss here is that of 'timespace' – the literal translation of the term 'chronotope' designed by Bakhtin in the 1930s (Bakhtin, 1981: 84; Bemong & Borghart, 2010: 4–5). Chronotope refers to the intrinsic blending of space and time in any event in the real world, and was developed by Bakhtin, as we shall see, as an instrument for developing a fundamentally historical semiotics.[1] As such, and in spite of the daunting Greekness of the term, it has had an impact on scholarship. The same cannot be said (yet) of the second concept I shall discuss, 'scale' – developed initially to point toward the non-unified, layered and stratified nature of meaningful signs and their patterns of circulation. A small amount of work has been done using scale as a conceptual tool, often studies of globalization.

In what follows, I shall first set the discussion in a broader issue: that of 'context' and contextualization. I shall then introduce chronotopes and scales as potentially useful concepts, after which I shall merge them with the issue of contextualization and show how timespace complexity can (and does) enrich work in our fields of study.

## Complicating Context

Notions such as scale and chronotope help us overcome two persisting problems in the study of language in society. These problems persist in spite of decades of work offering solutions to them; such solutions, however, are usually relegated to the realm of advanced scholarship, while the problems are part of most 'basic' approaches to issues in our fields.

The first problem is that studies of language in society tend to apply a simple untheorized distinction in the 'levels of context' included in analysis: the *micro versus macro distinction*. Discourse analysis of spoken interaction, or the sociolinguistic analysis of individual variables in speech, would typify *micro-analysis*, while ideologically oriented critical discourse analysis and studies of language policy and language attitudes would typify the latter. A rough gloss could be while 'micro' approaches examine how people affect language, 'macro' approaches focus on how language affects people. The second problem, closely related to this, is the dominance of *one-dimensional models of meaning* (cf. Silverstein, 1992: 57). There is a widespread assumption that language in actual social use must yield *one* 'meaning', both as a locally emerging behavioral effect pushing participants in a conversation from one turn into the other and from opening to closing, and as a local denotational correlate of correct and intentional morphosyntactic work by a 'speaker'. This second problem presupposes a vast amount of shared resources among language users, including agreements about the conventions governing their deployment.

Note in passing that I used the term '*local*' here: in our common analytic vocabulary, 'micro' stands for 'local' and 'macro' stands for 'translocal' – spatial metaphors defining a particular scope of context. And 'local', in addition, also often occurs as a synonym for *synchronic:* the things that happen here-and-now in a particular speech event. Space and time are interchangeable features in the way we talk about analysis; I shall have occasion, of course, to return to this point.

There is a mountain of literature criticizing the 'micro–macro' distinction, very often targeting the inadequacies of 'micro' approaches, which, as I said, persist in spite of such critical work.[2] Most authors would argue that inadequacies occur precisely at the interstices of several 'levels' of context, as when the range of contextual–conversational inferences transcends the scope of what is purely brought about in the 'local' conversational context and needs to include broader sociocultural 'frames' of contextual knowledge (Goffman, 1974; Gumperz, 1992; Silverstein, 1992), or when what looks like a single and coherent activity – a multiparty conversation, for instance – proves upon closer inspection to contain several different, not entirely aligned or even conflicting, activities, calling into question the levels of 'sharedness' in purpose and orientation of the different participants (Cicourel, 1992; Goodwin, 2007; Goodwin & Goodwin, 1992; see also Goffman, 1964). So, what is 'brought about' as a joint collaborative activity such as a conversation may obscure deep differences in what is being 'brought along' by different participants, and consequently in what is 'taken along' by these participants after the activity. As all of us who have done some teaching know, people can walk away from seemingly focused speech events with divergent understandings of 'what was actually said'.

This has a direct bearing on our second problem, that of one-dimensional models of meaning, and the connection between both problems was clearly spelled out by Silverstein (1992), drawing on the new wave of studies of language ideologies moving in at that time. Silverstein distinguished between two views of interaction, one centered on intentionally produced and organized denotation (a one-dimensional view), and another centered on what was achieved *indexically* by means of a complex mode of communicative behavior in which pragmatic and metapragmatic (ideological) aspects are inseparable – a multidimensional view in which vastly more is achieved by participants than merely denotational alignment. The language-ideological dimension of semiosis, we have since learned, moves the field of analysis in very different directions: Saussurean language is substituted by a multiplex 'total linguistic fact' (about which more in a moment); the analysis of communication shifts from intention to *effects*, of which denotation is just one; and such effects are necessarily unstable and indeterminate – hence 'creative'.

The nexus of the two problems I identified earlier is *indexicality*: language-ideologically 'loaded' semiotic features (indexicals) come in as a 'translocal' but 'locally' enacted layer of *historical* meaning. Indexicality, in Silverstein's conception, brings into profile the historical dimension of Goffman's frames: when we perform interpretive work, we draw on relatively conventionalized (and therefore historical) sets of metapragmatically attributive meaning – 'tropes' (Silverstein, 1992: 69; also Agha, 1997, 2007) – that are triggered by indexicals providing presupposable pointers to 'those implicit values ... of relational identity and power that, considered as an invokable structure, go by the name of "culture"' (Silverstein, 1992: 57; also Agha, 1997). The interstices between distinct 'levels' of context disappear because each 'local' (micro) act of contextualization operates by means of locally (in)validated invocations of 'translocal' (macro) meanings:

> The point is that social life as *interactions* that constantly call up culture (and its deployability or realization in them) and reinvest it with their historicity, is the object of this wider construal of 'contextualization'. (Silverstein, 1992: 57; also Agha, 1997)

And the Gumperzian 'contextualization cues' – the target of Silverstein's critique – reemerge as semiotic features (indexicals) prompting 'local' interpretations grounded in 'translocal' historically configured ascriptions of genre, key, footing and identity often captured under the term 'register' (Agha, 2005, 2007; Silverstein 2003, 2006a). This is why uniquely situated activities such as talk in school can, and do, contribute not just to learning but also to membership of social class and other 'macro' social categories: 'Collective socio-historical schemas are continuously reconstituted in within the flows and contingencies of situated activity' (Rampton, 2006: 344; Wortham, 2006).

Meaning in context here appears as a more broadly conceived complex of *valuations* – indexicals point to what *counts as meaning* in a specific semiotic event. To make this point relevant for what follows, let us underscore that *value* and *history* are central here: we best see 'meaning' as *value effects* derived from local enactments of historically loaded semiotic resources (cf. Blommaert, 2005b: Chapter 4; cf. also Agha, 1997: 495). The 'local' and 'micro', therefore, are not 'synchronic' but profoundly historical, and the micro–macro distinction (our first problem) has become irrelevant, since every instance of 'micro' contextualization would at once be an instance of 'macro' contextualization. As for the one-dimensional view of meaning as a singular and linear outcome of interaction (our second problem), it is replaced by a multidimensional package of effects, some of which are 'locally' enacted with others occurring later in forms of re-entextualization (Blommaert, 2001b; Silverstein & Urban, 1996a). What is 'taken along' from one semiotic event is 'brought along' into the next one. And *this* is our object of study: the total linguistic (or semiotic) fact

> is irreducibly dialectic in nature. It is an unstable mutual interaction of meaningful sign forms, contextualised to situations of interested human use and mediated by the fact of cultural ideology. (Silverstein, 1985a: 220)

This object has become a complex non-linear and multidimensional thing; the context in which it operates has likewise become a complex dialectics of features pointing at once to various 'levels'. Owing to this fusion of 'micro' and 'macro', this total linguistic/semiotic fact is intrinsically historical: a reality to which Voloshinov directed our attention long ago. Which brings us to Bakhtin.

## Chronotope and Scale

Recall that I emphasized value and history, because these notions lead us right to the core of Bakhtin's view of language and are indispensable in our discussion of chronotope. Let me briefly elaborate both.

Bakhtin's concept of language is a sociolinguistic one, containing not just 'horizontal' distinctions such as dialects (linguistic variation) but also 'vertical' ones such as genres, professional jargons and the like (social variation). To be more specific, Bakhtin sees language in its actual deployment (as e.g. in a novel) as a repository of 'internal stratification present in every language at any given moment of its historical existence' (Bakhtin, 1981: 263). At any moment of performance, the language (or discourse, as Bakhtin qualifies it) actually used will enable an historical-sociological analysis of different 'voices' within the social stratigraphy of language of that moment: Bakhtin's key notion of heteroglossia – the delicate 'dialogical' interplay of socially (ideologically, we would now say) positioned voices in e.g. a novel – is the building block of a 'sociological stylistics' (Bakhtin, 1981: 300), and as he demonstrated in the various essays in *The Dialogical Imagination*, this sociological stylistics is necessarily *historical*.[3] In actual analysis, it operates via a principle of indexicality, in which the use of genre features such as 'common language ... is taken by the author precisely as the *common view*, as the verbal approach to people and things normal for a given sphere of society' (Bakhtin, 1981: 301; cf. also Rampton, 2003). Form is used to project socially stratified meaning ('verbal-ideological belief systems'; Bakhtin, 1981: 311), and this indexical nexus creates what we call 'style', for it can be played out, always hybridized, in ways that shape recognizable meaning effects 'created by history and society' (Bakhtin, 1981: 323).

The step from history to value is a small one. The stratified sociolinguistic diversity which is central to Bakhtin's view of language – its historically specific heteroglossic structure – means that *understanding* is never a linear 'parsing' process; it is an *evaluative* one. When Bakhtin talks about understanding, he speaks of 'integrated meaning that relates to value – to truth, beauty and so forth – and requires a *responsive* understanding, one that includes evaluation' (Bakhtin, 1986: 125). The dialogical principle evidently applies to uptake of speech as well, and such uptake involves the interlocutor's own historically specific 'verbal-ideological belief systems' and can only be done from within the interlocutor's own specific position in a stratified sociolinguistic system. Nothing, consequently, is 'neutral' in this process – not even time and space, as his discussion of chronotope illustrates.

Bakhtin designed the chronotope to express the inseparability of time and space in human social action, and he selected the 'literary artistic chronotope' where 'spatial and temporal indicators are fused into one carefully thought-out, concrete whole', in such a way that the chronotope could be seen as 'a formally constitutive category of literature' (Bakhtin 1981: 84). Identifying chronotopes enabled Bakhtin to address the co-occurrence of events from different times and places in novels. He saw chronotopes as an important aspect of the novel's heteroglossia, part of the different 'verbal-ideological belief systems' that were in dialogue in a novel.

I make this point in order to dispense with two, in my view misguided, interpretations of the chronotope: one in which chronotopes are used as *descriptive* tools, shorthand for the ways in which time and space are actually represented in discourse (e.g. Crossley, 2006; Wang, 2009), and another one in which the chronotope is seen as the cognitive theory behind Bakhtin's work, a memory structure not unlike schemata (e.g. Keunen, 2000). Both interpretations miss what is perhaps the most productive aspect of the chronotope concept: its connection to *historical and momentary agency*. In Bakhtin's analyses, chronotopes invoke and enable a plot structure, characters or identities, and social and political worlds in which actions become dialogically meaningful, evaluated and understandable in specific ways. Specific chronotopes produce specific kinds of person, actions, meaning and value. Decoding them is in itself a chronotopic phenomenon, in addition, in which other historicities convene in the here-and-now historicity of understanding.

We shall see how productive this can be for our scholarship. For now, let us gloss Bakhtin's chronotopes as 'invokable histories', elaborate frames in which time, space and patterns of agency coincide, create meaning and value, and can be set off against other chronotopes. Which is why the sub-title to Bakhtin's essay on 'Forms of time and of chronotope in the novel' was 'Notes towards a historical poetics' – Bakhtin's problem was that novels are not just historical objects (Dickens wrote in the mid-19th century) but also articulate complexly layered historicities, the historical ideological positions of narrator, plot and characters, in the form of chronotopes.

Chronotopes presuppose the non-uniformity of historical spacetime in relation to human consciousness and agency, and they share this presupposition with that other concept I must discuss here: scale. The origins of the latter concept lie elsewhere, in Braudel's majestic study *La*

*Méditerranée* (1949). Braudel distinguished three 'levels' of history: the very slow history of climate and landscape (but also including 'mentalities'; Braudel, 1969 [1958]: 51) which he called *durée*, an intermediate cyclical history of 'conjunctures', and the day-to-day history of 'événements'. The three levels correspond to different speeds of development, from the very slow change in climate to the very rapid pace of everyday events. These distinctions also coincided with different levels of human consciousness and agency: most individuals are not acutely aware of the bigger and slower historical processes of which they are part, while they are aware of events and incidents punctuating their lives; and while no individual can alone and deliberately change the climate, individuals influence and have a degree of agency over their everyday historical context; and while individual people can influence their own lives with individual actions that take hardly any time (as when they commit a murder), it takes enormous numbers of people and actions spread over a very long time span for the climate to change. Processes developing at the level of the *durée*, consequently, were seen by Braudel as developing on another 'scale' as those happening in the here-and-now, and note that Braudel's distinction between levels of history includes a range of theoretical statements involving levels of human consciousness and agency. A 'comprehensive' history, according to Braudel, had to include all of these different scales, since every historical moment was and is a nexus of all of these scales.

Braudel's concept of history was refined and expanded by Immanuel Wallerstein in an attempt to develop what he called 'World-System Analysis' – a new social science that addressed the many intricate forms of historical linkage and exchange that characterize the emergence of an increasingly globalizing capitalist world (Wallerstein, 2004). Wallerstein rejected the focus on time alone and opted instead for a (by now familiar) unitary notion of timespace, with more 'scales' than in Braudel's framework (Wallerstein, 1998). The details of Wallerstein's scalar stratigraphy need not concern us here – the point to take on board is that, like Braudel, Wallerstein connects timespace 'levels' with levels of human awareness and agency; an individual vote for a political party during elections is an action on a different scale than that party winning the elections, which is again different from that party forming a government and implementing a neoliberal austerity program.

As mentioned at the outset, while chronotopes have had a relatively rewarding career in scholarship in our fields, scales are relatively underused so far. When that notion was introduced in sociolinguistic work, it was presented as a concept that might do exactly what Braudel and Wallerstein used it for: to make fine stratigraphic distinctions between 'levels' of sociolinguistic activity, thus enabling distinctions as to power, agency, authority and validity that were hard to make without a concept that suggested vertical – hierarchical – orders in meaning making (Blommaert, 2007, 2010; Collins *et al.*, 2009; Wortham, 2006, 2009). In the next section, I will bring chronotopes and scales together and examine how they can contribute to a complexity-oriented, realistic account of context and contextualization which, in turn, affects our views of language and meaning.

## Chronotope, scale and context

I propose to see chronotopes as that aspect of contextualization by means of which specific chunks of history can be invoked in discourse as meaning-attributing resources or, to refer to earlier terminology, as *historically configured and ordered 'tropes'*. As for scales, I propose to see them as defining the *scope of communicability* of such tropes, and in line with what was argued earlier, we can also call this their scope of creativity (see Briggs, 2005). Both are useful to distinguish between two dimensions of context and contextualization: that of the *availability* of specific contextual universes for invocation in discursive work (chronotope); and that of their *accessibility* for participants and audiences involved in discursive work (scale). These two dimensions, I have argued in earlier work, are essential sociolinguistic qualifications of discourse-analytic notions of 'context'; contexts are actual and concrete resources for semiosis, and they are subject to differential distribution and inequality in rights-of-use (Blommaert, 2005b: Chapter 3; see also Blommaert & Maryns, 2002; Briggs, 1997, 2005). Let me now clarify these points.

In its simplest form, chronotopes as historically configured tropes point us to the fact that specific complexes of 'how-it-was' can be invoked as relevant context in discourse. Events, acts, people and themes can be set and reset, so to speak, in different timespace frames, in such a way that the setting and resetting enable and prompt indexicals ordered as socioculturally recognizable sets of attributions. I am staying quite close to Bakhtin's chronotopic analyses here, where the invocation of a particular timespace (e.g. that of ancient Greek adventure stories) triggers an ordered complex of attributions that defines the plot (what can happen, and how), the actors (who can act, and how), the moral or political normative universes involved in what happens, the trajectories of plot and character development and the effects of what happens. We get *generic types* (Bakhtin, 1981: 251) or in Agha's terms, *figures* of personhood, of action, of sociopolitical values, of effect; and these figures are then performed through speech by means of indexicals – essentially random features which have now been ordered in such a way that they converge on the 'figures' invoked by the particular timescale setting and create a logic of deployment and of expectation (Agha, 2005: 39, 2011). The 'type' is converted into recognizable 'tokens'. To provide a trivial example, a narrative starting with 'once upon a time' – the fairy tale genre trigger – prompts a timeless and geographically unidentifiable place in which princes, giants, witches, wizards and dwarfs can be expected alongside imaginary animals (dragons, unicorns) and animated objects (talking trees or moving rocks), with magic, a simple good–bad moral universe and a happy ending as expected features ('happy ever after'). Bakhtin argued that such chronotopic organization defined the specific genres we culturally recognize. All of the features of such a fairy tale have been centered on indexical-ordering 'figures', and we follow the logic of performance by deploying them in the right order – a disruption of one feature (e.g. the 'good prince' suddenly becoming ugly or arrogant) can disrupt the entire order.

Specific features can operate as *tropic emblems*, because they instantly invoke a chronotope as outlined above and bring chunks of history to the interactional here-and-now as relevant context. They invoke the 'type' of which the actual enactment is a 'token'. Thus, mentioning 'Stalin' can suffice to invoke a Cold War chronotope in which Stalinism equals the enemy and in which dictatorial, violent and totalitarian attributions define the 'figure' of the Stalinist leader; images of Che Guevara can be used to reset (or 'align', to use Agha's term) contemporary moments of social activism in an older historical lineage of left-wing rebellion, creating an indexical 'pedigree' if you wish, very much in the way that '-isms' ('communism', 'liberalism') do – it creates an endless *durée* and/or 'stops time' by denying the relevance of intervening patterns of change and development (Lemon, 2009).

Ethnic and ethnolinguistic labels can have such emblematic effect, invoking chronotopes of 'tradition' not necessarily anchored in chronology or concrete historical facts, in which nationalist political-ideological positions, the moral righteousness of ethnic struggles, and essentializing attributes such as (pure) language or religion can be part of the ethnic 'figure'. Woolard (2013) documents precisely that, in her study of how personal experiences related to Catalan identity and language are captured in three different chronotopes by different respondents, with different chronotopical positions being directed at (and contrasted in reference to) the emblematic notion of 'Catalan'. We see how contesting the emblematic notion of 'Catalan' (invoking the chronotope described above) is contested by means of different chronotopes framing what 'Catalan' *actually means*, always with reference to the 'typical' (or dominant) chronotope. Note how this play of chronotopes is *argumentative*: it creates apart from all the other effects already reviewed also an *epistemic-evaluative* effect of truth, importance and relevance. More on this in a moment.

The chronotopic organization of language as a field of experiential and political discourse proves to be an important part of the language-ideological apparatuses by means of which we decode our sociolinguistic lifeworlds and the ways in which we fit into them (Inoue, 2004). Irvine (2004: 105) sees a deep connection between 'ideologized visions of available genres and linguistic styles' (or registers) and temporalities motivating them as coherent frames; and Eisenlohr (2004), in a perceptive paper, shows how such language-ideological temporalities underpin the construction of diasporic identities – with complex lines of affiliation to the Mauritian here-and-now and to a distant Indian past mediated through Hindi and Hindu ritualizations. Differences between 'being from here' and merely 'residing here' are articulated by invoking different historicities of origin, movement, stability and change. Contemporary forms of European nationalism place people's 'national' belonging in an unbroken line of unspoiled ethnolinguistic transmission reaching back into an unspecified past (the 'empty time' of 'ancestral' languages, Inoue, 2004: 5) and see the contemporary usage of 'pure' language (the institutionalized variety of it) as the contemporary normative enactment of that *durée* (Blommaert & Verschueren, 1992; Silverstein, 1996a, 1998). This is a powerful trope, and the rupture of this lineage (for instance by colonization or totalitarianism) leading to language loss can be downplayed by nostalgic appeals to the *durée* of ideal unbroken transmission ('heritage') combined, by absence of the 'complete' language, with the emblematic display of small 'typical' bits of the 'ancestral' language (Cavanaugh, 2004; Karrebæk & Ghandchi, 2014; also Moore, 2012; Silverstein, 1998).

That last point brings us to issues of scales and accessibility. We have seen how chronotopes, as invokable 'tropic' chunks of history, have powerful normative language-ideological dimensions. Their invocation and deployment come down to a *mise en intrigue* in which persons, acts, patterns of development and assessments of value can be laid down. Chronotopes are the stuff of Foucaultian discourses of truth, one could say. The delicate play of chronotopes, for instance in narrative, enables us to create epistemic and affective effects that *make sense* within the invoked context-of-use, and to strategize about outcomes in an argument (as Agha, 1997, demonstrates in presidential debates). Knowledge of such invokable histories – their availability, in other words – is a cultural resource and an asset which allows us to construct, for precisely targeted effects, elaborate patterns of different sociocultural materials in our discourses (e.g. Perrino, 2011; Schiffrin, 2009). Such knowledge makes us understandable.

Knowledge itself, however, is not enough; it makes us *understandable* but not necessarily *understood*. Available resources are not always accessible to all and differences in accessibility result in differences in meaning effect – misunderstanding, disqualification as irrelevant or untrue, 'pointless' or 'trivial'. Aspects of accessibility have a direct bearing on the scope of communicability: if I have access to the best possible and most widely understood ('typical') resources, chances are that my words will be heard (as 'tokens') by many; if I lack access to such resources, I lack such chances (cf. Agha, 2011). The issue of Bakhtinian 'voice' is thus not just a matter of *what* exactly has gone into the actual voice, but also – and predicated on – *who* has the capacity to create voice, to be a creative meaning-maker in the eyes of others and who has access to the resources to make sense of these meanings (Agha, 2011; Hymes, 1996; Wortham, 2006). I may have lived through important historical events – contexts available to me – but if I lack the actual resources for narrating these events in a way that makes their importance resonate with interlocutors – a matter of accessibility – I will probably end up talking to myself. The actual outcome of communication, thus, is an effect of the degrees of availability and accessibility of adequate contexts creatively invoked in discourse – of *chronotopes combined with scales*. And while the former is a cultural given, the second is a sociolinguistic filter on it.

Thus, trying to invoke a chronotope – e.g. the history of one's country – requires access to the genred and enregistered features that index the genres of 'historiography'. (Bakhtin, after all, was interested in the actual *forms* of time defining the novel.) In a long study on a Congolese painter who produced a grassroots-literate 'History of Zaire' (Blommaert, 2008), I explained why this document escaped the attention of professional historians (even when it was given, decades earlier, to a distinguished professional historian). Thsibumba, the author, had no access to critical resources defining the genre: he lacked access to structured information (an archive) and had to rely on his own locally inflected memory; furthermore, he lacked crucial literacy skills from the register of 'historiography'. The effect was that his 'History of Zaire' remained buried at the lowest scale of communicability: in the drawers of a single addressee, who could at best understand it as an anthropological artifact of restricted interest, but not a documentation of 'History' to be communicated on the scale level Tshibumba aspired to: the world of professional historians. It took an anthropologist such as I to 'upscale' his History by re-entextualizing it for another audience, but that took a very significant amount of re-ordering work.

Scale, thus, is best seen as the scope of actual understandability of specific bits of discourse (Blommaert *et al.*, 2015), and whenever we see chronotopes being invoked in discourse, we see them through the scalar effect of recognizability – that is, they can only be recognized by us when they have been performed by means of the register criteria their 'type' presumes. And note that such recognitions can occur simultaneously at different scale levels, when different audiences recognize different indexical orders in the same discourse. That in itself tells us something about the author and the audience: their positions in the stratified sociolinguistic economy that produced the discourse, enabling access to the resources required to create meanings that communicate with different people. Bakhtin's insistence on meaning as socially defined value derived from a stratified sociolinguistic system pushes us to this point: the historical analysis of novels, for Bakhtin, involved questions about how particular novels emerged out of particular social positions. We are capable now of adding this mature sociolinguistic dimension to most of the interpretations of chronotope.

## Timespace Complexity

If we accept the preceding points, the analysis of meaning contains at least to sub-questions: (a) *what* do we understand; and (b) how come we understand it *as such*? To return to earlier remarks, answers to both questions will involve aspects usually called 'micro'- as well as 'macro'-contextual, and to the earlier definition of the total linguistic/semiotic fact, we can now add that it is not just mediated by the fact of cultural ideology but also by the fact of sociolinguistic stratification. We will be confronted, in every actual example of discourse, by a complex construction of multiple historicities compressed into one 'synchronized' act of performance, projecting different forms of factuality and truth, all of them ideologically configured and thus indexically deployed, and all of them determined by the concrete sociolinguistic conditions of their production and uptake, endowing them with a scaled communicability at each moment of enactment. These dense and complex objects are the 'stuff' of the study of language in society (cf. Blommaert & Rampton, 2011; Silverstein, 2014).

Analysis of such objects must not seek to reduce their complexity but to account for it. Preceding developments in our field of study have dismissed the simple linear objects of linguistics as the (exclusive) conduits of meaning, and have replaced them by multiplex, layered, mobile and non-linear – hence indeterminate and relatively unpredictable – objects which still demand further scrutiny in our quest for precision and realism.

Part of that further scrutiny, I have suggested, is to imagine our object as shot through with different timespace frames provoking scaled meaning effects simultaneously understandable at different scale levels for different audiences, and continuing to do so long after they were effectively performed, with different effects at every moment of enactment.

## Notes

(1)   Brandao (2006) discusses the Einsteinian lineage of Bakhtin's chronotope; Holquist (2010) reviews its philosophical foundations. Since I shall focus on how Bakhtin's work can speak to contemporary theoretical and analytic concerns in linguistic anthropology, I consider these issues beyond the scope of this essay.

(2)   The most comprehensive early discussion of these inadequacies, tremendously relevant but rarely used these days, is probably Cicourel's *The Social Organization of Juvenile Justice* (1967); see also Silverstein (1992), Hanks (1996), Duranti (1997) and Blommaert (2001a and 2005b) for extended discussions. Two collections of essays, now slightly dated, provide broadly scoped discussions of context: Auer and DiLuzio (1992) and Duranti and Goodwin (1992).

(3)   It is a truism but very often overlooked or underplayed, for instance by Holquist: Bakhtin worked in an era in which the intellectual milieu was circumscribed by Marxism and in which a lot of work – including so-called 'dissident' work – developed in a critical dialogue with various degrees of Marxist orthodoxy. Evidently, Voloshinov's (and Bakhtin's?) *Marxism and the Philosophy of Language* (1973) is a case in point. Bakhtin's inclinations toward history and sociology (and the necessity of a *historical* sociology) are reflexes of Marxist scholarship.

# 12 Marxism and Urban Culture[1]

Since late March 2015, the Antwerp Grand Place offers a remarkable sight to the thousands of tourists passing to admire the city hall and the monumental fountain in front of it: dozens of individual citizens stand there seemingly alone, several meters separating each from the other. They carry no slogans or banners, rarely even emblems of parties or organizations. There is no shouting or chanting, no fists in the air. Some are quietly reading a book, others chat with bystanders or plainclothes police officers. For this is a protest action called 'the upstanding citizen'. It started as an individual initiative after an unauthorized sit-in there, protesting against racist remarks by the Antwerp Mayor, resulted in the mass arrest of over 200 people and the prohibition of follow-up protests. The City's rules only allow demonstrations that have been approved by the Mayor; they define a demonstration as something that happens in a group, and the latter is defined as several people doing things 'together'. 'The upstanding citizen' mode avoids all of those: while the action is obviously collective, people are not acting collectively – they defy the spatial and activity templates that defines a 'demonstration' by avoiding the proximity rules and recognizably joint activity modes defining collective behavior – shouting, chanting, jointly making symbolic gestures. Much to the frustration of the Mayor and his senior police officers, 'the upstanding citizens' appear at irregular intervals – it is an unpredictable event – and the person who initiated it does not make any overt appeal or invitation to others in view of joining him. He merely puts an announcement on his Facebook page, saying that he will visit the Grand Place at, say, 6 pm on Tuesday. Scores of others follow him each time. No law or regulation has been violated, while the city's political and historical-architectural center is converted into a space of overt but unpunishable contestation.

Such forms of creative, subversive and ludic interventions in public space are the stuff of this wonderfully edited collection of essays in which authors explore the purchase of central issues and concepts from the work of, mainly, Henri Lefebvre and David Harvey, with an occasional foray into the oeuvres of Engels, Bauer, Gramsci, Thompson, Soja and the Situationalists, in a joint (and largely successful) attempt to revive Marxist perspectives on 'the urban' as a field of cultural production, of humanist freedom and of dis-alienation. The book suggests a preceding enthusiastic and engaging dialogue between its authors, which makes its contributions lively, sometimes riveting, and the collection compelling. Much is achieved in this book, and I can indulge in what follows in some thoughts and observations triggered by the studies in this volume.

Before I do so, let me summarize the main intellectual line developed in the book and nicely sketched in Benjamin Fraser's introductory chapter. The conceptual point of departure is Marx's classic distinction between exchange value and use value – value within a market, and value outside the market, one could say. It was the genius of Lefebvre to apply this distinction to a political view of the city, which – in a critique of functionalist urbanists such as Corbusier – he saw increasingly becoming captured in a logic of exchange value. Cities were becoming, in the age of industrial capitalism, the locus where a giant workforce needed to be kept healthy, politically inert and fit for labor; cities were an instrument of capitalist power. The post-industrial stage, in turn, saw cities converted into capital itself, with speculative real-estate exchange value dominating the logic of infrastructuring. Against this reality, Lefebvre pitted a concept of '*l'urbain*', in which the city was not a mere built-up space or an exchange-valuable infrastructure, but a process of production driven by use-value. His *Le Droit à La Ville* (1968) codified this view: the city was, for him, a place where community life took place, consisting of an infinite multitude of ties between people, invested by interests but not driven by the quest for profit, but rather by the opportunities to achieve what Gortz (1989) later called 'self-production': becoming the *homo faber* whom the young Marx so passionately described in the Manuscripts (for Marx's humanism, see Erich Fromm, 1961). Achieving this level of humanity, for Lefebvre, was a fundamental right – hence '*le droit à la ville*'. This reconceptualization heralded an era of critical thought on urban spaces in scholarship as well as policy, and David Harvey did massive work identifying the tremendous critical potential lodged in this view. Needless to say that much of the politics of spatial contestation since 1968, with Occupy as its most recent articulation, has its roots in Lefebvre's reconceptualization of 'the urban'.

Note, of course, that Lefebvre's application of the Marxian distinction between different types of value to his view of 'the urban', eventually leads to a *cultural* bias (Lefebvre, 1958; see also Hobsbawm, 2011). While modes of self-production have material dimensions, their outcomes are largely immaterial – a social *ambiance* which Lefebvre emphasized as necessarily 'ludic', playful, but of fundamental importance for achieving the humanity he saw as the ultimate aim of Marxism. The authors in this book are, thus, not off-mark when they engage with the ways in which cities have been depicted in movies, novels or contemporary forms of carnivalesque demonstration. Note, at the same time, that Lefebvre's Marxism was for precisely those reasons long considered as heterodox (hence, revisionist) 'new left' by the non-Gramscian other half of Marxism. The authors in the book subscribe to this 'new left' tendency – the book title says it all – and the range of authors from whom they draw inspiration, surveyed above, testifies to this. There is one exception: in an otherwise empirically stimulating paper on the Austromarxists' dream of 'Red Vienna', Kimberly DeFazio sides with Engels' conclusion that only a revolutionary change in fundamental economic relationships will solve the urban problem, dismissing *en route* any approach that does not accept revolutionary action as the sole means of transformation as un-Marxist. It is a pity that she passes the same verdict on people who never dismissed revolution as an aim and instrument of historical change but merely described the complex transformations of capital, labor and capitalist society – think of André Gortz and E.P. Thompson as cases in point (Thompson, 1978). But let us return to the issue of the city.

Lefebvre consistently stressed the importance of a 'total science' of the city, decrying the ways in which institutionalized divisions between 'social sciences' and 'humanities' had become obstacles to holistic analyses of complex and dynamic phenomena such as cities and the patterns of human activity they involve. It is one of the achievements of this book that it manages to dissolve the distinction between what is 'cultural' (and hence, a matter for humanities) and what is 'social' (and hence, objects of social science). The cultural is fully social here, and even if we read chapters on eminently 'humanities' objects such as novels or movies, the analysis demonstrates how such cultural objects are in no way 'superstructural' – in a definition of the term that made it synonymous with 'superficial' – but often the stuff that generates, sustains and determines crucial social processes of group and community formation, the articulation of sociopolitical and economic interests, the construction and ratification of identities, and so forth. Evidently, this folding of the cultural into the social generates a third sphere: the political. Here again, the intellectual lineage within Marxism is clear: Thompson, in most of his work, famously claimed that there is no proletariat without shared experiences of capitalist expropriation and exploitation converging onto structured patterns of what we would now call identities. The bourgeoisie, likewise, controlled its membership more by means of symbolic than hard capital – Bourdieu's work, but also much of Erving Goffman's, established that in great detail (see also Bourdieu, 1984; Goffman, 1971; Moretti, 2013).

It is this great detail that I wish to briefly engage with in what follows. The question of detail is not a question only of analytical accuracy, it is a conceptual and ontological issue that revolves around the locus of 'culture' and of 'the urban'. In the book, such loci are, to some extent, stereotyped: we see typically 'urban' images in typically 'cultural' objects such as movies, texts, architecture and forms of political carnival. Thus 'culture' and 'the urban' are unproblematically clear in this book, so it seems. In actual fact they are not.

Let me start with the 'cultural'. If the cultural equals the social (and thence, the political), then the locus of culture is the everyday re-enactment, over and over again, of socially patterned activities that are perceived to be meaningful by others (hence, driven by shared complexes of norms and expectations). It was this fundamental observation (and ontological principle) that propelled the likes of Herbert Blumer, Aaron Cicourel, Howard Becker and Erving Goffman to consider the micro-politics of everyday social practices, not because they considered the microscopic to be the privileged locus of whatever we understand by the term 'society', but because such micro-practices are just not 'micro': they are effectively 'macro' – the only realistic specter we can have on big things such as 'society' or 'culture'. 'Culture', thus, is not just lodged in a novel, a poem or a painting, but also in a routine greeting, a downcast gaze or a raised middle finger. And the experiential basis of 'social' units such as class gains a clear empirical footing: whatever we call 'social' rests on degrees of sharedness in recognizing what others do; or even more practically, in the ways in which we are able to make sense of social situations by means of such degrees of sharedness. Briefly returning to our 'upstanding citizen' protests in Antwerp, we can see how such actions can be read, and understood as being politically meaningful, by reference only to locally valid cues about what counts as 'demonstration' and what does not count – insignificant actions become significant ones through the recognizable 'frames' they articulate (at least, recognizable to *some*).

I am saying nothing new here – I merely reiterate the fundamental assumptions of Symbolic Interactionism (see, in particular, Blumer, 1969; and Cicourel, 1972; see also Blommaert, 2015b). From a Marxist perspective, I find them quite productive, if for nothing else, because they compel us to turn a term such as 'praxis' – often, to my profound frustration, used in a lapidary and loosely generalizing way – into an empirical program. Let us go out and look for those moments of practice that can be read, and dissected, as 'praxis' and, as such, the ideology-infused moments in which 'society' and 'culture' enter reality. In my own work, I have attempted to take these principles into analyses of the actual, dense and complex semio-tizations of urban spaces by their inhabitants and users by means of what is now called 'linguistic landscapes' (Blommaert, 2013). People produce tremendous quantities of (what Benjamin Fraser, in the introductory chapter, calls) 'Humanities texts' in the spaces they inhabit, turning them from mere space into social space (and thence, into politicized space); they do so by means of shop window signs, posters, banners, stickers, graffiti, post-its on window and doors, scribbled signs on the pavement and so forth. Such forms of semiotic activity, individually as well as collectively, lead us to insights into their histories of production and their potential uptake by selected audiences (no single sign is meant for *everyone*), and show us how space is demarcated into actual zones of ownership, legiti-mate usage and contested presence – by means of eminently 'cultural' materials: written and designed messages communicating with specific addressees. They teach us that social and cultural spaces are spaces defined by real or virtual copresence (a feature central to Goffman's work, of course) and, hence, by patterns of communication that do not offer themselves easily to *a priori* definition or *a posteriori* generalization.

Attention to this level of praxis, thus, de-stereotypes the 'cultural' and disperses it over a tremendous amount of everyday events and practices; it also destereotypes 'the urban', I would argue, for such forms of praxis occur in areas we typically define as urban as well as in areas seen as 'peri-urban' or even 'rural'. And they occur in a tremendous multitude in that new space, often overlooked in current studies – the virtual space, which now crosscuts and connects 'urban' as well as 'non-urban' spaces in ways we still need to get our heads around, but of which we can assume that they render strict distinctions (and thus, definitions) of what is 'urban' and what is not quite problematic. 'Urban culture' – the term from the book title – may (and does) occur in phenomenally similar ways in spaces we would rarely call 'urban'. And to the extent that Lefebvre's *'droit à la ville'* concerned the fundamental right to a specific level of humanity, a discon-nection between, on the one hand, 'the urban' as the complex of rights to this kind of humanity and, on the other hand, the actual – stereotyped – cities known by names such as Mumbai, Paris or München might be nec-essary if we wish to preserve the fundamental humanist (and Marxist) sense attributed by Lefebvre to *'l'urbain'*.

I make these remarks not as a targeted criticism of *Marxism and Urban Culture*; as I emphasized above, the book does a remarkable job in re-opening a field of inquiry in which I merely sketched some other lines and opportunities. The fact that I felt invited to do so testifies to the stimulating nature of the book: it engages one in an intellectual space of significant interest and relevance. The editor and the authors are to be credited for it.

## Note

(1)  Review article of *Marxism and Urban Culture*, ed. Benjamin Fraser. Lanham, MD: Lexington Books, 2014.

# 13 On Scope and Depth in Linguistic Ethnography: A Commentary[1]

## Theory

One rather uncontroversial feature of ethnography is that it addresses complexity. It does not, unlike many other approaches, try to reduce the complexity of social events by focusing *a priori* on a selected range of relevant features, but it tries to describe and analyze the complexity of social events *comprehensively*. That is, good ethnography is *iconic* of the object it has set out to examine, it describes the sometimes chaotic, contradictory, polymorph character of human behavior in concrete settings, and it does so in a way that seeks to do justice to two things: (a) the perspectives of participants – the old Boasian and Malinowskian privilege of the 'insiders' view'; and (b) the ways in which micro-events need to be understood as both unique and structured, as combinations of variation and stability – the tension between phenomenology and structuralism in ethnography. While these two concerns are constant and define the long history of 20th-century ethnography, a third one was added from the 1960s and 1970s onward in the work of Fabian, Bourdieu, Clifford and others: (c) a concern for the situated and dialogical character of ethnographic knowledge itself – reflexivity.

Together, these points circumscribe a wide space of ethnographic theorizing which, even if it had its origins in early 20th-century 'modern' anthropology (Malinowski, Boas, Sapir, Mead), quickly extended far beyond that disciplinary space owing to people such as Gregory Bateson and Alfred Schutz, and later people such as Aaron Cicourel, Pierre Bourdieu, Clifford Geertz, Carlo Ginzburg and Harold Garfinkel, to name just a few. Ethnographic *theory* is not confined to statements on language (and when we now consider a project such as *linguistic* ethnography, it is good to keep that in mind). It gradually came to stand for a complex of theoretical statements on the nature of social knowledge, both that of 'subjects' and that of ethnographers. Ethnography is shorthand for a particular fundamental methodological position in the social sciences. When Gumperz, Hymes and others developed their 'ethnography of communication', they did it as a reaction against Chomskyan hegemonies in the study of language. The reaction, note, was fundamental: it was a statement about *what could be known about language as a social and cultural object*, or even better, *about knowledge of language necessarily being social and cultural knowledge*. Gumperz' (1972) introduction to *Directions in Sociolinguistics* as well as Hymes' superb 'Models of the interaction of language and social life' in the same book (Hymes, 1972) are very informative on this issue. So, 'the interactional approach to language behavior' which Gumperz defined as 'the unifying theme' of *Directions* was not the development of a *method*, but something that crystallized 'new theoretical insights and changes in research orientation' (Gumperz, 1972: 1). These changes had a long pedigree, important parts of which had been codified by Hymes in his *Language in Culture and Society* collection (Hymes, 1964).

I am saying all of this not to establish a dogma – ethnography was ever since its incipience very much an open and exploratory, even experimental, platform and not a school – but to frame some of the comments I have on the papers in this issue. I warmly welcome the issue and congratulate the contributors for their effort. It comes at a moment where the interest in ethnography is growing outside its prototypical fields of study and areas of popularity, and it will serve those who are currently trying to grasp what ethnography is about. Rampton does particularly good service to this constituency in his lead paper. He sketches a historical moment in which people concerned with issues of language and society, from a variety of disciplines and branches of scholarship, converge on ethnography and linguistics, 'more for their utility than for their pedigree'. Using this utilitarian principle, he then carefully carves out a space in which a project of linguistic ethnography could make sense, and he does so with an acute awareness that disciplinary boundaries are also real, institutionally sanctioned boundaries, and that a discourse of disciplines belongs to the realm of academic accountability these days. I will come back to the manifest advantages and problems of that approach below.

## Pedigree and Theory

One problem with defining linguistic ethnography in terms of disciplines and influential approaches is that we end up with a pedigree anyway – which is what happens toward the end of Rampton's paper. It is about pedigrees after all, and let me dwell on the issue of pedigree for a moment. We always define our current activities in relation to those of predecessors and whenever we quote someone, we are creating a history to our own theoretical activity. Thinking historically while we think theoretically, as Hymes never failed to point out, can prevent us from making elementary mistakes – wasting our time on questions that have been inspiringly or conclusively addressed long ago, or absolutizing conceptual or disciplinary distinctions that are historically and institutionally contingent and have no intrinsic intellectual value.

The frame I drew above should explain why I disagree with Sealey's opening statement that there is no inevitable link between what is now called linguistic ethnography and a particular theoretical perspective. There is indeed, even if such a link should not be read as a suggestion of a 'school' with some kind of orthodoxy, and even if the theoretical perspective is one at a very deep level of theorizing: there is a shared ontology and there is a shared epistemology to ethnography. The specific theoretical vocabularies as well as the particular research tools deployed are of secondary importance. In an ethnographic perspective one should never have to argue for the fact that social events are contextualized, connected with other events, meaningful in a more-than-unique way, and functional to those who perform the practices that construct the event. One should also not have to argue for the situated nature of any knowledge of such practices, and consequently, for the importance of *subjectivity* in ethnography – whether we call it (*pace* Bourdieu) an objectified subjectivity or (*pace* Fabian) inter-subjectivity. And one should not have to argue, consequently, for the fact that ethnographic knowledge is interpretive and hypothetical and escapes any attempt at positivist circumscription. These fundamental assumptions set ethnography apart from many other social scientific branches and these assumptions are firmly theoretical. The observation that hardly anyone agrees on particulars, or that many people would not want their work to be qualified as ethnographic even if they subscribe to soundly ethnographic principles is hardly surprising: the same applies to every branch of the study of language and society (just try to do the same exercise with sociolinguistics or discourse analysis).

This lack of consensus in itself does not deny the existence of ethnographic theory, of course. What it points toward is that theories have differing scope. If one is interested in socialism, one can use Marx as well as Tony Blair. The difference between both is that Marx is likely to provide more general and more widely applicable theoretical statements than Tony Blair; the difference is also that Marx has influenced Blair while the opposite is not true. Both provide theory, but while Marx can be said to provide a general theoretical outlook – a *methodology* – that enables and informs all sorts of concrete questions and inquiries, Blair's proposals would at best qualify as *method*: applicable to just a specific set of data with little validity beyond it. Ethnography, too, would best be seen as a general theoretical outlook, while things that are often (wrongly) metonymically seen as 'ethnography', such as fieldwork with participant observation and interviews, are just methods.

We must be insistent on this point, because I see traces in the papers by Sealey and Wetherell, and to some extent also in Rampton's opening paper, of confusion with regard to what it is we are talking about. There is a degree of stereotyping of ethnography going on, in which the scope and depth of ethnography are reduced to manageable (read: discipline-d) levels, and excellent opportunities to engage with theory are missed. Sealey's use of the term '(linguistic) ethnographers' is a case in point. On the one hand, the label is used flatly descriptively, in a way that suggests a firmly established discipline, while on the other hand theoretical statements and projects appear in a fragmented way, and so apparently become comparable with equally fragmented statements from within other theoretical complexes (see e.g. the puzzling comparison between Hymes and Popper on objectivity). The suggested clarity of the label is not supported by the bits of dialogue in which it is placed. And thus while Sealey makes valid and useful points, the foundations on which they are based demand clarification: who exactly are these ethnographers, and what exactly do they stand for? In Wetherell's paper – again a very useful reflection on important issues – the disciplines appear as equivalent closed spaces that need to be opened up and linguistic ethnography is defined as a finite set of research topics. This is a world in which distinguished scholars proclaim that discourse analysis is a theory of discourse, not of society or of the human mind, a world in which theories only seem to matter when they are *specific* theories – that is, methods. The possibility of general theories being useful without disturbing the disciplinary harmonies is not examined. In Rampton's paper, the passage where he separates 'culture' from 'language' as two different objects, of 'ethnography' and 'linguistics' respectively, invites questions. If we take a lineage from Boas to Sapir, Whorf, Hymes and Silverstein, we see that all of them use language and culture as one single object. I will return to this point below. For now, let me note that this is an *ontological* issue, that is, again, an issue that operates at a very deep level of theory and cannot be usefully framed in terms of established disciplines. Disciplines occur at a particular level of implementation of theories; fundamental and general theoretical assumptions are not contained by them, they cover and inform several disciplines and lower-level theories.

So perhaps if linguistic ethnography emerges out of a concern for utility rather than pedigree, utility may be enhanced by attending carefully to pedigree. There are more reasons for that.

## Pedigree as Argument

Pedigree is a practical tool, practical even in a culture of academic accountability in which we are forced to situate and identify ourselves perpetually in relation to benchmarks of recognizability. I drew the little historical frame in the beginning also to reassure those who currently work toward increased legitimacy for ethnographic research in our fields of study that there is quite a lot that they can draw upon, and that much of that is very respectable, even venerable. In other words, we have an *argumentarium* of considerable standing – very good theory grounded in very good empirical work – and that saves us the trouble of reinventing theories of language in society. We can *revisit* such theories, and indeed are compelled to seek a perpetual upgrading of them, but we should realize that we can do all of that from relatively solid foundations.

To give one example, I was intrigued, in Whetherell's paper, to see an appeal for incorporating psychology along language and culture in linguistic ethnography. Incidentally, this triad – language, culture, psychology – defined much of the early formative period of scholarship. Edward Sapir, as we know, lectured on 'the psychology of culture' (see the edition of his lectures, Sapir, 2002) and his views on the connections between language, culture and psychology were influential in the further development of the field of what is now linguistic anthropology. Even today, many people whose work would firmly qualify as ethnographic are deployed in psychology departments (e.g. John Lucy), and Michael Silverstein's chair in Chicago is in 'Anthropology, Linguistics, and Psychology'. What I am saying is that many of the problems we now detect have been addressed before, and we have discourses that may be helpful in solving them.

This also counts for the ontological issue mentioned earlier: what is the particular 'language' that linguistic ethnography examines? Again, taking stock of past discussions and ways of arguing can be informative. I have already pointed toward the way in which in linguistic anthropology fused 'language' and 'culture' into one object; the name of that object would be 'language', because 'culture' was someone else's province. Yet language would be 'cultura*l*' – intrinsically cultural – and the use of 'culture' in conjunction with 'language' was an unproblematic rhetorical move (Silverstein's (1977) classic paper 'Cultural prerequisites to grammatical analysis' can be read as an illustration). In Sapir's (1921) *Language*,

'language' and 'culture' thus occur in two different shapes and meanings: one, in the opening chapter, where language itself is defined as a fundamentally cultural object; and another, in the penultimate chapter 'Language, race and culture', where Sapir demonstrates the non-congruence between languages and cultures. Language and culture are abstract, theoretical nouns in the first chapter, while they are concrete and countable nouns in the second (*a* language and *a* culture). The concrete and countable cultures were the privileged object of ethno*logy*: the more abstract stage of anthropological work, where work on cultural forms culminated in the comprehensive description and comparative analysis of specific cultures. And Sapir's critique was ethnographic: he argued that work on cultural-language forms should not lead to the suggestion that concrete language groups and cultural groups coincide.[2]

It is easy to misrepresent the issues here: similar words suggest similar objects and when minds are set on seeing different objects, they will see them. But historically, the point should be clear: the 'original' linguistic-ethnographic object was a fusion of language and culture. Language was extracted as an autonomous object by people such as Leonard Bloomfield who, in line with the old philological tradition, suggested that knowledge of abstract linguistic structure would enable one to use language as a cultural tool: study the grammar carefully and you will miraculously be able to use any genre, style and register in the language, and do so in a socio-culturally competent way. People such as Margaret Mead opposed this view. For Mead, knowledge of a language was *cultural* knowledge – what else could it be when the purpose is to use that language to get to the cultural heart of a community? Mead's position on language use as a cultural phenomenon was significantly more sophisticated than that of Bloomfield: she was a Sapirian *pur sang* in her fundamental view of language (see Blommaert, 2006b, for a discussion of Bloomfield's and Mead's views; my judgment of Mead is more merciful than that of Scollon and Scollon in this issue).

Thus, debates on whether or not to separate language, culture, society have been held in the past, and we may find relief in reading such debates. The debates also had outcomes, and one was the emphasis on *function* in linguistic-anthropological work (Hymes, 1996). Function was the bridge between language structure and sociocultural patterns, and function needed to be seen as an open question, as the thing to be ethnographically determined. It is this emphasis on function that sets ethnographic approaches to language apart from many linguistic approaches to it, and as mentioned earlier, a focus on function is one of the things that one should no longer have to argue for in an ethnographic perspective. It is our quest for functions of language-in-use that has made all of us turn to context (how does language actually work in a specific set of sociocultural circumstances?), and the nexus analysis proposed by Scollon and Scollon is a splendid synthesis of decades of work on language–context relations, in which we see the dense and unpredictable layering of contexts and in which we see that an ethnographic object is always a composite, complex and layered one.[3]

## Building Blocks

My apology of pedigree is not meant to invalidate the attempts to construct an intellectual space called linguistic ethnography. Far from that, it is intended to boost the theoretical discussions that need to be held in this process. Here is ethnography again, and as always in the past, it is an open and experimental site in which people explore and try different ways of analyzing language in society. Such experiments are rare and valuable, and my point has been that we can be helped by thinking historically while we think theoretically. The pedigree I referred to will not solve any of the problems that researchers currently struggle with. But it may refine the questions we ask, make them more precise and specific, and it may expand the participation framework of the debate to include scholars of the past who faced similar issues. It's about 'using all there is to use' – which is the title of a chapter in Hymes' (2003) latest book, a book, incidentally, in which an ethnographic endeavor has become fully philological, again demonstrating the flexibility and openness of method in an ethnographic paradigm.

## Notes

(1)  This text is a concluding commentary to *Journal of Sociolinguistics* 11 (5), 2007, special issue 'Linguistic Ethnography', eds Karin Tusting and Janet Maybin.
(2)  See Hymes (1996) for a renewed critique of simple language-culture views, and note that Bourdieu's ethnography emerged out of a similar critique of ethnology – see Blommaert (2005b) for a discussion.
(3)  Work on language ideologies and indexicality represents another development of this same problem. Here, too, the emphasis is on the complex connections between linguistic form and cultural and social – contextual – effects. Agha (2007) is a landmark in this field.

# References

Agha, A. (1997) Tropic aggression in the Clinton – Dole presidential debate. *Pragmatics* 7 (4), 461–497.

Agha, A. (2005) Voice, footing, enregisterment. *Journal of Linguistic Anthropology* 15 (1), 38–59.

Agha, A. (2007) *Language and Social Relations*. Cambridge: Cambridge University Press.

Agha, A. (2011) Large and small forms of personhood. *Language and Communication* 31 (3), 171–180.

Appadurai, A. (1996) *Modernity at Large*. Minneapolis, MN: University of Minnesota Press.

Ardener, E. (1971) Social anthropology and the historicity of historical linguistics. In E. Ardener (ed.) *Social Anthropology and Language* (pp. 209–242). London: Tavistock.

Auer, P. (1995) Ethnographic methods in the analysis of oral communication: Some suggestions for linguists. In U. Quasthoff (ed.) *Aspects of Oral Communication* (pp. 419–440). Berlin: Walter de Gruyter.

Auer, P. and Di Luzio, A. (eds) (1992) *The Contextualization of Language*. Amsterdam: John Benjamins.

Backhaus, P. (2007) *Linguistic Landscapes: A Comparative Study of Urban Multilingualism in Tokyo*. Clevedon: Multilingual Matters.

Bakhtin, M.M. (1981) *The Dialogic Imagination* (ed. Michael Holquist). Austin, TX: University of Texas Press.

Bakhtin, M.M. (1986) *Speech Genres and Other Late Essays*. Austin, TX: University of Texas Press.

Barni, M. and Extra, G. (eds) (2008) *Mapping Linguistic Diversity in Multicultural Contexts*. Berlin: Mouton de Gruyter.

Bauman, R. (1995) Representing native American oral narrative: The textual practices of Henry Rowe Schoolcraft. *Pragmatics* 5 (2), 167–183.

Bauman, R. and Briggs, B. (1990) Poetics and performance as critical perspectives on language and social life. *Annual Review of Anthropology* 19, 59–88.

Bemong, N. and Borghart, P. (2010) Bakhtin's theory of the literary chronotope: Reflections, applications, perspectives. In N. Bemong *et al.* (eds ) *Bakhtin's Theory of the Literary Chronotope: Reflections, Applications, Perspectives* (pp. 3–18). Ghent: Academia Press.

Ben-Rafael, E., Shohamy, E., Hasan Amara, M. and Trumper-Hecht, N. (2006) Linguistic landscape as symbolic construction of the public space: The case of Israel. *International Journal of Multilingualism* 3, 7–30.

Bloch, M. (1953) *The Historian's Craft*. New York: Vintage Books.

Blommaert, J. (1996) Frame and perspective in the analysis of discourse: On being critical of more than just discourse. Paper presented at Conference on 'Frame and Perspective in Discourse', University of Groningen, November 1996.

Blommaert, J. (1997) Whose background? Comments on a discourse-analytic reconstruction of the Warsaw Uprising. *Pragmatics* 7 (1), 69–81.

Blommaert, J. (ed.) (1999a) *Language Ideological Debates*. Berlin: Mouton de Gruyter.

Blommaert, J. (1999b) The debate is open. In J. Blommaert (ed.) *Language Ideological Debates* (pp. 1–38). Berlin: Mouton de Gruyter.

Blommaert, J. (1999c) Reconstructing the sociolinguistic image of Africa: Grassroots writing in Shaba (Congo). *Text* 19 (2), 175–200.

Blommaert, J. (2000) Analysing African asylum seekers' narratives: Scratching the surface. Working Papers in Urban Language and Literacies 14, King's College, London.

Blommaert, J. (2001a) Context is/as critique. *Critique of Anthropology* 21 (1), 13–32.

Blommaert, J. (2001b) Investigating narrative inequality: African Asylum seekers' stories in Belgium. *Discourse and Society* 12 (4), 413–449.

Blommaert, J. (2001c) The other side of history: Grassroots literacy and autobiography in Shaba, Congo. *General Linguistics* 38 (1), 135–157.

Blommaert, J. (2004) *Workshopping: Professional Vision, Practices and Critique in Discourse Analysis*. Ghent: Academia Press.

Blommaert, J. (2005a) Bourdieu the ethnographer: The ethnographic grounding of habitus and voice. *The Translator* 11 (2), 219–236.

Blommaert, J. (2005b) *Discourse: A Critical Introduction*. Cambridge: Cambridge University Press.

Blommaert, J. (2005c) Situating language rights: English and Swahili in Tanzania revisited. *Journal of Sociolinguistics* 9 (3), 390–417.

Blommaert, J. (2006a) Ethnopoetics as functional reconstruction: Dell Hymes' narrative view of the world. *Functions of Language* 13 (2), 255–275.

Blommaert, J. (2006b) From fieldnotes to grammar: Artefactual ideologies and the textual production of languages in Africa. In G. Sica (ed.) *Open Problems in Linguistics and Lexicography* (pp. 13–60). Milan: Polimetrica.

Blommaert, J. (2007) Sociolinguistic scales. *Intercultural Pragmatics* 4 (1), 1–19.

Blommaert, J. (2008) *Grassroots Literacy: Writing, Identity and Voice in Central Africa*. London: Routledge.

Blommaert, J. (2010) *The Sociolinguistics of Globalization*. Cambridge: Cambridge University Press.

Blommaert, J. (2012) Supervernaculars and their dialects. *Dutch Journal of Applied Linguistics* 1 (1), 1–14.

Blommaert, J. (2013) *Ethnography, Superdiversity and Linguistic Landscapes: Chronicles of Complexity*. Bristol: Multilingual Matters.

Blommaert, J. (2014) *State Ideology and Language in Tanzania, Second and Revised Edition*. Edinburgh: Edinburgh University Press.

Blommaert, J. (2015a) Chronotopes, scale and complexity in the study of language in society. Tilburg Papers in Culture Studies, paper 121. Tilburg University, the Netherlands.

Blommaert, J. (2015b) Pierre Bourdieu and language in society. Tilburg Papers in Culture Studies, paper 153. Tilburg University, the Netherlands.

Blommaert, J. and Bulcaen, C. (2000) Critical discourse analysis. *Annual Review of Anthropology* 29, 447–466.

Blommaert, J. and Dong J. (2010) *Ethnographic Fieldwork: A Beginner's Guide*. Bristol: Multilingual Matters.

Blommaert, J. and Huang, A. (2010) Semiotic and spatial scope: Towards a materialist semiotics. Working Papers in Urban Languages and Linguistics, no. 62. London, Gent, Albany & Tilburg.

Blommaert, J. and Maryns, K. (2002) Pretextuality and pretextual gaps: On (re)defining linguistic inequality. *Pragmatics* 12 (1), 11–30.

Blommaert, J. and Rampton, B. (2011) Language and superdiversity. *Diversities* 13 (2), 1–22.

Blommaert, J. and Slembrouck, S. (2000) Data formulation as text and context: On the (aesth)etics of analysing asylum seekers' narratives. Working Papers on Language, Power and Identity 2 (June), Ghent University. See http://bank.ugent.be/lpi

Blommaert, J. and Van de Vijver, F. (2013) Combining surveys and ethnographies in the study of rapid social change. Working Papers in Urban Language and Literacies, paper 108. King's College, London.

Blommaert, J. and Verschueren, J. (1992) The role of language in European nationalist ideologies. *Pragmatics* 2 (3), 355–375.

Blommaert, J., Collins, J., Heller, M., Rampton, B., Slembrouck, S. and Verschueren, J. (eds) (2001) *Discourse and Critique*. Special double issue, *Critique of Anthropology* 21 (1–2).

Blommaert, J., Collins, J. and Slembrouck , S. (2005) Spaces of multilingualism. *Language and Communication* 25 (3), 197–216.

Blommaert, J., Westinen, E. and Leppänen, S. (2015) Further notes on sociolinguistic scales. *Intercultural Pragmatics* 12 (1), 119–127.

Blumer, H. (1969) *Symbolic Interactionism: Perspective and Method*. Englewood Cliffs, NJ: Prentice Hall.

Blumer, H. (2000) Public opinion and public opinion polling. In S. Lyman and A. Vidich (eds) *Selected Works of Herbert Blumer: A Public Philosophy for Mass Society* (pp. 147–160). Urbana, IL: University of Illinois Press (original work published 1947).

Bourdieu, P. (1982) La mort du sociologue Erving Goffman, découvreur de l'infiniment petit. *Le Monde*, 4 December. See http://www.homme-moderne.org/societe/socio/bourdieu/varia/mortEGoffman.html

Bourdieu, P. (1984) *Distinction: A Social Critique of the Judgment of Taste*. Cambridge, MA: Harvard University Press.

Bourdieu, P. (1986) *Distinction: A Social Critique of the Judgment of Taste*. London: Routledge.

Bourdieu, P. (1988) *Homo Academicus*. Stanford, CA: Stanford University Press.

Bourdieu, P. (1990) *The Logic of Practice*. Cambridge: Polity Press.

Bourdieu, P. (1991) *Language and Symbolic Power*. Cambridge: Polity Press.

Bourdieu, P. (1993) L'espace des points de vue. In P. Bourdieu (ed.) *La Misère du Monde* (pp. 13–15). Paris: Seuil.

Bourdieu, P. (1994) Public opinion does not exist. In P. Bourdieu, *Sociology in Question* (pp. 149–157). London: Sage (original work published 1972).

Bourdieu, P. (2000) Making the economic habitus: Algerian workers revisited. *Ethnography* 1 (1), 17–41.

Bourdieu, P. (2004) Algerian landing. *Ethnography* 5 (4), 415–443.

Bourdieu, P. and Passeron, J.-C. (1970) *La reproduction: Eléments pour une théorie du système d'enseignement*. Paris: Minuit.

Bourdieu, P. and Winkin, Y. (2002) Preface. In A. Cicourel, *Le raisonnement médical: Une approche socio-cognitive* (pp. 9–19). Paris: Seuil.

Bourdieu, P., Passeron, J.-C. and De Saint Martin, M. (1994) *Academic Discourse: Linguistic Misunderstanding and Professorial Power*. Stanford, CA: Stanford University Press (original work published 1965).

Brandao, L.A. (2006) Chronotope. *Theory, Culture and Society* 23 (2–3), 133–134.

Braudel, F. (1949) *La Méditerranée et le monde méditerranéen à l'époque de Philippe II.* Paris: Armand Colin.

Braudel, F. (1969) Histoire et sciences sociales: La longue durée. In F. Braudel, *Ecrits sur l'Histoire* (pp. 41–83). Paris: Flammarion (original work published 1958).

Briggs, C. (1986) *Learning How to Ask.* Cambridge: Cambridge University Press.

Briggs, C. (1997) Notes on a 'confession': On the construction of gender, sexuality and violence in an infanticide case. *Pragmatics* 7 (4), 519–546.

Briggs, C. (2005) Communicability, racial discourse, and disease. *Annual Review of Anthropology* 34, 269–291.

Bulcaen, C. and Blommaert, J. (1997) *Eindrapport VFIK Project 307: Begeleiding van migrantenvrouwen en -meisjes in centra voor residentieel welzijnswerk.* Antwerp: IPrA Research Center.

Burke, K. (1969) *A Rhetoric of Motives.* Berkeley, CA: University of California Press (original work published 1950).

Caplan, P. (1997) *African Voices, African Lives: Personal Narratives from a Swahili Village.* London: Routledge.

Castells, M. (1996) *The Rise of the Network Society.* London; Blackwell.

Cavanaugh, J. (2004) Remembering and forgetting: Ideologies of language loss in a Northern Italian town. *Journal of Linguistic Anthropology* 14 (1), 24–38.

Cheung, F.M., Van de Vijver, A.J.R. and Leong, F.T.L. (2011) Toward a new approach to the assessment of personality in culture. *American Psychologist* 66, 593–603.

Cicourel, A. (1964) *Method and Measurement in Sociology.* New York: Free Press.

Cicourel, A. (1967) *The Social Organization of Juvenile Justice.* New York: Wiley.

Cicourel, A. (1972) *Cognitive Sociology: Language and Meaning in Social Interaction.* Harmondsworth: Penguin Education.

Cicourel, A. (1992) The interpenetration of communicative contexts: Examples from medical encounters. In A. Duranti and C. Goodwin (eds) *Rethinking Context* (pp. 291–310). Cambridge: Cambridge University Press.

Cicourel, A., Witzel, A. and Mey, G. (2004) 'I am not opposed to quantification or formalization or modeling, but do not want to pursue quantitative methods that are not commensurate with the research phenomena addressed' (interview). *Forum Qualitative Sozialforschung/Forum Qualitative Research* 5 (30), 1–19. http://www.qualitative-research.net/index.php/fqs/rt/printerFriendly/549/1186

Clifford, J. (1988) *The Predicament of Culture: Twentieth-century Ethnography, Literature and Art.* Cambridge, MA: Harvard University Press.

Collins, J. (1998) *Understanding Tolowa Histories.* New York: Routledge.

Collins, J. (2014) Constructing English language learners: An analysis of register processes and state effects in the schooling of multilingual migrant students. Tilburg Papers in Culture Studies, paper 96. Tilburg University, the Netherlands.

Collins, J. and Blot, R. (2003) *Literacy and Literacies: Texts, Power and Identity.* Cambridge: Cambridge University Press.

Collins, J., Slembrouck, S. and Baynham, M. (eds) (2009) *Globalization and Language Contact: Scale, Migration and Communicative Practices.* London: Continuum.

Cook-Gumperz, J. (ed.) (1988) *The Social Construction of Literacy.* Cambridge: Cambridge University Press.

Creese, A. and Blackledge, A. (2010) Towards a sociolinguistics of superdiversity. *Zeitschrift für Erziehungswissenschaften* 13, 549–572.

Crossley, S. (2006) A chronotopic approach to genre analysis: An exploratory analysis. *English for Specific Purposes* 26 (1), 4–24.

Cusset, F. (2008) *French Theory: How Foucault, Derrida, Deleuze & Co Transformed the Intellectual Life of the United States*. Minneapolis, MN: University of Minnesota Press.

Darnell, R. (1998) *And Along Came Boas. Continuity and Revolution in Americanist Anthropology*. Amsterdam: John Benjamins.

De Saussure, F. (1960) *Cours de Linguistique Générale*, ed. C. Bally and A. Sechehaye (3rd edn). Paris: Payot.

Drew, P. and Hutchby, I. (1995) Conversation analysis. In J. Verschueren, J.-O. Östman and J. Blommaert (eds) *Handbook of Pragmatics: Manual* (pp. 182–189). Amsterdam: John Benjamins.

Duranti, A. (1997) *Linguistic Anthropology*. Cambridge: Cambridge University Press.

Duranti, A. and Goodwin, C. (eds) (1992) *Rethinking Context: Language as an Interactive Phenomenon*. Cambridge: Cambridge University Press.

Eco, U. (1979) *A Theory of Semiotics*. Bloomington, IN: Indiana University Press.

Eisenlohr, P. (2004) Temporalities of community: Ancesteral language, pilgrimage and diasporic belonging in Mauritius. *Journal of Linguistic Anthropology* 14 (1), 81–98.

Fabian, J. (1983) *Time and the Other. How Anthropology Makes Its Object*. New York: Columbia University Press.

Fabian, J. (1986) *Language and Colonial Power*. Cambridge: Cambridge University Press.

Fabian, J. (1990a) *History from Below*. Amsterdam: John Benjamins.

Fabian, J. (1990b) *Power and Performance*. Madison, WI: University of Wisconsin Press.

Fabian, J. (1991a) Rule and process. In J. Fabian, *Time and The Work of Anthropology* (pp. 87–109). Chur: Harwood (original work published 1979).

Fabian, J. (1991b) *Time and The Work of Anthropology*. Chur: Harwood.

Fabian, J. (1995) Ethnographic misunderstanding and the perils of context. *American Anthropologist* 97 (1), 41–50.

Fabian, J. (1996) *Remembering the Present*. Berkeley, CA: University of California Press.

Fabian, J. (2001) *Anthropology with an Attitude*. Stanford, CA: Stanford University Press.

Fairclough, N. (1992) *Discourse and Social Change*. Cambridge: Polity Press.

Foucault, M. (2001) 'L'oeil du pouvoir'. In *Dits et Ecrits II* (pp. 190–207). Paris: Gallimard (original work published 1977).

Fromm, E. (1961) *Marx's View of Man*. New York: Continuum.

Gee, J. (1996) *Social Linguistics and Literacies*. London: Taylor & Francis.

Gieser, T. (2008) Embodiment, emotion and empathy: A phenomenological approach to apprenticeship learning. *Anthropological Theory* 8, 299–318.

Ginzburg, C. (1990) *The Cheese and the Worms*. Harmondsworth: Penguin.

Goffman, E. (1964) The neglected situation. *American Anthropologist* 66 (6), 133–136.

Goffman, E. (1971) *Relations in Public: Microstudies of the Public Order*. New York: Basic Books.

Goffman, E. (1974) *Frame Analysis: An Essay on the Organization of Experience*. New York: Harper & Row.

Goodwin, C. (1994) Professional vision. *American Anthropologist* 96 (3), 606–633.

Goodwin, C. (2007) Participation, stance and affect in the organization of activities. *Discourse and Society* 18 (1), 53–73.

Goodwin C. and Goodwin, M.H. (1992) Context, activity and participation. In P. Auer, and A. DiLuzio (eds) *The Contextualization of Language* (pp. 77–99) Amsterdam: John Benjamins.

Gorski, P. (2013) Bourdieu as a theorist of change. In S. Gorski (ed.) *Bourdieu and Historical Analysis* (pp. 1–15). Durham, NC: Duke University Press.

Gorter, D. (2006) Introduction: The study of the linguistic landscape as a new approach to multilingualism. In D. Gorter (ed.) *Linguistic Landscape: A New Approach to Multilingualism* (pp. 1–6). Clevedon: Multilingual Matters.

Gortz, A. (1989) *Critique of Economic Reason*. London: Verso.

Greimas, A.J. (1990) *Narrative Semiotics and Cognitive Discourses*. London: Pinter.

Gumperz, J. (1968) The speech community. *International Encyclopedia of the Social Sciences* (pp. 381–386). New York: Macmillan. [Reprinted in A. Duranti (ed.) (2001) *Linguistic Anthropology: A Reader* (pp. 43–52). New York: Wiley.]

Gumperz, J. (1972) Introduction. In J. Gumperz and D. Hymes (eds) *Directions in Sociolinguistics: The Ethnography of Communication* (pp. 1–25). New York: Holt, Rhinehart & Winston.

Gumperz, J. (1982) *Discourse Strategies*. Cambridge: Cambridge University Press.

Gumperz, J. (1992) Contextualization revisited. In P. Auer and A. DiLuzio (eds) *The Contextualization of Language* (pp. 39–53). Amsterdam: John Benjamins.

Hanks, W. (1996) *Language and Communicative Practice*. Boulder, CO: Westview.

Hanks, W. (2005) Pierre Bourdieu and the practices of language. *Annual Review of Anthropology* 34, 67–83.

Haviland, J. (1996a) 'We want to borrow your mouth': Tzotzil marital squabbles. In C. Briggs (ed.) *Disorderly Discourse* (pp. 158–203). New York: Oxford University Press.

Haviland, J. (1996b) Text from talk in Tzotzil. In M. Silverstein and G. Urban (eds) *Natural Histories of Discourse* (pp. 45–78). Chicago, IL: University of Chicago Press.

Haviland, J. (1997) Shouts, shrieks, and shots: Unruly political conversations in indigenous Chiapas. *Pragmatics* 7 (4), 547–573.

Heller, M. (2000) *Linguistic Minorities in Late Modernity*. London: Longman.

Hobsbawm, E. (2011) *How to Change the World*. New Haven, CT: Yale University Press.

Holquist, M. (2010) The fugue of chronotope. In N. Bemong *et al.* (eds) *Bakhtin's Theory of the Literary Chronotope: Reflections, Applications, Perspectives* (pp. 19–33). Ghent: Academia Press.

Huang, A. (2010) London Chinatown: A sociolinguistic ethnography of visuality. PhD dissertation, University of Jyväskylä.

Hymes, D. (ed.) (1964) *Language in Culture and Society: A Reader in Linguistics and Anthropology*. New York: Harper & Row.

Hymes, D. (1966) Two types of linguistic relativity (with examples from Amerindian ethnography). In W. Bright (ed.) *Sociolinguistics: Proceedings of the UCLA Sociolinguistics Conference, 1964* (pp. 114–167). The Hague: Mouton.

Hymes, D. (1972) Models of the interaction of language and social life. In J. Gumperz and D. Hymes (eds) *Direcions in Sociolinguistics: The Ethnography of Communication* (pp. 35–71). New York: Holt, Rinehart & Winston.

Hymes, D. (1975) Breakthrough into performance. In D. Ben-Amos and K. Goldstein (eds) *Folklore: Performance and Communication* (pp. 11–74). The Hague: Mouton.

Hymes, D. (1980) *Language in Education: Ethnolinguistic Essays*. Washington, DC: Center for Applied Linguistics.

Hymes, D. (1981) *In Vain I Tried to Tell You. Essays in Native American Ethnopoetics*. Philadelphia, PA: University of Pennsylvania Press.

Hymes, D. (1983) *Essays in the History of Linguistic Anthropology*. Amsterdam: John Benjamins.

Hymes, D. (1986) Models of the interaction of language and social life. In J. Gumperz and D. Hymes (eds) *Directions in Sociolinguistics: The Ethnography of Communication* (pp. 35–71). London: Basil Blackwell (original work published 1972).

Hymes, D. (1992) The concept of communicative competence revisited. In M. Pütz (ed.) *Thirty Years of Linguistic Evolution* (pp. 31–57). Amsterdam: John Benjamins.

Hymes, D. (1996) *Ethnography, Linguistic, Narrative Inequality: Toward an Understanding of Voice*. London: Taylor & Francis.

Hymes, D. (1998) *Reading Takelma Texts*. Bloomington, IN: Trickster Press.

Hymes, D. (ed.) (2002) The use of anthropology: Critical, political, personal. In *Reinventing Anthropology* (pp. 3–79). Ann Arbor, MI: University of Michigan Press (original work published 1969).

Hymes, D. (2003) *Now I Know Only So Far: Essays in Ethnopoetics*. Lincoln, NB: University of Nebraska Press.

Hymes, D. (2004) *In Vain I Tried To Tell You: Essays in Native American Ethnopoetics*, 2nd edn. Lincoln, NB: University of Nebraska Press.

Ingold, T. (2000) *The Perception of the Environment: Essays on Livelihood, Dwelling and Skill*. London: Routledge.

Inoue, M. (2004) Introduction: Temporality and historicity in and through language ideology. *Journal of Linguistic Anthropology* 14 (1), 1–5.

Irvine, J. (1995) The family romance of colonial linguistics: Gender and family in nineteenth-century representations of African languages. *Pragmatics* 5 (2), 139–153.

Irvine, J. (2004) Say when: Temporalities in language ideology. *Journal of Linguistic Anthropology* 14 (1), 99–109.

Jackson, M. (1989) *Paths Toward a Clearing: Radical Empiricism and Ethnographic Inquiry*. Bloomington, IN: Indiana University Press.

Jakobson, R. (1960) Closing statement: Linguistics and poetics. In T. Sebeok (ed.) *Style in Language* (pp. 350–377). Cambridge, MA: MIT Press.

Jefferson, G. (1996) A case of transcriptional stereotyping. *Journal of Pragmatics* 26 (2), 159–170.

Johnstone, B. (2008) *Discourse Analysis* (2nd edn). London: Blackwell.

Juffermans, K. (2010) Local languaging: Literacy products and practices in Gambian society. PhD Dissertation, Tilburg University.

Karrebæk, M. and Ghandchi, N. (2014) The very sensitive question: Chronotopes, insecurity and Farsi heritage language classrooms. Tilburg Papers in Culture Studies, paper 118. See https://www.tilburguniversity.edu/research/institutes-and-research-groups/babylon/tpcs/item-paper-118-tpcs.htm

Keunen, B. (2000) Bakhtin, genre formation, and the cognitive turn: Chronotopes as memory schemata. *CLCWeb: Comparative Literature and Culture* 2 (2), article 2. See http://docs.lib.purdue.edu/clcweb/vol2/iss2/2/

Kress, G. (2009) *Multimodality: A Social Semiotic Approach to Contemporary Communication*. London: Routledge.

Kress, G. and Van Leeuwen, T. (1996) *Reading Images: The Grammar of Virtual Design*. London: Routledge.

Kroskrity, P. (ed.) (2000) *Regimes of Language*. Santa Fe, CA: School of American Research Press.

Landry, R. and Bourhis, R.Y. (1997) Linguistic landscape and ethnographic vitality: An empirical study. *Journal of Language and Social Psychology* 16, 23–49.

Lefebvre, H. (1958) *Le Marxisme*. Paris: Presses Universitaires de France.

Lefebvre, H. (1968) *Le Droit à la Ville*. Paris: Antropos.

Lefebvre, H. (2000) *The Production of Space*. Oxford: Blackwell (original work published 1991).

Lemon, A. (2009) Sympathy for the weary state? Cold War chronotopes and Moscow others. *Comparative Studies in Society and History* 51 (4), 832–864.

Maryns, K. (2004) The asylum speaker: An ethnography of language and communication in the Belgian asylum procedure. PhD Dissertation, Ghent University.

Maryns, K. and Blommaert, J. (2001) Stylistic and thematic shifting as a narrative resource: Assessing asylum seekers' repertoires. *Multilingua* 20 (1), 61–84.

McCall, M. and Becker, H. (1990) Introduction. In H. Becker and M. McCall (eds) *Symbolic Interactionism and Cultural Studies* (pp. 1–15). Chicago, IL: University of Chicago Press.

Meeuwis, M. and Blommaert, J. (1997) A monolectal view of code-switching: Layered code-switching among Zairians in Belgium. In P. Auer (ed.) *Codeswitching in Conversation*. London: Routledge.

Meeuwis, M. and Brisard, F. (1993) Time and the diagnosis of language change. Antwerp Papers in Linguistics 72. University of Antwerp, Antwerp.

Möller, J.S. and Jörgensen, J.N. (eds) (2011) *Language Enregisterment and Attitudes*. Copenhagen: Copenhagen Studies in Bilingualism.

Moore, R. (1993) Performance form and the voices of characters in five versions of the Wasco coyote cycle. In J. Lucy (ed.) *Reflexive Language* (pp. 213–240). Cambridge: Cambridge University Press.

Moore, R. (2000) Endangered. In A. Duranti (ed.) *Language Matters in Anthropology: A Lexicon for the Millennium* (pp. 65–68). Special issue of *Journal of Linguistic Anthropology* 9 (1–2), 1–276.

Moore, R. (2012) 'Taking up speech' in an endangered language: Bilingual discourse in a heritage language classroom. *Working Papers in Educational Linguistics* 27 (2), 57–78.

Moretti, F. (2013) *The Bourgeois*. London: Verso.

Myers-Scotton, C. (1993) *Social Motivations for Codeswitching*. Oxford: Clarendon.

Ndege, S. (2002) The Meru folktale: An ethno-poetic study. PhD Dissertation, Ghent University.

Ochs, E. (1979) Transcription as theory. In E. Ochs and B. Schieffelin (eds) *Developmental Pragmatics* (pp. 43–72). New York: Academic Press.

Ochs, E. and Capps, L. (2001) *Living Narrative: Creating Lives in Everyday Storytelling*. Cambridge, MA: Harvard University Press.

O'Connell, D. and Kowal, S. (1995) Transcription systems for spoken discourse. In J. Verschueren, J.-O. Östman and J. Blommaert (eds) *Handbook of Pragmatics: Manual* (pp. 646–656). Amsterdam: John Benjamins.

Pachler, N., Makoe, P., Burns, M. and Blommaert, J. (2008) The things (we think) we (ought to) do: Ideological processes and practi²ces in teaching. *Teaching and Teacher Education* 24, 437–450.

Pan Lin (2009) Dissecting multilingual Beijing: The space and scale of vernacular globalization. *Visual Communication* 9 (1), 67–90.

Perrino, S. (2011) Chronotopes of story and storytelling events in interviews. *Language in Society* 40, 90–103.

Prigogine, I. and Stengers, I. (1984) *Order out of Chaos: Man's New Dialogue with Nature*. New York: Bantam Books.

Rampton, B. (1995) *Crossing: Language and Ethnicity Among Adolescents*. London: Longman.

Rampton, B. (1996) *Crossing*. London: Routledge.

Rampton, B. (2003) Hegemony, social class and stylization. *Pragmatics* 13 (1), 49–83.

Rampton, B. (2006) *Language in Late Modernity: Interaction in an Urban School.* Cambridge: Cambridge University Press.

Rampton, B. (2014) Gumperz and governmentality in the 21st century: Interaction, power and subjectivity. Tilburg Papers in Cultural Studies, paper 117. Tilburg University, the Netherlands.

Reay, D. (2004) 'It's all becoming a habitus': Beyond the habitual use of habitus in educational research. *British Journal of Sociology of Education* 25 (4), 431–444.

Sapir, E. (1921) *Language: An Introduction to the Study of Speech.* New York: Harcourt Brace.

Sapir, E. (1929) The status of linguistics as a science. *Language* 5, 207–214.

Sapir, E. (2002) *The Psychology of Culture: A Course by Edward Sapir,* ed. J. Irvine. Berlin: Mouton de Gruyter.

Schegloff, E. (1988) Description in the social sciences 1: Talk-in-interaction. *Papers in Pragmatics* 2 (1/2), 1–24.

Schiffrin, D. (2009) Crossing boundaries: The nexus of time, space, person and place in narrative. *Language in Society* 38, 421–445.

Scollon, R. (2001) *Mediated Discourse Analysis: The Nexus of Practice.* London: Routledge.

Scollon, R. (2008) Discourse itineraries: Nine processes of resemiotization. In V. Bhatia, J. Flowerdew and R. Jones (eds) *Advances in Discourse Studies* (pp. 233–244). London: Routledge.

Scollon, R. and Scollon, S.W. (2003) *Discourses in Place: Language in the Material World.* London: Routledge

Scollon, R. and Scollon, S.W. (2004) *Nexus Analysis: Discourse and the Emerging Internet.* London: Routledge.

Scollon, R. and Scollon, S.W. (2009) Breakthrough into action. *Text and Talk* 29 (3), 277–294.

Scott, J.C. (1990) *Domination and the Arts of Resistance: Hidden Transcripts.* New Haven, CT: Yale University Press.

Shohamy, E. and Gorter, D. (eds) (2009) *Linguistic Landscape: Expanding the Scenery.* London: Routledge.

Silverstein, M. (1977) Cultural prerequisites to grammatical analysis. In M. Saville-Troike (ed.) *Linguistics and Anthropology (GURT 1977)* (pp. 139–151). Washington, DC: Georgetown University Press.

Silverstein, M. (1985a) Language and the culture of gender. In E. Mertz and R. Parmentier (eds) *Semiotic Mediation* (pp. 219–259). New York: Academic Press.

Silverstein, M. (1985b) The pragmatic poetry of prose: Parallelism, repetition, and cohesive structure in the time course of dyadic conversation. In D. Schiffrin (ed.) *Meaning, Form, and Use in Context* (pp. 181–199). Washington, DC: Georgetown University Press.

Silverstein, M. (1992) The indeterminacy of contextualization: When is enough enough? In P. Auer and A. Di Luzio (eds) *The Contextualization of Language* (pp. 55–76). Amsterdam: John Benjamins.

Silverstein, M. (1996a) Monoglot 'standard' in America: Standardization and metaphors of linguistic hegemony. In D. Brenneis and R. Macaulay (eds) *The Matrix of Language* (pp. 284–306). Boulder, CT: Westview.

Silverstein, M. (1996b) The secret life of texts. In M. Silverstein and G. Urban (eds) *Natural Histories of Discourse* (pp. 81–105). Chicago, IL: University of Chicago Press.

Silverstein, M. (1997) The improvisational performance of culture in realtime discursive practice. In R.K. Sawyer (ed.) *Creativity in Performance* (pp. 265–312). Greenwich, CT: Ablex.

Silverstein, M. (1998) Contemporary transformations of local linguistic communities. *Annual Review of Anthropology* 27, 401–426.

Silverstein, M. (2003) Indexical order and the dialectics of sociolinguistic life. *Language and Communication* 23, 193–229.

Silverstein, M. (2004) Cultural concepts and the language–culture nexus. *Current Anthropology* 45 (5), 621–652.

Silverstein, M. (2005a) Axes of –E vals: Token vs. type interdiscursivity. *Journal of Linguistic Anthropology* 15, 6–22.

Silverstein, M. (2005b) The poetics of politics: 'Theirs' and 'ours'. *Journal of Anthropological Research* 61 (1), 1–24.

Silverstein, M. (2006a) Old wine, new ethnographic lexicography. *Annual Review of Anthropology* 35, 481–496.

Silverstein, M. (2006b) Pragmatic indexing. In K. Brown (ed.) *Encyclopaedia of Language and Linguistics* (2nd edn), Volume 6 (pp. 14–17). Boston, MA: Elsevier.

Silverstein, M. (2009) Does the autonomy of linguistics rest on the autonomy of syntax? An alternative framing of our object of study. Plenary paper, XXXVI Finnish Linguistics Conference, Jyväskylä, May (ms).

Silverstein, M. (2014) How language communities intersect: Is 'superdiversity' an incremental or transformative condition. Tilburg Papers in Culture Studies, paper 107. See https://www.tilburguniversity.edu/research/institutes-and-research-groups/babylon/tpcs/item-paper-107-tpcs.htm

Silverstein, M. and Urban, G. (eds) (1996a) *Natural Histories of Discourse*. Chicago, IL: University of Chicago Press.

Silverstein, M. and Urban, G. (1996b) The natural history of discourse. In M. Silverstein and G. Urban (eds) *Natural Histories of Discourse* (pp. 1–17). Chicago, IL: University of Chicago Press.

Stocking, G. (1992) *The Ethnographer's Magic and Other Essays in the History of Anthropology*. Madison, WI: University of Wisconsin Press.

Stocking, G.W. Jr (ed.) (1983) *Observers Observed. Essays on Ethnographic Fieldwork*. Madison, WI: University of Wisconsin Press.

Tedlock, D. (1983) *The Spoken Word and the Work of Interpretation*. Philadelphia, PA: University of Pennsylvania Press.

Thompson, E.P. (1978) *Poverty of Theory*. London: Merlin.

Urban, G. (1996) Entextualization, replication, and power. In M. Silverstein and G. Urban (eds) *Natural Histories of Discourse* (pp. 21–44). Chicago, IL: University of Chicago Press.

Valchev, V.H., Nel, J.A., Van de Vijver, A.J.R., Meiring, D., De Bruin, G.P. and Rothmann, S.R. (2013) Similarities and differences in implicit personality concepts across ethno-cultural groups in South Africa. *Journal of Cross-Cultural Psychology* 44, 365–388.

Verschueren, J. (1995) The pragmatic perspective. In J. Verschueren, J.-O. Östman and J. Blommaert (eds) *Handbook of Pragmatics: Manual* (pp. 1–19). Amsterdam: John Benjamins.

Vertovec, S. (2006) The emergence of super-diversity in Britain. Centre on Migration, Policy and Society, working paper 25. Oxford University.

Voloshinov, V. (1973) *Marxism and the Philosophy of Language*. Cambridge, MA: Harvard University Press.

Wacquant, L. (2004) Following Pierre Bourdieu into the field. *Ethnography* 5 (4), 387–414.

Wallerstein, I. (1998) The time of space and the space of time: The future of social science. *Political Geography* 17 (1), 71–82.

Wallerstein, I. (2004) *World-Systems Analysis: An Introduction.* Durham, NC: Duke University Press.

Wang, H. (2009) The chronotopes of encounter and emergence. *Journal of Curriculum Theorizing* 25 (1), 1–5.

Woolard, K. (2013) Is the personal political? Chronotopes and changing stances towards Catalan language and identity. *International Journal of Bilingual Education and Bilingualism* 16 (2), 210–224.

Woolard, K., Schieffelin, B. and Kroskrity, P. (eds) (1998) *Language Ideologies: Theory and Practice.* New York: Oxford University Press.

Wortham, S. (2006) *Learning Identity: The Joint Emergence of Social Identification and Academic Learning.* Cambridge: Cambridge University Press.

Wortham, S. (2009) Moments of enduring struggle: Review of Ben Rampton (2006) Language in late modernity: Interactions in an urban school. *Linguistics and Education* 20 (2), 200–208.

# Index